Arthur Thomas Fisher

Outdoor Life in England

Arthur Thomas Fisher

Outdoor Life in England

ISBN/EAN: 9783337095369

Printed in Europe, USA, Canada, Australia, Japan

Cover: Foto ©Lupo / pixelio.de

More available books at **www.hansebooks.com**

OUTDOOR LIFE

IN

ENGLAND

BY

ARTHUR T. FISHER
(*Late 21st Hussars*)
AUTHOR OF 'STABLE AND SADDLEROOM,' 'ROD AND RIVER,' ETC.

LONDON
RICHARD BENTLEY AND SON
Publishers in Ordinary to Her Majesty
1896
[*All rights reserved*]

TO
MY WIFE.

PREFACE.

A NEW book and a new ship may, in many respects, be said to resemble each other. Purpose, design, material, and labour, are requisite for their construction. Each bears its cargo and its bill-of-lading. Author and publisher, owner and underwriter, alike desire prosperity to the 'outward bound.'

My previous literary efforts have received such kindly recognition by the public that I venture to launch the present volume, in the hope that it may experience a welcome similar to that accorded to its predecessors. Before it leaves my hands I think it is incumbent on me to offer some few words by way of preface, in explanation of its object and construction.

Although the main portion of the work has reference to objects of natural history, it has not been my intention to write a treatise on that subject. I do not presume to pose as a naturalist, but merely as a lover of Nature, and as such it is my desire to attract the attention of others to the many objects of interest around them which they may have hitherto disregarded, and thus, it may be, help them to care for and love them. With this purpose in view, I have abstained from adhering to any recognized arrangement or order. In describing the plumage of birds, their measurements, etc., I have had recourse to the works of the best authorities on such subjects, and I have endeavoured to make the description as brief and simple as possible, in order to assist the reader to readily identify a specimen without the necessity of having to wade through one more lengthy.

I have referred to but a few of the commoner wild-flowers—merely those which are more interesting by reason of some legend attaching to them, or the supposed or real possession of some special medicinal virtue—most of which may be found growing either by the roadside or in the fields of nearly every county.

I have devoted but comparatively few pages to 'British Field Sports,' not by reason of any indifference to them, but because they form the subject of so many volumes at the present day that a longer treatise would be superfluous. I have more fully dealt with fishing in a previous work, 'Rod and River.'

Since watercress-farming has, of late years, become an industry of such importance, I have thought that some account of the cultivation of the plant might prove of interest.

The compilation of the present work has afforded me much pleasurable occupation. Should its perusal, as I trust it may, afford the reader any additional interest in 'Outdoor Life,' I shall be content.

OUTDOOR LIFE IN ENGLAND

DWELLERS IN FIELDS

PART I.

The Brute Creation—Love of Animals—English Wild Animals—The Wild-Cat—Bettws-y-Coed—Gradual Extinction of Wild-Cats in Britain—Wild Domestic Cats—Colour of the True Wild-Cat—The Badger—Badgers and Foxes—Foxes and 'Scent'—Fox-scented Plant—A Cold-scenting Country—Foxes and Poultry—A Foxy Story—Varieties of Foxes—John Peel—Fox-hunting on Foot—Scotch Greyhound Foxes—Foreign Foxes—English Foxes—Killed in the Open—Foxes and Rabbits in the Same Earth—Fox-cubs at Play—Vulpecides—Tame Foxes—Impudence of Foxes—Cocktails—Gradual Decrease of Hares in England—Former Days at Ashdown—A Distant Hare—Hares and their Ways—A 'Star' Leveret—Timidity and Ferocity of Hares—Solitary Habits of Hares—Travelling Powers of Hares—Positions selected by Hares to 'form'—Hare-hunting—Daring of Hunted Hares—Hare and Fox Hunting—Mr. Jeffreys' Harriers—Hare-shooting—Recipe for preparing a Hare for Cooking—Utility of Hares—Poaching Hares—Poachers' and Keepers' Wires—Treasure Trove—Netting Hares in Gateways—Hare-calls—Rabbits for Sport—Rabbits for Pleasure—Acute Senses of Hearing and Smell—Prolificacy of Rabbits—Breeding Season of Rabbits—Soil suitable for

I

Rabbits—Liver Disease of Rabbits—Disease caused by Overcrowding—Re-stocking a Manor with Rabbits—Counties most suitable for Rabbits—Assertion that Rabbits once domesticated do not burrow—White Wild Rabbits—Black Wild Rabbits—Tame Rabbits—Rabbit-farming—Effect of Rabbits on Pasture-lands—Condition of Rabbits when born—Hedge Rabbits stated not to burrow—Wood Rabbits and Ferreting—Rabbits at Play—Notice to quit—Rabbit-poaching—Distribution of Rabbits to the Poor—Necessity for paunching Rabbits soon after killing—Disposal of Game in a Larder—Crossing of English Rabbits with Foreigners.

THE extent to which we are indebted to what is termed the brute creation can hardly be over-estimated. Our comfort, happiness—indeed, our very existence—is dependent on theirs. Each living thing contributes its share towards maintaining the balance of Nature; the smallest, and apparently the most insignificant, object is frequently capable of performing the most important duties, and of this the microscope affords us constant proof. Each day reveals the existence of creatures hitherto unknown. So long as the world remains, the labours of the naturalist can never cease, and each new discovery leaves us more awestruck than before at the infinite power of the Creator. And all these things, from the greatest to the least, were brought into being for our benefit. They, surely, claim our deepest interest.

The man who cannot love animals but half lives; life to such an individual must be a very colourless and dreary affair. Yet there are people so constituted, who, being unable to love anything but themselves, are deserving of our commiseration, comparing unfavourably in their selfishness with the very creatures they ignore, which, as we are aware, are capable of exhibiting the strongest and most disinterested affection towards those who treat them kindly. We may, however, console ourselves with the reflection that with the majority of us a love for animals is inherent, and the better we understand their ways and habits the more they excite our interest.

Contrasted with other larger, less-populated countries, and, indeed, with what it was formerly, England possesses comparatively few wild animals; and it is sad to reflect that several of these are in danger of becoming extinct by reason of constant persecution. The black rat may be said to have completely vanished, having been supplanted by the more modern brown species, and it is very much to be doubted if we have not suffered considerably by the exchange. The wildcat is but rarely seen nowadays. Much the same may be said of the marten. The polecat is far from common; and although the badger still makes its home in the outlying woods in some of our wilder districts, it runs the risk of being ere long exterminated.

Once only has it been my good fortune to see a veritable wild-cat. I was fishing in a somewhat wild part of North Wales. Finding that the fish were not rising in the river I was on, I decided to try another neighbouring stream, and to join a friend whom I had left there in the morning. In order to avoid a long detour, it was necessary for me to force my way through some rough woodlands. When crossing a clearing, a wild-cat sprang out of the ferns and trotted leisurely away, giving me ample opportunity to observe it. In colour it was a dirty yellow, striped with gray; its size some three or four times greater than a large domestic cat. It appeared to be horribly mangy, and smelt most abominably. Had it been in good condition, it might possibly have been a very handsome animal; but, as it then was, it gave me the impression of strongly resembling a man-eating tiger, disgusting and sickening me. I remember, when a boy, to have been told that wild-cats were not uncommon in the Gwydr forest near Bettws-y-Coed in North Wales, and there may be some few still there. This was, however, in the days when Bettws was a less fashionable resort than now, and less accessible to tourists. Beautiful it must always be, though the presence of a railway-station and a smart hotel are less in keeping with the rocks, valleys, and streams than the humbler but no less hospitable Royal Oak, which, when I first knew the place, with the exception of some two or three clean though unpretentious lodging-houses, was the one and only resting-place for tourists and travellers. Jardine states that wild-cats were to be still found in Cumberland and Westmorland, in some of the wilder parts of those counties; that they were abundant in Scotland, and were formerly so in the South of England, though at the time he wrote they had become extinct in this latter portion of the country. I should, however, very much doubt if they are nowadays other than extremely rare anywhere in these islands, by reason of the great depredations which they commit where game is abundant. Keepers look upon cats generally as their natural enemies, and when it is considered what terrible poachers they are, this is hardly to be wondered at. When once a domestic cat takes to poaching, there is but one cure, viz., a charge of shot, for she becomes absolutely useless to her owner as far as her helping to keep down the rats and mice is concerned, and is for ever straying and wandering about in the woods. Such animals have, doubtless, bred in a wild state, and been often mistaken for the true wild-cat, though far inferior in size. The wild-cat is generally yellow in colour, with dark gray stripes; at times it is of a bluish gray, with darker gray stripes, but I believe that the former is the truer colour.

There are few of our wild animals which more undeservedly bear an evil reputation than the badger. It is a verification of the saying, 'Give a dog a bad name.' No more harmless or inoffensive animal exists, nor one more persecuted. Happily, the custom of badger-baiting has gone out of fashion. It seems incredible that the mere bullying of any living creature could ever have afforded amusement to any but those whose minds were too brutalized to perceive that there could be any cruelty in such 'sport.' The mind of the true sportsman recoils from such performances. In this respect the present generation are superior to their forefathers, who were ignorant and degraded enough to extract pleasure from encouraging animals to fight with each other, 'cock-fighting,' 'badger-baiting,' 'bull-baiting,' and 'dog-fighting' constituting some of the chief pleasures of the English country squire. In these more enlightened and humane days we feel almost tempted to doubt that such things could ever have been, still more so that the term 'sport' should have been so degraded. It is most sincerely to be hoped that such 'pastimes' may never be resuscitated. The poor badger led a sorry life then, and it is quite time he was left alone in peace. So far from doing harm, he is a most useful and peaceable creature, though he is credited with all kinds of malpractices. He may dig a few holes, but he is otherwise sinless. He generally elects to make his home in wild, out-of-the-way places, and so his excavations and interesting underground passages are matters of but slight consequence. He lives principally on roots, worms, snails, and such-like. His enemies accuse him of killing rabbits and game generally. The latter is a most unfair and calumnious charge, for he is *not* a carnivorous beast. He is most interesting, useful, and cleanly withal. By the last-named good quality he renders the greatest service in preventing the spreading of mange amongst foxes, for as he not infrequently takes up his abode in a fox earth, his cleanly habits tend to promote the health and general well-being of his fellow-lodgers, who are apt to suffer severely at times from their utter disregard of all sanitary laws.

So far from being harassed and suppressed, badgers ought rather to be encouraged. In the district in which I reside I am sorry to say that much ignorance still prevails regarding the habits of the badger, and I have heard it positively asserted, and in all good faith, even by intelligent people, that he is guilty of every possible enormity. I have tried to enlighten them on the subject, but they are too obstinate to be convinced, and from time to time I hear of parties being organized for the purpose of digging out any badgers which may have taken up their quarters on some one or other of the outlying farms.

I have heard it stated that the ham of a badger is considered a great delicacy; I must also admit that I have heard this statement most flatly denied. I should imagine that a badger would be as nauseous an animal for food as could be found in the whole world of nature, always excepting a skunk.

A badger is essentially a nocturnal animal; he is rarely, if ever, to be seen outside his earth in the daytime. When night comes, and all respectable people are thinking of going to bed, he rouses himself and shambles off in quest of food. His shape is not conducive to rapid travelling, though it is surprising what a pace he can go when pressed by dogs. Like the rest of his race, he smells horribly; nevertheless, he is most scrupulously clean in his household arrangements. It is asserted that the odour of a fox is singularly offensive to his nostrils. Now, a badger's earth is just as suitable a dwelling as the heart of a fox can desire, and the latter, knowing full well how detestable his natural aroma is to a badger, is not slow to avail himself of the fact, and so purposely fouls the mouth of the earth, a proceeding which is so intolerable to the cleanly badger, that he holds his nose and makes a bolt of it, whereupon in goes the fox and takes possession of the 'furnished apartments.' I am unable to verify the truth of this statement; but my belief in the wily craftiness of a fox is very strong, and I believe him to be an animal capable of any dirty trick. Nevertheless, I have, for all that, good reason to love him well. I trust I may have been able to show that there is every reason why we should endeavour to preserve, rather than exterminate, our badgers, if only for the good they do and their usefulness in hunting countries. If for no other reason, a badger is the only species of bear which remains to us, and so is surely deserving of our support and protection.

There is a saying amongst hunting men, and it is true enough, that when the scent of a fox is very apparent, there is but little chance of a gallop. I am not going to write a chapter on 'scent,' for it is a subject which no one has ever yet succeeded in understanding. I am inclined to believe that its strength or weakness depends, in a great measure, on electricity, and hounds can 'own' it or not according as it is nearer to, or higher from, the ground. In the former case, they can perceive it and we cannot; in the latter, it is apparent to our nostrils, but too high for theirs. This may be a very unscientific way of putting it, but I do not profess to be scientific. There is, however, no gainsaying the fact that hounds can hunt a fox over some soils better than others, and under some conditions of atmosphere with perfect ease, whereas under others they cannot, to use a hunting phrase, 'own a yard of it'; and I have never, under any circumstances, known hounds able to hunt out a line when the scent of the fox was apparent to human nostrils.

I have frequently fancied that I could detect the smell of a fox, and more especially has this been the case when shooting rabbits in gorse-coverts. For some years I held the lease of a large gorse-covert, in which I managed to preserve a goodly number of rabbits, and could always show two or three litters of foxes as well.

It was not to be wondered at that I should have supposed this scent, so like that of a fox, to have been due to the presence of one of those animals. I noticed that it was almost always apparent in some two or three places. Happening to mention the circumstance to an acquaintance, he informed me that he had heard that there was a plant, common in the district, bearing a scent very similar to a fox. I was subsequently able to satisfy myself that I had been mistaken in supposing that it proceeded from the latter, and so concluded that it must have been the plant referred to; but what description of plant it may be I have, I regret to say, not had further opportunity of ascertaining, as the gorse-covert has since been doomed to destruction by the person from whom I rented it, much to my own regret, and, I may doubtless add, to that of the foxes.

Our neighbourhood is somewhat overstocked with foxes; the wildness of the country is peculiarly suitable for them. The many gorse-coverts which stud the downlands afford warm lying, and the abundance of rabbits enables them to keep the larder well supplied without any very great exertion. The woodlands are heavy, and the country generally none too good scenting, and so they increase and multiply considerably, despite the number killed annually by the hounds; but, as may be inferred, it is no easy matter to account for a fox under such conditions, and unless the scent is unusually good, and the hounds get quickly on the line of a fox when he breaks away, he has every chance of saving his brush.

It is amusing to see the trouble which the village people take to prevent the foxes making free with their hen-roosts. Wherever poultry is kept, the gardens and premises are adorned with pieces of white rag tied to sticks, posts, railings, anywhere and everywhere, all of which precautions are taken to avoid the trouble of shutting up the fowls at night. The result may be readily imagined, for after a time the foxes care no more for the rags than they do for the sticks to which they are tied; and so it happens that many a fat hen is carried off, her remains being probably discovered in one of the many withy-beds or gorse-coverts on the outskirts of the village when the hounds go there to draw. The owners bewail their misfortune, and send in their claims to the masters of the neighbouring packs, who are ever generous and just in such matters. Nevertheless, it always appears to me to be somewhat hard on the masters of hounds to be called upon to settle claims for such poultry as can be safely housed. With turkeys and guinea-fowls, etc., the case is different; but whenever the opportunity offers, I never fail to endeavour to impress on the claimants for reimbursement for poultry they assert to have been taken by foxes, that, if they are too lazy to shut up their cocks and hens, they do not deserve compensation. I have never yet lost a single head of poultry by foxes, notwithstanding the fact that the foxes cross the field in which my poultry are kept in order to avail themselves of the bridge which connects the two sides of the village. At times they presume to come under the windows of my house, as their tracks in the snow have testified. It is unnecessary for me to add that I take the precaution of having my poultry safely housed at night.

A few years ago I happened to be on a visit to a relation who was, at the time, master of one of the North-Country packs of foxhounds. The cubbing season was nearly over, and although an unusual number of foxes had been accounted for, there still remained far too many for sport, the breeding season having been exceptionally favourable. One morning, after two cubs had been broken up, and the hounds were drawing another covert, an old dog-hound was observed self-hunting in the distance, and close on to a fox which he ran into and rolled over single-handed in the most masterly style, just in time to prevent his entering the covert. Not wishing to give any more foxes to the hounds that morning, the master gave orders for this one to be kept intact, declaring his intention of having it stuffed, and a place reserved in the case for the head of the hound when it died. That evening, when the fox was brought to the house, the master was enjoying the comforts of an armchair after the fatigues of the day, and was already half-way to dreamland, when the servant, announcing its arrival, asked where it was to be put. 'Oh,' replied his master, but half awake, 'put it—put it in the larder,' and the next minute he was snoring loudly. It was past midnight, and the remainder of the household had retired to rest, leaving the sleeper still snoring in his chair, when we were suddenly awakened by the banging of doors, a volley of execrations in a familiar voice, followed by a loud thump on the roof of one of the outbuildings, then more execrations, more banging of doors, and all was still. In the morning we were enlightened as to the cause of the disturbance. It appeared that, on waking up, my host proceeded, as usual, to make the tour of the downstairs premises in order to satisfy himself that all was safe for the night. On passing through one of the passages, he was aware of the most overpowering smell of a fox, and discovered the cause to proceed, as he naïvely remarked, 'from the larder, of all places.' To seize the unoffending corpse by the brush, and open the back-door, was no sooner decided upon than carried out, but what to do with it was another matter. The dogs might, perhaps, get at it! The moon was shining brightly on the roof of an outhouse; the suggestion was readily accepted, and the next moment the corpse was ruthlessly sent spinning through the air, and fell with a loud thump, dislodging half a dozen tiles, which clattered down on to the stone-paved yard. Eventually the fox found its way into the hands of the local taxidermist, and now forms an interesting ornament to the inside of the house from which it was previously so unceremoniously ejected.

To many people a fox is merely a fox; but there are varieties of the species even in this country. There is the pure-bred English variety, the well-known little red rascal, and there is also the well-known large North-Country fox which inhabits the mountainous districts of Cumberland. All British sportsmen are familiar with the name of John Peel, and many of them are doubtless under the impression that the hero of the popular song was a hard-riding huntsman of the old school. Good sportsman as he undoubtedly was, John Peel invariably hunted on foot, and his hounds were what is termed a trencher-fed pack; that is to say, they were, if not the property of different people, at all events fed and housed by them, and so, on hunting mornings, it was necessary for them to be collected from the various farmhouses where they were 'walked,' as it is termed in hunting parlance. Thus Ranter, Ruby, Bellman, True, and Co., had to be sent back to their respective homes after the day's work was over, probably often without escort, and with the inducement to be 'off to kennel' of a crack from the thong of a hunting-whip.

In those days the more hilly districts were

hunted with foxhounds on foot, such a method being rendered necessary to keep down the foxes, owing to the unrideable nature of the country. I have been told that this style of hunting still exists in some parts of the North Country, though I have never been present at any of these gatherings. From what I have been informed respecting them, it would appear that it often takes the best part of a day to kill a fox by such means, and the destruction of the animal must be effected rather by wearing it down than by pace, for which purpose, in order to admit of the field keeping up with them, the hounds used must necessarily be slow.

Although I have hunted with more than one pack over the Border, I have never had the good fortune to see a specimen of the Scotch greyhound foxes. I have been informed that they are immense, long-legged animals, possessed of great speed and strength.

A great number of our foxes at the present time are not the pure English breed. Where the supply has been short, foreign foxes have now and again been imported and turned down, and such an admixture of blood has not been an acquisition, the result being the production of an animal very inferior in pluck and constitution to our own indigenous breed. Continental foxes, like Continental horses, are what is termed 'soft,' and inferior in the stamina and activity which is so characteristic of those bred in these islands.

I am inclined to the belief that where our foxes have been crossed with foreign blood they are less ruddy in colour.

There are few handsomer animals than a well-conditioned English dog-fox, surely, seen at his very best, when, roused from his late slumbers by the approach of the hounds, he jumps up out of the fern with a whisk of his brush, dashes across the woodland ride in the bright sunlight of a February morning, and, stealing away from the covert, makes his point across the green pastures of the shire for his home far away in the beech-woods in the distant hills.

But how sadly changed his appearance an hour later, as, with lolling tongue and heaving sides, he struggles along under the hedgerow! No wretched welsher ever looked more utterly disreputable and miserable. Despite the excitement and pleasure of, it may be, the best and quickest thing of the season, who cannot find it in his heart to wish to save the life of the wretched victim for whose blood the hounds, even now trailing over the last fence, are so furiously thirsting? Game to the last, he tries to double back on the far side of the hedge. Alas! it is too late. A hound has viewed him, turns him into the field, and all is over. To quote Whyte-Melville's well-known lines:

' 'Twas a stout hill fox when they found him;
Now 'tis a hundred tatters of brown.'

It is by no means an uncommon occurrence to find foxes and rabbits inhabiting different parts of the same earth. Our vulpine friend, ever alive to his own interests, is by no means averse to taking up his quarters in a rabbit-hole. Such an arrangement suits his convenience admirably, for not only is he thus spared the trouble of digging out a house for himself, but the requirements of the family larder, where rabbits are plentiful, can be supplied with the smallest amount of trouble.

As the number of rabbits which a single fox is capable of consuming annually is very considerable, it might reasonably be supposed that the rabbits should object to occupy quarters in such close proximity to their natural foes. Fortunately for them, however, with a perversity which is apparently common to man and foxes alike, the latter seem to desire what they have not got in preference to such things as they possess, and so it comes to pass that the neighbouring coverts offer greater attractions for them than those in which they reside, and it may be that the sport afforded by their 'home coverts' lacks the charm which surrounds a more indiscriminate system of poaching.

It is a pretty sight to watch a litter of fox-cubs playing about in the summer evenings—such soft, woolly little animals, full of life and mischief. There were two such happy families within a couple of hundred yards of each other last summer on a farm close to the village in which I reside. Alas! some evil-minded vulpecide contrived to poison the whole of one litter of five. A hare loaded with strychnine was discovered in the earth. I regret to say that the culprit has never been detected. It was a sad sight which the poor little stiffened corpses presented. Popular suspicion attached itself to the keeper of a neighbouring shooting. The man bears an evil reputation, but I am inclined to think that it was rather the work of one of his numerous enemies, as there was no apparent object which he could have for the perpetration of such a dastardly act; and, moreover, I am well aware that, whatever his faults may be, he is careful to preserve foxes for his master. The earth was in dangerous proximity to the farmstead, in which a large number of fowls are reared.

When taken in hand young enough, foxes are very easily tamed, and are most amusing pets, though after a time they are not always to be trusted. One which belonged to some members of my family was exceptionally tame, and used to play fearlessly with the dogs, to one of which it was occasionally coupled. The hounds (foxhounds) were kennelled in another part of the yard, and it was amusing to see him put his head out of his kennel and bark at them as they passed by. Poor little animal! he, like all such pets, came to a sad end by eating a poisoned rat which was accidentally given to him. My earliest recollections are in connection with a tame fox which we as children were in the habit of feeding. A large, beautiful animal he was, too, and lived to a good old age.

Of what a fox is capable may be conjectured by the following anecdote, which, together with an illustration, appeared in one of the principal sporting papers a few years ago : A hunted fox, when passing a farmyard, was seen to snap up and carry off a goose, though at the time the hounds were within but a field of him. On another occasion I happened to be returning from fishing, in the dusk of a September evening, through a stubble-field, at the end of which some few shocks of corn had been purposely left standing. When half across the field, I heard the cries of a leveret in distress, proceeding apparently from the direction of the shocks. I supposed that it must have been caught in a wire. As I neared the place the cries ceased, and it being too dark to see clearly, I lighted a match, and looked in amongst the sheaves, when out darted a fox. I was unable to see if it was carrying anything, but just caught sight of its brush as it whisked round the sheaves on the far side, and bolted off, as I suspected, into a small patch of osiers close at hand. Following it up as quickly as I could, and lighting another match, I heard it break away again, evidently still retaining its hold of the leveret, whose cries were audible until lost in the far distance. A pretty determined piece of poaching, as a September leveret is generally fairly well grown, and, judging from its cries, this one must have been of a good size. The sides of the surrounding hills were teeming with rabbits, and so it may be inferred that foxes evidently prefer to sup on leverets. This very fox, doubtless, had his home in one of the many adjacent gorse-coverts, but was unable to resist the temptation of poaching off his own manor.

I believe it to be a well-acknowledged fact that foxes and dogs at times cross breed with each other. It is stated that the advances in such cases emanate from the vixen, not from the dog, the former coming down into the neighbourhood of the villages. The result of such an intermixture is generally known as a cocktailed fox, from the peculiar way such hybrids carry their brushes.

For some years past English hares have been gradually decreasing in numbers. This is doubtless due, in a great measure, to the Ground Game Act. I was recently informed that, on a manor on the Berkshire hills, formerly the annual scene of one of our principal coursing meetings, and where in those days the hares were so plentiful as to necessitate the thinning of the ground previous to the day's sport, the present supply is insufficient for a coursing meeting at all. I shall never forget the number of hares which had collected in one turnip-field, after the neighbouring downland had been cleared one morning. I was riding up to the meeting, and, being somewhat late, took the shortest route, unintentionally passing close to the ground into which the superfluous hares had been driven. It really seemed as if there were almost as many hares as turnips. Nor will this appear to be any exaggeration to those persons who may have had experience of a Scotch hare drive, or a coursing meeting in the days to which I refer.

I am not particularly enamoured of coursing as a sport, but the remembrance of those meetings is very pleasant. The fresh, pure air of the downland, the ocean of grass, and the kindly hospitality, all combined to render such outings most enjoyable. Then there was the sport itself, even to an outsider not without interest, which deepened as the final ties approached. The number of hares which were killed during the four or five days the meeting lasted was very great. The list of events was a lengthy one, and the 'ties' and 'byes' very rapidly multiplied the original number.

I remember the then honorary secretary of the meeting attracting my attention to the distance at which, under favourable conditions, a hare was visible on the hillsides of the downlands, and his narrating how on one occasion, when riding over the ground with one of the officials previous to a meeting, they noticed what appeared strangely like a hare, though the distance which intervened was too great to admit of such a supposition being possible. As they approached the object, it seemed still more strongly to bear out the resemblance, and eventually, on their reaching it, it got up and galloped away. My informant was the late John Bowles, Esq., of Milton, in Berkshire, whose veracity was, of course, beyond doubt. I fear to state the distance he mentioned from memory, lest I should do so incorrectly, it being so many years ago that I cannot feel certain of being accurate, but it was well-nigh incredible. I only regret, as do all who knew him, that he is no longer living for me to refer to. Of course, the fact of the hare being visible at an extraordinary distance must have been due to a peculiar condition of the atmosphere.

Hares love to squat on the hillsides out of the wind. An east or west wind are those to which they least object, but when a cold north or a rain-laden southerly wind prevails, they betake themselves off to the hedgerows and coverts. The barest-looking ground is often selected by them to lie on, and a hole scratched out on the leeward side of a molehill, or a broken bank, affords comfortable shelter, and there, unless disturbed, they will sit throughout the day, asleep with wide-open eyes, or survey the world around them until it is time to caper off to supper in the turnips. The ears of a hare are singularly adapted for hearing, the size and position of their eyes enabling them to see around and behind them. Strange to say, however, it is easier to approach a hare from in front than from any other direction ; this fact is perhaps due to the position of the eyes, which are situated somewhat on the side of the head, and backward, rather than forward. I think it is Jesse who states, in his ' Gleanings of Natural History,' that it has been asserted that if, when roused, a hare goes away with one ear cocked and the other laid down, she will always beat the dogs, whereas if, as is more usually the case, both ears are laid down, the chances are against her making good her escape ; but I have never proved the truth of this assertion.

Unlike rabbits, hares are born with their eyes open, and are covered with hair. They seem to breed during the greater part of the year. As a rule, they produce two at a birth, though three are by no means uncommon. One naturalist mentions a case in which a hare gave birth to no fewer than seven young ones.

Some few years ago, a labourer, whom I occasionally employed as a hedger, brought a live leveret to me, stating that it was one of three which had been born outside his garden, and informed me that whenever three were produced at a birth they invariably had a white star mark on their foreheads. I was somewhat sceptical as to the truth of this latter statement, but have since ascertained that some naturalists assert it to be a fact. I kept the leveret until it had developed into a full-grown hare, when I gave it away. It grew very tame, and would sit out under the large wire run in front of its house and play with the dogs. The latter used to lie about in the sun close to the cage, the hare drumming at them with its fore-feet. I have often seen a happy family composed of several spaniels round the cage, two cats sitting on the top, several white fantail pigeons, and, not infrequently, some pied-wagtails fearlessly running about on the grass within a few yards.

We are accustomed to regard a hare as one of the most timid of all animals, and in a state of Nature this is the case. When, however, they are kept in confinement, and have been tamed, they not only lose their shyness to a very great extent, but are at times capable of exhibiting an amount of ferocity hardly credible; and instances have been recorded of their having completely beaten off a dog. A relation of mine was well acquainted with a lady in one of our Northern towns who kept two hares, which she had succeeded in taming, and which were very much attached to her. On her return home, after a prolonged absence of some three or four months, and visiting her pets, they had, apparently, not only lost their affection for her, but attacked her in so savage and determined a manner that she was forced to beat a retreat. I have every reason to believe in the absolute truth of this statement.

Unlike rabbits hares prefer solitude. It is an

almost unknown thing to put up two hares which have 'seated' together. Even the young ones, as soon as they are weaned, appear to separate themselves, and will lie couched some fifty or sixty yards away from the doe. In hilly countries hares prefer to lie as near to the top of a hill as the weather permits of their doing. The reason for this is probably because the length of their hind-legs enables them to travel uphill better than down. When, however, they are forced to take downhill, feeling their inability to descend in a straight line, they invariably travel in an oblique direction. If pressed hard down a very steep incline, they are apt, at times, to turn head over heels. It is unusual to find hares 'seated' under a hedgerow, except in stormy weather, when no other protection is at hand. As a rule, they prefer to make their 'forms' in the centre of a field, probably for greater security. In mild, drizzly weather they generally move up to the higher grounds, or seek the shelter of a gorse bush.

As everyone is aware, a hare is capable of giving a pack of hounds infinitely more trouble to kill than a fox. It is the exception for a hare to run straight away from hounds for any great distance, though occasionally it will take a line as straight as that of a fox. The account of a run with some harriers in one of our Eastern counties, in which, after affording a rattling gallop, the hare took out to sea in the Wash, was recorded in the *Field*. The pack referred to was kept by a relation of mine. For those people who are able to appreciate the hunting and working of hounds, hare-hunting affords greater opportunities for witnessing the intricate difficulties of hunting by scent than any similar description of sport. The man who is able to handle harriers well and successfully should be able to circumvent a fox, although the tactics of the two animals pursued are different; for whereas a forward cast will generally succeed in hitting off the line of a fox, when hounds are at fault, nine times out of ten it is on one of the backward casts that the true line of a hare will be found. It may well be said that the direction a lost hare has taken will most surely be the one which appears least likely. It is the constant 'doubling' on scent which renders hare-hunting so difficult. The best pack of harriers I have ever seen at work is one belonging to Mr. Jeffreys. In colour they are black and tan, owing to a strong infusion of the bloodhound cross. These hounds, which are notorious, are excellently well handled by their owner, who contrives to account for an incredible number of hares in the course of the season. They are somewhat light-limbed, very speedy, and possess the most wondrous noses. No matter what the weather or country may be, they can pick up a scent where other hounds could not run for a yard, and even in the driest fallow or road in March; I should say that they could kill a fox, if entered to such a quarry, equally well.

Hare-shooting is but poor sport, and very inferior, even under the best circumstances, to good rabbit-shooting—at all events, in my own estimation. To miss a hare within easy distance in the open is inexcusable, and to shoot at one at a doubtful range still more so. To have to carry it when shot is not a labour of love. Under such circumstances it is better not to shoot at all. Many a time have I had reason to abuse myself for having been foolish enough to shoot a hare when there was no one present with me to carry it. I am very much inclined to the opinion that, unless coursed or hunted, a hare is by no means deserving of the repute in which it is held for table purposes, and there is, moreover, comparatively little of its flesh worth eating. The following method of preparing a hare may possibly be found useful, viz. : After skinning the animal, immerse it in vinegar and water with a few juniper-berries for twelve or, better still, twenty-four hours previous to roasting. By this means it will be found to be little if at all inferior to a coursed or hunted hare.

> 'Si vespertinus subitò te oppresserit hospes,
> Ne gallina malùm responset dura palato,
> Doctus eris vivam misto mersare Falerno :
> Hoc teneram faciet.'
> HORACE : *Satirarum*, II. iv.

Hare skins are useful for a variety of purposes. The country people make them into waistcoats, chest-protectors, etc. The fur from the face and ears forms an admirable body, either natural or dyed, for certain trout-flies, such as the 'rough olive dun,' 'blue dun,' 'sedge flies,' etc. The hind-feet are most useful for oiling guns and such-like articles. They were in former days much used by those ladies who preferred to supply the complexion which they lacked by a liberal use of the rouge pot; and the bones of the hind-legs, when scraped and polished, are capable of being converted into very handsome cigarette-holders. So, all things considered, a hare may be said to be a most useful animal.

Besides hunting, coursing, or shooting, various illegitimate methods are employed in capturing hares, most commonly that known as 'wiring,' to my mind detestable in every sense of the word. A person well skilled in setting a hare-wire can make pretty certain of success. It is, however, a practice usually confined to the poaching fraternity, who are far more skilful in the use of a wire than keepers. An experienced eye can very readily detect the difference between a poacher's and a keeper's wire, whether the latter is set for hares or rabbits. An old hand can utilize a bramble with nearly as certain effect as a wire, and with far less fear of detection, always provided that there happens to be a bramble growing near enough to the run of a hare for the purpose. It is somewhat difficult to explain, without the aid of an illustration, the difference between a wire set by a keeper and that set by a poacher; but if the two are compared, the difference is very perceptible. Keepers twist their wires far too much, as a general rule, and although they present a very much neater appearance, they are not nearly as destructive; their wires, too, are generally hand-twisted. A skilful poacher never twists his wires by hand, and is careful not to touch the wire more than he can help during its manufacture, using for the purpose of twisting the strands a weight which is attached to each separate one, and by moving which the necessary degree of twist is imparted, ever taking care to make the twist as slight as possible. A poacher is well aware of the value of an old wire, always provided it is sound and good, preferring it to a new one. The general effect of the wire when set may to an inexperienced eye appear clumsy, but a closer inspection will show the care and skill with which it has been laid. Keepers, as a rule, set wires to catch rabbits or hares for their employers, whereas poachers do so for themselves. On one occasion, when shooting with a friend, we took up some thirty or forty rabbit-wires which had been set by a poacher; and the next day my friend found a basket containing upwards of forty more, all of which he gave to an old man in his employ. Curiously enough, we afterwards discovered that these wires had been set by the grandson of the man to whom they were given, who, of course, was not a little pleased to have his property restored to him.

Another method of taking hares adopted by poachers and the lower class of gipsies, is to place a net across a gateway through which hares are known to pass, and then to send a trained lurcher into the adjoining fields to beat up the hares. Calling hares by means of a hare-call, and then shooting them or suddenly slipping a lurcher on them, are plans occasionally pursued. An ordinary tobacco-pipe, provided it has a mouth-piece, makes an excellent call-pipe. The call is produced by pressing the mouthpiece against the lips, which must be nearly closed, sucking in the air, placing the ball of the thumb on the bowl of the pipe, and again quickly removing it. It is easy to produce the required sound with a very little practice.

Since writing the foregoing, I witnessed the following, which I think may perhaps interest the reader : On the afternoon of Easter Day, 1895, I was walking in the water-meadows in front of my house in company with my wife and a friend who had two well-broken retrievers with him. My wife left us, returning home by a bridge which spans the river intervening between my house and the meadows, and which is at that point some forty or fifty yards in width, the current being strong and deep. For some days previously I had noticed a hare in the meadow, and on this occasion she jumped up some two hundred yards from where we were standing in the centre of the field, raced round the meadow, and eventually made straight for the river. The dogs had remained perfectly steady at heel, though fully aware of what was going on. Without the slightest hesitation she plunged boldly out into the stream, swam rapidly across, and scampered up the bank, when, seeing my wife, who had been watching the performance, she turned aside and bolted away through the garden. I regret to say that she has not since reappeared in the meadows. It was strange that she should have elected to swim so broad a river in preference to making her escape by either of the two sides of the field which lay open to her, more especially since she had not been chased or unduly disturbed in any way. The meadow is a large one, bounded on one side by the river in question, and on another by a small tributary stream. The animal did not appear particularly frightened either before or after her voyage. She may, perhaps, have been suffering from the insanity to which March hares are proverbially supposed to be addicted! It was certainly a somewhat eccentric and unaccountable performance.

Without rabbits the majority of sportsmen would be nowhere. Not only do they afford excellent sport, but they very materially assist in filling the game-bag on an ordinary estate. I think I may safely assert that no other of our British wild animals is able to equal the rabbit in prolificacy. That they are terribly destructive is too sadly true ; but they are cheery, happy little creatures, and their presence is capable of adding considerably to the homeliness and interest of any park, which, if devoid of rabbits, always seems to be wanting in life. It is pleasant to see them capering away when disturbed, their little white ' scuts ' bobbing up and down, and still more so to watch them at play in the summer evenings ; but it is necessary to keep concealed and well below the wind, it being far easier to approach them in the open with the wind in one's face than to stalk them under covert with a side or down wind. Their senses are very acute, more especially those of hearing and smelling. The larder of a country house is but ill furnished without a supply of rabbits; fortunately there are but few months in the year when they are not procurable. It has been estimated that the descendants of but a single couple of rabbits, provided they all attain to maturity, will in the space of four years reach nearly a million in number. This is, however, an impossibility, inasmuch as not more than half of each litter live to grow to any size. That rabbits do increase and multiply exceedingly is indisputable. They have several litters annually, the number of these depending much upon the weather. If the spring is mild and open, they begin to breed as early as the end of February, and continue to do so until the end of September, and frequently still later on into the autumn.

They are, perhaps, at their best for the table during the earlier months of winter, after a few frosts. About March their ears become covered with a minute kind of black flea, and when these appear it is a sign that they are commencing to breed, and are therefore less suitable for food. Their size and quality depend very greatly on the nature of the ground which they inhabit, a light dry, sandy soil being the best; the drier and lighter the better they will thrive, always provided that there is an ample supply of food. In wet, low-lying lands they never attain to any great weight, and are, moreover, very subject to become what is termed by the country people 'coed,' which is, I believe, a corruption of the word 'cothered,' meaning a diseased state of the liver. It is easy to ascertain when a rabbit is thus affected, inasmuch as the animal presents a thriftless, lanky appearance, and if grasped by the hand across the loins it will be observed that there is an absence of flesh and firmness in that region. Any doubt there may be on the subject may very readily be removed when the animal is paunched, as the liver will be seen to be covered with white spots—*i.e.*, tubercles. Of course, rabbits thus diseased are unfit for food. Nevertheless, numbers are doubtless sold in the markets which are in this condition, but from which the livers have been purposely removed. The disease is more prevalent during a wet season. I do not know if rabbits suffering from it ever recover, but I should consider it highly improbable. Rabbits in warrens which are overstocked and have become tainted are also liable to this disease. Sir R. Payne-Gallwey, in his valuable work on shooting, states that it is a wise plan to kill down every rabbit on an estate from time to time, and to restock with animals from a different district; I am inclined to believe that such a system is most advisable, and conducive to the propagation of good healthy stock. It takes a very short time to restock a manor with rabbits. Many years ago, on the estate of a relation of mine situated in Lincolnshire, there were absolutely no rabbits. Being desirous of restocking the ground, he procured some rabbits from one of the Midland counties, and turned them down. In the course of a very few years they had increased in number to such an extent as to ruin the pasturage of the park, and it has since then been a matter of the greatest difficulty to keep them at all within reasonable limits. The soil, being of a light, sandy nature, is most suitable, and they are notorious for their size and the excellent quality of their flesh, fetching a high price in the market. Lincolnshire, Cambridgeshire, Norfolk, and Suffolk are, perhaps, of all our counties, most suitable for rabbit-breeding; next to these the chalky downlands of Kent, Sussex, Hants, and Wilts. Such soils provide the conditions which are essential for the purpose, being light, dry, and easily burrowed.

I have recently seen a statement to the effect that rabbits which have once been domesticated relinquish their burrowing propensities, an assertion which I do not believe to be true; indeed, I am well aware that such is not the case, having had every opportunity of witnessing the havoc wrought by some three or four tame rabbits which, after having been kept in confinement for a considerable time, were permitted their liberty in the back of a small garden in one of our Northern towns. In a very short space of time they had formed burrows in every direction, and succeeded in so completely undermining one of the walls as to render it unsafe. It is the natural habit of a rabbit to burrow, and I do not for an instant believe that any amount of domestication would eradicate this tendency if the animals were subsequently enlarged. I refer, of course, to pure wild rabbits, which may have been domesticated, and not to the lop-eared and other fancy breeds. Where white rabbits have been turned down in a park, they make burrows in the same way as their commoner coloured brethren. There are generally a few specimens of the black variety to be found on every manor. I am, however, inclined to consider their flesh inferior to that of the common grey rabbit.

Despite their size, tame rabbits are never of a very delicate flavour, and much the same may be said of those kept in movable hutches.

Much has been written on the subject of rabbit-farming by means of hutches. Under exceptionally favourable conditions it is, I believe, possible to make it a profitable industry. I have been informed that, after three or four years, unless the ground available is of large extent and the hutches constantly shifted, the soil becomes tainted and disease makes its appearance ; and this appears to me to be highly probable. It is, too, very doubtful whether the ground could not be more profitably utilized. For a time such a system would prove useful for the purpose of improving a rough pasture, as rabbits are close feeders, and the manure might also serve to enrich the ground ; but during the period of actual occupation the latter would be unsuitable for other grazing purposes, since neither cattle nor sheep will feed well on a tainted soil, though in process of time a finer and better description of grass is said to be produced from pastures which have been eaten down by rabbits.

Unlike hares, rabbits, when born, are blind and hairless. The buck, like the jack hare, evinces the same antipathy to the young ones during the earlier stages of their existence, and will not hesitate to destroy them unless the doe is careful to conceal them.

The well-known naturalist Ray asserts that hedge-rabbits do not burrow to the same extent as the warreners, as they are called. It may appear presumptuous to gainsay the opinion of such an authority, but I am very much inclined to doubt the assertion, for that hedge-rabbits burrow freely is indisputable. Where the undergrowth is thick and affords suitable covert, they are more in the habit of sitting out than other rabbits, and that they should do so is hardly to be wondered at. The drier and softer the lying in hedgerows, the more frequently they will 'form.' Wherever long, soft grass exists beneath the shelter of a holly or gorse-bush the 'form' of a hedge-rabbit may generally be found. The condition of the bank of any old hedgerow which has been tenanted by rabbits, when cleared for the purpose of 'pleaching' or 'laying' the fence, as it is termed, reveals the extent to which hedge-rabbits are capable of burrowing.

In those woodlands where rabbits are abundant, it becomes necessary, in order to destroy them, to have recourse to the use of ferrets; for with the fall of the leaf they take to their burrows, and but comparatively few of them show themselves during the day-time. Should a fall of snow intervene it is easy to form a pretty accurate estimate of the stock, the numerous tracks plainly indicating where the merry conies disported themselves in the moonlight during the previous night.

It is most amusing to watch rabbits at play in the summer evenings, from the concealment afforded by some neighbouring bush. At the least sign of danger they sit up on their hind-legs, with ears erect and their large, soft, dark eyes wide open. Can any sight be prettier? Who could be heartless enough to take the life of these creatures under such circumstances? Strange though it may appear, should one of these very rabbits dash across the hill, or get up in the open field in front of me, I am quite sure that, if I had a gun with me, I should do my best to knock it over. Such a feeling is, I suppose, indicative of one's sporting instincts. Circumstances alter cases. To shoot any game sitting is an undoubtedly low action, and unworthy of a true sportsman.

The instant a rabbit has reason to become apprehensive of danger, he strikes hard on the ground with his hind-leg in order to give warning to his brethren and kinsfolk to be on the lookout and prepare to make tracks, which they do to the utmost of their ability. Confidence being once more restored, they come hopping out again from the edges of the covert, now and again stopping to nibble a few mouthfuls of grass ; then a few long hops and another halt, until they have proceeded as far as they think prudent.

Where the soil is light and keepers are slack in the performance of their duties, rabbits get terribly poached, it being the easiest thing in the world for a man single-handed, with the aid of a dog, to procure as many as he may desire. The dog hunts the rabbit to ground, or else shows the hole where one may be, and an iron bar or an ordinary hedgestake very soon works a passage down to the rabbit large enough for the dog to work in, or for the insertion of an arm, when out comes the wretched bunny. A quick, dexterous twist with the hand ends his woes, and the next minute he is reposing in the depths of a hare-pocket, or hidden away 'to be left till called for.' If anyone is seen approaching, it is an easy matter to throw away the stick and brush down the dog with a wisp of grass.

The occasional gift of rabbits to the poorer village people is most acceptable to them. Such little kindnesses are ever well bestowed, and much appreciated. They form a welcome addition to the daily fare, and I know, from experience, that the man who is liberal with his rabbits need have little fear of poachers. At one time I rented some shooting which was bounded by an open road over the downs. It was merely rough and furzy rabbit-shooting. On the other side of the road was a similar shooting belonging to a friend of mine, but who was none too liberal in the distribution of his rabbits amongst the villagers. My own rabbits were rarely, if ever, interfered with, whereas those on his side were poached in the most indiscriminate manner. There were no keepers employed on either side, and from the situation and aspect of the other shooting, rabbits should have been far more plentiful than on my own land. I conclude that the village people, knowing that they were sure to get rabbits given them by me, thought it as well to leave my shooting alone, and being equally sure that they were not likely to get any from my friend, thought it as well to help themselves, and did so, as I am aware, having more than once witnessed the performance, which I, of course, duly reported.

I may as well here remark, for the benefit of the uninitiated, that the sooner a rabbit is paunched after being killed, the better. Good as rabbits are when properly treated and dressed, they are well-nigh uneatable if allowed to remain unpaunched, even for a single night. Of course, as every sportsman is well aware, it is the general custom for keepers to thus prepare them before they are taken to the house. Even then a careless or ignorant servant may completely ruin them by hanging them too closely together. This last remark applies equally to all game, which should ever be kept well separated in the larder.

It has of late years been frequently the custom to cross our English rabbits with foreign blood, with a view to increasing their size, and this it undoubtedly does; all the same, I very much doubt if such crossings have improved their sporting qualities. Although I fully believe in the value of fresh blood from time to time, I nevertheless consider that a more sporting animal is produced without such foreign infusion, even though it may be inferior in size and weight, and infinitely handsomer. It has been stated that rabbits are not indigenous to Great Britain. This may be the case. But it is so many centuries since they were imported, and they have taken so readily to us and thriven so remarkably well, that I think we may regard them as truly British.

DWELLERS IN FIELDS.

PART II.

Polecats—Probable Origin of Ferrets—Stoats and Weasels—Curious Recovery of a Lost Ferret—A Gipsy Ferret—A Lost Ferret—Ferrets in Houses—Method of keeping Rats out of a House—Martens—Squirrels—Rats—Poisonous Effect of Rat-bites—The Black Rat—The Brown Rat—Goldsmith on the Brown Rat—Black and Brown Rats—Disappearance of the Black Rat—Rats and Snakes—The Water-vole—Fights between a Brown Rat and a Water-vole—Appearance of Water-voles indicative of Bad Sport when Fishing—Persecution of the Water-vole—Rodents—Shrews—Varieties of Shrews—Superstitions regarding Shrews—A Shrew Ash—Superstitious Days—A Gipsy's Curse—A 'Rampike' Tree—Origin of the Word 'Shrew'—Persecution of Shrews—Mortality amongst Shrews—The Common Shrew—Pugnacity of Shrews—Peculiarities observable in the Teeth of Shrews—Distinguishing Characteristics of the Common Shrew—Characteristics of the Water-shrew—The Oared Shrew—Shrews compared with the Mole—The Mole—Utility of Moles—Foxes feeding on Moles—Underground Dwellings of Moles—Mole-catching—The Hedgehog—Superstition regarding the Hedgehog—Gipsy Method of cooking Hedgehogs—Indian Method of cooking Fowls—Torpidity of Hedgehogs during Winter—Cruelty to Hedgehogs—Hedgehog not an Ugly Animal—Varieties of Wild Animals in Britain—The Otter—Trapping Otters—

Tame Otters—Training Otters—Accusations made against Otters—Otters asserted not to be Fish-poachers—' Quodding ' for Eels—Otters Fish-poachers—Toughness of Otter's Skin—Sport and Cruelty—Powers and Pluck of Otters—The Ear of an Otter—Size of Otters—Derivation of Word 'Otter'—Inland and Sea Otters the same—British Bats—Common British Bats—The Great Bat—Greater Horseshoe Bat—Smaller Horseshoe Bat—Long-eared Bat—The Common Bat—Common and Rare British Bats—Barbastelle Bat—Whiskered Bat—Reddish-gray Bat—Daubenton's Bat—Notch-eared Bat—Mouse-coloured Bat—Bechstein's Bat—Serotine Bat—Hairy-armed Bat—Parti-coloured Bat—Probable Importation of some of our Rarest Bats—The Cheiroptera—A Mixed Bag—Descriptive Table of British Bats.

OF all the many enemies of the rabbit, the polecat is, perhaps, the one which it has most cause to fear. Fortunately, these animals are by no means as common as formerly, for although, like the rest of their species, they do good in helping to keep down rats, mice, and such-like vermin, they are terrible poachers. Bewick states that a couple of polecats are capable of exterminating the entire stock of rabbits in a warren. The same naturalist asserts that, in addition to the depredations these animals commit by killing game, poultry, etc., they also do not scruple to take eels, in proof of which he narrates the following anecdote, the truth of which he vouches for : ' During a severe storm one of these animals was traced in the snow from the side of a rivulet to its hole, at some distance from it. As it was observed to have made frequent trips, and as other marks were to be seen in the snow which could not easily be accounted for, it was thought a matter worthy of great attention. Its hole was accordingly examined, the foumart (*i.e.*, the polecat) taken, and eleven fine eels were discovered to be the fruits of its nocturnal excursions. The marks in the snow were found to have been made by the motion of the eels in the creature's mouth.' Jardine states that a polecat will not scruple to kill even turkeys and geese. It is doubtless very strong, active, and courageous. They are more common in the wilder districts of Britain, more especially in the Northern counties; keepers, not unnaturally, grant them but scant mercy, and ere long they will probably become extinct. There is no created thing without its use, though we may at times find it somewhat difficult to realize the fact, there being some forms of animal life which, so far as our limited knowledge extends, appear to be incapable of doing anything but harm. But even the polecat is not without some good qualities, despite its destructive propensities, for it not only destroys a certain amount of other vermin, but enables us to benefit by its very ferocity, inasmuch as our breed of ferrets has been very considerably improved by being crossed with the polecat. Such ferrets are ever the best, though perhaps less tractable than the white variety. It is asserted by naturalists that our ferrets were imported from Spain, to which country they came from Africa. Were it not that the stoat changes its colour, very much according to the season, that it is an animal more or less unaffected by cold, it would seem probable that our breed of ferrets may have had its origin in a cross between the polecat and the stoat. Ferrets are, however, very sensitive to cold, and require to be carefully housed during severe weather in order to keep them in health. This has reference more particularly to the white ferrets than to those which, having been crossed with the polecat, are similar to that animal in colour, and are more generally powerful and hardy.

Keepers and others are very apt to confound the stoat, or ermine, as it is sometimes termed, with the weasel, although the difference between the two is very marked. The weasel, called by the country-folk 'wizzle,' is not nearly as large as the stoat; though similar in shape, its colour is more decidedly ruddy than the stoat, nor does it change its colour. The habits of both animals are much the same, but the stoat is the more powerful. Both do good by destroying rats and mice, etc., and both do harm, being inveterate poachers, destroying game and poultry whenever they get the chance. It is asserted by some authorities that they do not hunt by scent. This can hardly be the case, since they will follow a rabbit or leveret through dense covert, and steadily hunt it down, when they seize it by the back of the head, and speedily destroy it. Apart from size and change of colour, they differ very greatly in two particulars, the tail of the stoat being much longer than that of the weasel, and invariably, even when the fur has changed to white, tipped with black. The stoat is the true ermine, whose skin is esteemed so valuable. It is, however, not the British species which is used by the furriers, but one which is imported from Northern Europe, the fur of the foreign variety being far whiter and superior in every respect to that of the British, which is, moreover, not sufficiently plentiful at any period of the year to supply demand. A somewhat curious incident occurred when I happened to be rabbit-shooting with a friend during the earlier part of the present season. We were trying some small gorse-bushes, situated on the side of a hill, when a stoat was observed making away across the valley. One of the party fired at it, but missed it, and before he could approach near enough to give it another barrel it effected its escape. Some weeks previously an old man, who was employed as a warrener, had lost one of his best ferrets in this valley, and although he had constantly searched and set traps in the hopes of recapturing it, he had been unsuccessful. Almost immediately after the stoat had escaped from the gorse - bush, we observed a great commotion amongst some of the dogs in that identical bush, and supposed that they had caught a rabbit. On one of the beaters proceeding to the spot, he discovered that it was the lost ferret, which was doing its best to protect itself from the dogs. Fortunately it was but very slightly injured, and rapidly recovered. It was strange that both the stoat and the ferret should have been together in the same bush.

Some three summers ago, when the hay was being made in a small water-meadow belonging to me, a labourer informed me that he had noticed one of my ferrets in the bank of a hedgerow which bounded the field. Not having any ferrets of my own, I was somewhat at a loss to understand how a ferret could have found its way into a field which was on all sides surrounded by streams. Searching the hedgerow, I discovered a small polecat ferret threading its way through the bushes. Observing me, it bolted into a rathole, but on my whistling to it it reappeared, and after several attempts I succeeded in catching it. I was holding it somewhat carelessly with my right hand, while talking to the man who had accompanied me, forgetting that my left hand was quite close to the ferret, which seized me by the thumb, biting me severely, and refused to let go its hold until it had been pretty sharply tapped on the muzzle. I concluded that it belonged to the old warrener previously referred to, whose cottage was within a quarter of a mile distant. I accordingly sent it over to him. He afterwards informed me that the ferret was not his property, but had belonged to some gipsies who had been encamped near the village some few weeks previously; that he had known of its being loose, and had tried repeatedly, though unsuccessfully, to catch it. I suspected that it was probably a good animal of its kind, from the fact of its having belonged to the gipsies, and it proved to be one of the very best ferrets I ever used. I gave it to the old man with the understanding that I was always to have the use of it when I required it, but I regret to say that it was used for the purpose of driving some rats out of the floor of a barn, and, being overmatched by them, met its death, greatly to my sorrow, for it was remarkably gentle and tame, and we were able to use it constantly without a muzzle, as it never laid up and would come readily to call.

On a previous occasion I had employed the same old warrener to ferret out some rabbits which had taken up their quarters in one of the down hillsides about a mile away from the village. We had three ferrets at work, and all three had, apparently, laid up, having stupidly been put in unmuzzled. The evening was drawing on apace, and it was bitterly cold. Just as we were preparing to leave, having given up all hopes of recovering any of the three ferrets, and the position of the earth being such as to render it impossible for us to dig down to them, we succeeded in recapturing two out of the number. We waited till we could no longer see, and were compelled to leave the missing ferret to take its chance, in the hopes that we might recover it in the morning; but for two days nothing was to be seen of it. At the end of that time it was discovered in the back premises of the village butcher. It must have made its way over a long stretch of downland, and through part of the village. It had been doubtless attracted to that particular spot by the scent of the slaughter-house, having probably, in the first instance, made its way back to the village for warmth, or to return to its home.

It is a terrible thing to lose a ferret in a house where it has been found necessary to dislodge rats which may have taken up their abode therein, for there is no knowing when or where the animal may reappear, and so the whole establishment is kept in a state of excitement, fearful lest it should emerge in the night and fasten on some member of the household when asleep, and not a little apprehensive that it may become wedged in amongst some portion of the building, and, dying there, render the house uninhabitable for the time being. I once thus lost a ferret in my house, though I was fortunate enough to recover it alive by cutting a hole in the ceiling of one of the upper rooms. We had been considerably annoyed by the rats, and I was at a loss to know what to do, for I feared to again make use of ferrets in so ancient a building. Eventually I thought of a plan, which succeeded so admirably that I think it worth while to inform my readers. Being aware that, for a long time after a house has been ferreted, rats will not enter it, it occurred to me that this fact must, of course, be due in a great measure to the scent of the ferrets. I therefore procured some litter from a hutch in which ferrets were kept, and had it pushed as far as possible into every rat-hole we could find, afterwards closing up the holes with any suitable substance at hand. This plan had the desired effect, and for nearly two years not a single rat attempted to invade the premises.

The foregoing is a simple remedy. There was no smell whatever apparent from the litter, but had there been such it would have been far preferable to the annoyance and damage caused by the rats. I had previously tried the effect of poison, but the result was too dreadful for me to desire to repeat the performance, as the rats, dying behind the wainscots and panellings of the rooms, necessitated our leaving the house for a time.

I only wonder that this remedy which suggested itself to me is not generally adopted. It is doubtless satisfactory to destroy all the rats which may infest one's premises, but since 'prevention is better than cure,' it is surely far more so to keep them away altogether.

It is to be regretted that martens are becoming so scarce in England, for although it cannot be denied that they are excessively mischievous and dire poachers, they are such beautiful little animals that we can ill afford to spare them altogether. They are now rare, except in the wilder districts of Scotland and North Wales, etc. I fear that, despite their beauty, their vices exceed their virtues, and so the keepers do their best to exterminate them, and, it cannot be denied, with very sufficient reason. At one time it was supposed that there were two varieties of martens in Britain, viz., the pine or yellow-throated, and the common or beech-martin. Modern naturalists have, however, determined that both are one and the same animal. The fur of these animals, especially the foreign variety, is of considerable value, being dense, soft, and long. The tail is very similar to that of a squirrel. From the names 'pine' and 'beech' it might reasonably be supposed that the martens are chiefly addicted to living, like the squirrels, in trees. Such is not the case, as they really spend more of their time on the ground than in trees, and will, even when hunted by dogs, rather avoid than take to a tree, though when hard pressed they will do so.* The marten appears to be a link between the stoat and the squirrel, its shape partaking very much of both animals; but as far as its carnivorous propensities are concerned, its habits resemble those of the stoat. It is to be regretted that in this particular it is not equally blameless with the squirrel; it might, perhaps, under such conditions, be less liable to persecution. Not that the poor squirrel is by any

* A connection of mine, when living in Wales, used to hunt the marten, using a couple or two of foxhounds for the purpose.

means exempt from the latter, nor can I, with every desire to protect it, assert that it is entirely innocent of wrong-doing. But its sins are comparatively few; so beautiful and graceful an animal may surely be forgiven the minor offences of which it is guilty, and, after all, a hundred squirrels are not as destructive as a single hare or rabbit. And so I can find it in my heart to plead for these lovable little animals, and it grieves me sorely to see their dead bodies adorning the keeper's tree or the barn-door, in company of such miscreants as stoats, weasels, magpies, etc. The chief misdemeanour of which squirrels are guilty is the damage which they inflict on young trees, larches especially, for they wantonly attack the leading shoots, and so ruin the trees. Still, they might be spared where the trees are of such a description as to be exempt from their attacks. As a rule, when there are plenty of hazels, and nuts are abundant, they are less mischievous. It is at the time when their winter store is exhausted that their onslaughts on young trees are most severe. It has been asserted that squirrels lie dormant throughout the winter, but this everyone conversant with the habits of these animals is well aware is not the case. I have frequently seen them skipping about in the snow, even during the most severe weather, in the North of England. They doubtless do sleep a great deal in the winter months, but not to the extent generally supposed. The brush of a squirrel, like that of a fox, serves to keep him warm, and is doubtless given to these animals for that purpose as well as for adornment. Where there are trees suitable for the purpose, squirrels prefer to make their nests in some hollow trunk, but in fir-woods they build large untidy-looking nests of moss, grass, and leaves, etc. My memory reverts to the days when, as a boy, I used to roam through the fir-woods around Eridge Castle, in Kent. There was surely never such a place for all sorts of birds and animals, and it was the greatest delight to me to spend a half-holiday there. Game was most abundant, despite the number of jays, magpies, etc., and squirrels were more than plentiful. It was delightful to see them bound from one tree to another, across the grass rides of the woodlands, lighting on the spray of a fir-tree, which, apparently all too slender to bear them, swayed up and down with their light weight. There is to me always something very comical about a squirrel, as he stops to take stock of an intruder; then, scampering along a bough, stops again, with a merry twinkle in his eye, as if to say, 'You can't catch me,' though one longs to do so, and to play a game of romps with the agile, happy little creature, and to cuddle it up in one's arms, for it looks so soft and warm. I should feel myself a brute indeed were I capable of harming it. What greater cruelty can there be than to confine such a creature in a cage? Its every look and gesture betokens an intense love of freedom. Such an instrument of torture as a squirrel's cage is, too! I wish with all my heart that there were no such things as cages for birds or animals. Let them be tamed by all means, where it is possible to do so without permanent deprivation of freedom. 'Live, and let live,' should be the motto of every lover of Nature. Rats and mice and such-like vermin must, of course, be kept under, or we ourselves should be nowhere. I am afraid that, with respect to rats, I hold them in such intense abhorrence as to show them but scant mercy. They interest, though they sicken me. It has frequently been my ill-fortune to reside in districts where they have been unusually numerous. Whilst professing the most sincere love for birds and beasts generally, I can never resist killing a rat or a snake, and in so doing I consider that I am rendering a public service, especially if the snake be of a poisonous kind. And the bite of a rat is at times wellnigh as harmful as that of an adder, for although its effects may not be so rapidly manifested, they are frequently most serious. Much, of course, depends upon the health and habits of the person bitten, as also upon the substance upon which the rat may have been previously feeding. Some two or three instances of blood-poisoning from the bite of a rat have come to my knowledge during the past few years. Two of these cases nearly proved fatal. In one instance a farmer, observing a rat in a trap, incautiously put his hand on the spring in order to release it, without having taken the precaution to first despatch it, the result being that the rat bit him severely. He became seriously ill, and for many weeks was in a most critical condition. He happened to be a man of somewhat intemperate habits, and this fact doubtless aggravated the evil effects of the poison. In the same parish another farmer, a particularly temperate man, and apparently possessed of an iron constitution, when ferreting for rabbits, put his hand into a hole for the purpose of dragging out a rabbit, and was severely bitten by a rat. For a time his life was despaired of, and it was fully two years before he recovered his health; indeed, he has never completely done so.

As I have before remarked, it is very much to be doubted if, when the original English rat, the black variety, was exterminated by the present breed, the brown, we did not suffer considerably by the exchange. As may be supposed, from the fact of the brown rat having exterminated its predecessor, the former is the more powerful and larger of the two—and, it may be added, far less lovable, for the black rat was a really handsome animal, especially when compared with the present reptilious-looking quadruped—and, being larger and more powerful, the brown rat is capable of more harm. I can only remember having once seen a specimen of the black rat, and that was kept in confinement. I very much doubt if it would be possible to procure a single specimen of this rat at the present time. It would be, at all events, a very difficult matter. Such few specimens as may from time to time be procured, I believe, come from Scotland. I have spoken of this rat as the original British rat; such is, however, not exactly the case, since it is stated to have been brought over to this country from the Continent, having doubtless escaped from foreign merchant vessels when in port. Most naturalists, however, agree in considering that, whatever vices the black rat may have possessed, they were inferior to those of its successor.

Goldsmith states that the brown rat first made its appearance on the coasts of Ireland, having been brought thither by ships which traded between that country and Gibraltar; whereas Buffon asserts that it came to us from the southern regions of Asia; Jardine, that it is supposed to have been introduced from Persia and the East Indies about 1730, and gradually to have spread over the greater part of the Continent of Europe, as well as America, by means of the frequent commercial intercourse established between the nations of these regions. Other naturalists term it the Norwegian rat, by reason of its being supposed to have come from Norway. I think that this latter suggestion is the most probable, but from wheresoever it may have come to us, its presence is most undesirable. I think that, in addition to its many other sins, it may be credited with being the cause of numberless deaths annually by working its way into drains, and so allowing the escape of sewage and foul gases into dwellings, as well as by a similar process occasioning the contamination of wells, etc., to say nothing of the serious injury sustained by buildings by reason of their becoming undermined. Altogether it is a loathsome and dangerous animal, and does infinitely more harm than good. I for one should be only too glad to know that every brown rat in the country was exterminated.

Goldsmith writes of the brown rat as follows: 'In a very few years after its arrival, it found means to destroy almost the whole species [*i.e.*, the black rat], and to possess itself of their retreats. All other animals of inferior strength shared the same fate. The frog had been designedly introduced into Ireland some years before the Norway rat, and was seen to multiply exceedingly. The Irish were pleased at the introduction of a harmless animal, which served to rid their fields of insects; but the Norway rat soon put a stop to their increase, for, as they were of an amphibious nature, they pursued the frog to its lakes, and took it even in its own natural element. The Norway rat has the same disposition to injure us, with much greater powers of mischief than the black rat. . . . Scarcely any of the feeble animals escape its rapacity except the mouse, which shelters itself in its little hole, where the

Norway rat is too big to follow. Luckily, they eat and destroy each other, or else their fecundity would soon cause them to overrun the whole country. The large male rat generally lives in a hole by itself, and is dreaded by its own species as the most formidable enemy.'

In an editor's note in Goldsmith's work, it is asserted that the natural antipathy commonly supposed to exist between the black and the brown rats is an error, and that the latter do not necessarily exclude the former from their vicinity, but that the two species often live under the same shelter in contiguous burrows.

With such conflicting opinions, it would appear somewhat difficult to account for the disappearance of the black rat. I think, however, that it may be fairly assumed that the brown rat ousted and devoured his predecessor. These two animals not only differ very considerably in size and colour, but the tail of the black rat is proportionately longer and more slender. I do not think, from all I am able to gather regarding it, that the latter is as fearless of taking the water as the brown rat.

One's antipathies must increase with age. I can hardly credit nowadays that in my boyhood I kept a pet rat, or ever handled snakes with impunity ; but such was the case. The rat was caged in my desk at school, and I have a very distinct recollection of having filled the pockets of my jacket with slow-worms. Nothing would induce me to handle either the one or the other at the present time, still less could I be capable of feeling any affection for either. Nor do I think that residence in India sufficed to lessen the intense loathing which I entertain for rats and snakes. Were it not for these and such-like creatures, India would, in my estimation, be one of the most delightful of all countries; but the reptiles and rats are very real discomforts to those who, like myself, have a horror of them. Can anything compensate one for such drawbacks? Go where you will throughout the length and breadth of the land, there is no possibility of avoiding them. Some places are worse than others in these respects, but in each and all there is an inexhaustible supply of crawling, jumping, squirming reptiles, the majority of which are poisonous; their presence mars the enjoyment of sport. Walk through the jungle, and the chances are most favourable for encountering a lively cobra or two. Enter a snipe-djeel, and one can hear the water-snakes—huge yellow monsters—rattling away, and not infrequently are they visible; they may be harmless, but they are repulsive. For a time I endeavoured to conquer my repugnance to these detrimentals to sport, but after some unpleasant experiences, I was forced to yield, and not even the charms of the best of snipe-shooting had power to enable me to overcome the feelings of aversion and dread which for ever haunted me.

It is a relief to turn from the contemplation of rats proper, to the interesting and harmless water-vole, more commonly, but erroneously, termed the water-rat. The word 'vole' is supposed to have been derived from 'wold'—a field or plain. The appellation 'water-vole' is therefore inapt. 'Vole' has, however, come to be regarded as having reference to the genus *Arvicola*, of which *Arvicolæ amphibia* is represented by the water-vole. It is a harmless little animal, and free from any of the qualities which render the ordinary rat so detestable. It is not carnivorous, but lives entirely on vegetable food. Nothing can be prettier than to watch them feeding by the riverside, or, it may be, seated on the broad, flat leaf of a lily or some other water-plant in the summer evenings. The only crime which can be laid to their charge is that of undermining the banks of rivers, and in this respect they are capable of doing considerable damage; but they are less disposed to increase the number of their runs than other rats, and so, where their numbers are not excessive, they are, comparatively speaking, harmless. Their appearance is dissimilar to the ordinary rat in many ways. The head is rounder and blunter, the feet longer and softer, and the tail only some three or four inches in length; the feet are less naked and not flesh-coloured; their ears are also much smaller and shorter. They are plucky little creatures, and able to hold their own against the ordinary rat. During the last summer I

A BROWN RAT AND A WATER-VOLE

witnessed an encounter between a large brown rat and a half-grown water-rat.

The water had been allowed to run out of a pond belonging to me, and I was watching its rise as the pond was being refilled through the hatch in the bank of the adjacent river. Whilst so doing, I observed two rats scampering back to their holes in the sides of the pond—the one a large brown rat, the other a half-grown water-vole. The latter repeatedly attacked the former, but on each occasion—some four or five times—was overpowered by the superior weight of his antagonist and pushed into the water; but, nothing daunted, he renewed the attack. Eventually, on their seeing me, both disappeared amidst the long grass and sedges surrounding the pond.

I have observed that when the water-voles come out to feed by the river, especially when they are to be seen crossing and recrossing the stream, such times are unfavourable for catching fish. I do not know if others have noticed this to be the case, but I have found it to be so invariable that I have, at times, reeled up my line and gone home, believing it to be useless. It is not that the trout are scared in any way because the surface of the water may be constantly broken by their movements, but they are not on the feed.

The water-vole is a charming, interesting animal, and one which I should be indeed sorry to see exterminated. Were it not so frequently miscalled, it would probably suffer less persecution ; but the very name of rat is quite sufficient to warrant its destruction by those who are too ignorant to know better.

The front (incisor) teeth of the water-vole are similar to those of the ordinary rat, the squirrel, hare, rabbit, and mouse, all of which animals belong to the order called Rodentia, or Rodents. These teeth are singularly adapted for gnawing, their shape and action being like that of an adze —a tool much used by wheelwrights ; and it is by them that the rodents are distinguishable from all other animals. From the foregoing, it may be seen that the water-vole, although a rodent, is no more a rat than it is a squirrel, despite its similarity in appearance at first sight to a rat. A hare is a rodent, so also is a rabbit ; they are similar in shape, and their habits are, so far as their food is concerned, alike, but there the similarity ends The one burrows, the other does not ; and whereas the flesh of the one is white when cooked, that of the other is brown. There is thus a very marked difference between the two, apart from that which exists in colour and shape.

Thus it happens that the shrews are frequently miscalled shrew-mice, yet they are not mice, nor are they even rodents ; they belong to the order of Insectivora, and feed entirely on insects and worms. Their teeth are not adapted for gnawing as are those of the rodents. There are three species of shrew which have been observed in

Britain, viz., the common, the water, and the oared, and there is yet a fourth, the square-tailed shrew, but this last-named is of too rare occurrence to refer to ; indeed, the oared shrew is rare, though it is asserted to have been common in Fifeshire. The water-shrew is by no means frequently met with, and may be certainly classed as belonging to our rarer British quadrupeds.

In times past, when superstition was more rife in England than it is at the present day, the poor shrews were terribly persecuted, being regarded as venomous beasts; for not only was their bite believed to be fatal, but if one chanced to run over the limb of an animal, it was credited with causing the limb to become diseased. The following brutal remedy was supposed to be efficacious in such cases : A hole was bored with an auger in an ash-tree, and into this a live shrew was put ; the hole was then plugged up with wood. When an ash-tree had been thus treated, any branches gathered from it and waved over the affected limb were supposed to effect a cure. We may truly say, What brutes people were in those days! and what utter fools too! There is still a most unaccountable amount of superstition prevalent in many of our country districts. It perhaps lingers more in the Southern and Western counties. My own servants are terribly superstitious, and most firmly believe in ghosts, a belief which has occasioned me no little trouble at times, as my house has the reputation of being haunted. Nothing would induce them to go upstairs alone after dark if they could possibly avoid doing so. Not long ago the following story was told me by one of our leading farmers, of another farmer whom he had known intimately, and who lived in the next village. A gipsy woman begged of him on one of the village club days, and he gave her a piece of tin which had been taken from the top of a soda-water bottle. She at first, believing it to be a sixpence, thanked him most profusely; but afterwards, discovering she had been tricked, turned round and cursed him, telling him that he would die before the year was out. He was a man of a peculiarly robust constitution, a man who, as my informant described it, had never known a day's illness in his life. He, however, took it so much to heart that he became positively ill, and as the time for the completion of the year drew nigh he became so terrified, and, in consequence, so ill, that he really did die, and on the very last day of the twelve months, although there was absolutely nothing the matter with him but what had arisen from the nervous state into which he had thrown himself.

But to return to my subject. An ash-tree in which a shrew had been thus buried alive was also termed in some districts 'rampike,' and the same word was also used to denote any tree which was beginning to decay at the top from age. Drayton refers to this in the following lines :

> 'As the night-crow sometimes you might see,
> Croaking to sit upon some *rampick* tree.'

The word 'shrew' is said to be derived from the Saxon *screawa*, *i.e.*, a shrew or venomous mouse, and it occurs in Saxon only in reference to the shrew. 'Shrew' itself also bears the meaning of evil, or wicked. And so the poor shrew, the most harmless little creature imaginable, was tortured, tormented, and ruthlessly butchered, solely because of its name. Its life is all too short as it is, for numbers of them die annually, and their dead bodies may be frequently seen in the roads and footpaths towards the end of the summer. As their bodies, when thus found, bear no marks of violence, it has been supposed that they are very subject to some disease. It is strange that they are almost always to be found in the middle of some public footpath or road, for they are naturally very shy, timorous little animals, living in the hedgerows, woods, and fields, making burrows somewhat after the fashion of the mole, though on a minor scale, and in these they pass the winter. Unlike the mole, they are able to run very rapidly, but, like that animal, their feet are singularly well fitted for digging. The nest of the common shrew is made of grass, not in a burrow, but on the surface of the ground. Sometimes it may be found in a hole in a bank, but wherever it may be, it is always difficult to find, by reason of its being so well concealed. Bell states that shrews are very pugnacious, fighting desperately with each other, and to such an extent that, if two are placed in a box together, the stronger makes very short work of his companion.

If the incisor teeth of a shrew are examined, it will be observed that they are very peculiar, resembling double teeth with very long points to them, and that they are somewhat square in shape, like ordinary grinders with long necks, and curved downwards. The front teeth in the lower jaw are very small. The whole of the dental arrangement is peculiar, and requires to be seen to be easily understood. I have an excellent drawing of the jaws of a shrew before me, but I am unable to describe it without the aid of illustration. The fur is close and soft, the under parts of a pale gray, the upper parts brown, the muzzle very long and tapering, and the tail long and slender. The pale gray colour of the under parts of the body is continued along the length of the under jaw and as far as the eyes in the upper jaw, forming with the brown colour of the upper parts a decided line, towards which the nearer the gray approaches the lighter it becomes, until it appears almost white where it reaches the under jaw. The whiskers are very long, and the feet are flesh-coloured. The feet of the water-shrew are edged with white hairs, and the upper parts almost black, the under parts being nearly white. The texture of the fur is much the same in both species; it may be that it is slightly thicker in the water-shrew than in the common variety. The muzzle of the water-shrew is shorter and flatter, the feet are larger and broader; indeed, the whole animal is on a larger scale than the common shrew. Its habits are very similar to those of the water-vole, and are, as its name implies, aquatic. It can swim rapidly, and can dive and run about the bottom of a pool with the greatest ease. When swimming, its body is higher out of the water than that of the water-vole, and it seems to run along the top of the water like some of the water-beetles, rather than swim in it. When it dives, the air-bubbles which collect round its body give it the appearance of a crystal ball. Like the common shrew, it lives on worms and insects, though, unlike that animal, it seeks these under and in the water, as well as on the land.

The oared shrew I have never seen, but it is said to be larger than the water-shrew, and generally stronger. From the best illustrations which I have seen of this animal, it appears to be almost black above, and of a slaty colour beneath. Its habits are similar to those of the water-shrew. It is apparently extremely rare. Its tail, which is long and slender, is of a pale gray or white on the under side. Jardine states that it has been observed in Norfolk, Cambridgeshire, in Battersea fields, and near Glasgow. It is probably now well-nigh extinct.

In some respects the shrew resembles the mole. The common shrew, as I have observed, makes its burrows in a somewhat similar manner, although it generally constructs its nest on the surface of the ground. The feet of both animals are adapted for digging, and the texture and disposition of the fur is not unlike that of the mole, though much shorter. The muzzles of both animals are long and pointed. The incisor teeth of the mole are, however, different to those of the shrew, being of the ordinary shape; those in the lower jaw project, giving the appearance of being what is termed underhung. Perhaps the most remarkable characteristic of the mole is its extraordinary strength. I am disposed to believe that there is no quadruped in the world more powerful in comparison to its size. Anyone who has ever dissected a mole must have been struck with the immensity of its limbs and muscular development, and, indeed, this is necessary to enable it to construct its underground chambers and galleries. At times a mole may be observed at work close to the surface, yet ripping up the turf as easily as if it were sand. The formation of the animal is singularly well adapted for living and working underground, and in the dark. When found on the surface, it appears unable to see well in the daylight, although it is able to crawl along at a fair pace. I have repeatedly captured them in the day time, and found them very quick to take advantage of any cover available. They are strange-looking creatures, and their pink feet, or rather, I should say, hands, with the long tapering nails, give them a very uncanny appearance; but their fur is exquisitely fine, soft, and dense, and were they larger, their skins would be of great value to the furriers. As it is, the country people frequently make use of them for waistcoats, etc., and at times for bed coverlets. I have heard that these are considered of great value, especially when the centre is formed of the skins of white moles. The farmers pay, as a rule, twopence or threepence a head for moles. There are in most villages one or two individuals who are employed for the purpose of mole and rat catching. They bring the tails of the moles which they have captured to the farmer on pay-night as a voucher for the number killed.

Moles do a great deal of good, and a considerable amount of harm if they chance to make their way into a garden. In the fields their labours are not to be despised, always provided that the mounds which they throw up are afterwards levelled, and the fresh earth scattered over the surface of the ground. On farms where this is not attended to, the mounds become grass-grown, and speedily ruin the pasture. If the top of an old mole-hill is removed, it will almost invariably be found full of ants, and so partridges and pheasants frequent those fields for the sake of the ants, of which they are excessively fond, and which furnish them with the best of food. In those districts where ants are abundant pheasants will generally thrive well, not only because of the ants, but because the soil is generally dry and suitable for game-rearing. Some little knowledge of the habits of the mole is requisite to ensure its capture, and the professional mole-catchers know exactly where to set their traps. It is said that foxes are given to feeding on moles, and this is probably true, though I have never found any bones similar to those of a mole in the vicinity of a fox's earth. I do not, however, think that a fox would take the trouble to dig for a mole unless pressed for food, in which case it is very probable that he would speedily shift his quarters to 'fresh fields and pastures new.'

The underground apartments of the mole are very interesting and cleverly constructed, but in order to examine them thoroughly great care is required, as the chambers and galleries are very easily displaced by the spade in the process of digging down to them. They consist of one large chamber or hall, surrounded by a gallery; a similar gallery also encircles the upper portion of the central hall, and from these galleries passages are excavated in various directions. Although the mole is but imperfectly supplied with the sense of sight, its power of hearing is remarkably acute, and at the least alarm it speedily betakes itself through one of its many passages to its central hall. It feeds chiefly on worms, and its object in forming these passages is for the purpose of procuring its food. The mole-catchers, knowing this, are able to tell in which direction the new work is proceeding, and place their traps in the run; and so when the mole resumes his labours he releases the spring (whether the trap be of iron, or the older fashioned hazel-rod and snare), and is caught, much to his own dismay and to the satisfaction of the mole-catcher, who snips off his tail, transferring it to his waistcoat pocket, and reckons that he has increased his income by so many more pennies.

The hedgehog, or hedgepig, is another of our animals which is most unjustly maligned, numberless iniquities being laid to its charge. Prejudice is difficult to eradicate, and absurh though it may appear, the belief that it damages the udders of cows by sucking them is still prevalent in many of our rural districts. It is also accused of destroying eggs. I regret to say that I am unable to disprove this allegation as little as to prove its truth, and I fear it may not be altogether unfounded, inasmuch as the hedgehog, although classified by naturalists as being an insectivorous animal, is by no means exclusively so. Its principal food consists of insects, but it will eat well-nigh anything—worms, slugs, snails, and reptiles of all sorts. Those which I have kept from time to time were extremely fond of bread-and-milk. They are most useful in houses which are infested with black-beetles, and are very easily tamed; but they have an unfortunate habit of hiding themselves away in the most extraordinary places during the daytime, and are always turning up where least expected.

The right eye of a hedgehog, boiled in oil, and preserved in a brazen vessel, was formerly supposed to enable a person to see in the dark. What did they not believe in former days! Pallas the naturalist states that a hedgehog is able to eat the cantharides, or Spanish beetle, with impunity. The effects of this insect, when dried and used for blistering purposes, are well known, so the statement is therefore corroborative of the assertion that hedgehogs can eat anything. The hedgehog is also probably proof against the poison of an adder. As is well known, gipsies consider them a great delicacy, and not so very long ago I was informed by a person who had tasted one that they do so with good reason. The gipsy method of cooking a hedgehog is to envelop the body in clay, and bake it in the embers. When the clay breaks open the cooking is complete. A somewhat similar manner of preparing fowls is practised by the native cooks in India. The fowl (when killed) is plunged immediately into a vessel of boiling water, which process enables the skin to be readily removed. The carcase is then covered with a thick paste made of common flour and water, tied up in a cloth, and boiled. When brought to table the shell is removed, and the fowl covered with white sauce. This latter is necessary, for if omitted the appearance is far from appetising. Nevertheless, it is an excellent method of cooking a fowl, especially when likely to be tough or insipid, as is the case with the generality of Indian poultry.

During the winter months the hedgehog lies dormant, eating nothing until the spring is well advanced. Some dogs are very clever in the way they are able to tackle a hedgehog, and I have known them carry it to a pond, drop it in the water, and then, when it has been thus forced to unroll itself, seize and kill it ; but such performances ever afford me far more pain than pleasure, and though fully able to appreciate the pluck of a dog which can seize a hedgehog regardless of the wounds he receives, my sympathies are entirely with the latter animal, which I would ever endeavour to save from destruction or ill usage.

A hedgehog is by no means an ugly animal ; its bright eye bespeaks no little intelligence, and, as I have remarked, it is very easily tamed ; the pale gray colour of its under parts contrasts pleasingly with the rich brown spines and black feet and muzzle. It is towards the latter part of the summer that these animals are more commonly to be observed, and at that time they suffer no little persecution at the hands of the village boys, who are far too frequently most brutally cruel to all wild animals.

At the most, there are but fifty different varieties of wild animals in Britain at the present time, and of this number some are exceedingly rare. We have but one variety of the following, viz. : the hedgehog, mole, badger, squirrel, wild-cat, and otter. The last-named animal, though perhaps not often seen without the assistance of hounds, is by no means uncommon ; and it may be said that wherever there are streams with fish in them, there are sure to be otters ; every district suitable for the sport is nowadays hunted by a pack of otter hounds, and thus the otters, being preserved for sporting purposes, are subjected to less general persecution than formerly, Where, however, it is impossible to kill them with hounds by reason of the depth of the streams, they are at times destroyed by means of traps. It is by no means an easy matter to trap an otter, and to do so requires great care and no little patience, for an otter is an excessively wary animal, and its senses, especially that of smelling, are singularly acute. The run of an otter having been found, the steel trap, unbaited, is placed therein and covered over with brushwood, care being taken not to touch either trap or brushwood with the bare hand, for were this precaution neglected, the otter would be certain to detect the scent and turn aside out of the run. At first, seeing the brushwood in its accustomed path, it jumps over it. Day by day the trap is gradually moved farther away from the brushwood, until it is so placed that, on landing over the latter, it is caught. This is, I believe, the best way of capturing otters.

Traps baited with fish are sometimes used: but since an otter will not touch fish unless it is perfectly fresh, it is necessary to renew the bait very frequently, and this constant disturbance of the trap is not conducive to success. Otters are very easily tamed if taken in hand when they are young enough, and are very affectionate. It is but a year or two ago that a lady was observed walking down Oxford Street followed by a tame otter. They have been frequently trained to catch fish for their owners. At first the otter is fed on fish and water, and by degrees milk and vegetables are mingled with this food and less fish given it. Bread is then added, and no fish given at all until it has become accustomed to live on bread only, upon which diet it is stated to thrive well. It is then taught to fetch and carry, in the same manner as a dog; an imitation fish made of leather, and stuffed with wool, is then made use of, and it is taught to fetch and drop this when required. After the preliminary training is completed, a dead fish is thrown into the water for it to retrieve, and a live one being eventually substituted, its education is completed. It has been asserted that, when they are pressed for food, otters are capable of destroying poultry, rabbits, and even lambs; but I am forced to admit that I am disinclined to credit such a statement, and should require very conclusive proofs to enable me to attach any importance to it.

A friend of mine who is the owner of a well-known pack of otter-hounds, and an excellent sportsman to boot, has more than once tried to convince me that otters do not kill trout or other fish, provided they can procure eels. I wish I could agree with him, but I have had convincing proofs to the contrary. That they do kill eels I am well aware, and also that they are very partial to such fare; but I am also equally well aware that, in those rivers where eels and other fish are abundant, they contrive to kill a certain number of fish. On one salmon river with which I am well acquainted, the otters at times evinced a partiality for the salmon, despite the fact that some of the pools offered remarkably good sport to the eel-quodders. As some of my readers may not be acquainted with the sport of quodding for eels, I will endeavour to describe it. The fisherman is provided with a fairly long and very stiff rod, partaking rather of the character of a pole than a rod, to which a strong line is attached, and to the end of this line a large bunch of worms, threaded upon worsted, is fastened; a heavy lead which serves the purpose of shot, and a box with a lid, or a bucket, completes the equipment. The line thus baited is dropped into a likely spot for eels, care being taken to prevent its becoming slack. The eel sucks at the worms, and its movements are communicated to the fisherman—hence the necessity for keeping the line somewhat taut—who, when he considers that sufficient time has been allowed, pulls up the bait with a swift but steady motion, drops the eel into his box—which serves him for a seat—and resumes operations. By this method a large number of eels may be taken in an evening, especially during thundery weather, when, unlike other fish, eels are most inclined to feed.

Were otters to confine their poaching propensities to eels only, they would be entitled to the gratitude of all fishermen ; at least, such is my opinion, inasmuch as it is my firm belief that eels are by no means averse to eating the spawn of fish. I may malign them, but I have reason to believe them by no means blameless in this respect. I could, indeed, wish that otters were innocent of all harm, for they are most interesting animals, and very handsome. Their fur, which is thick and soft, is of great value to the furriers, though that of the British otter is not considered as suitable in this respect as the foreign. The toughness of its skin is remarkable. When an otter has been killed by the hounds, if its skin is examined, it will be found that not a single tooth has succeeded in penetrating it. As I hope to refer to the sport of otter-hunting later on I forbear to do so at the present time ; but I fear that all sport seems inseparable from cruelty, and that of otter-hunting is no exception. I trust, however, that I may not be thought desirous of condemning sport. On the contrary, I love it far too well to do so, but I find it impossible to honestly deny the existence of cruelty in a greater or less degree in every description of sport, and no amount of argument will ever cause me to alter my opinion.

An otter is a gallant beast, and will fight to the death, nor will he ever utter one cry of distress, no matter how severely he may be treated. He can swim with the greatest rapidity, well-nigh as quickly as a fish—indeed, were this not so, he would soon starve—and he can remain under water for a very long time. The ear of this animal is provided with a species of valve, which is doubtless used for the purpose of preventing the entrance of water, and enabling it to use its powers of hearing when diving. The otter frequently attains to a considerable size; one weighing twenty-four pounds was killed near my garden some three or four years ago by the otter-hounds, and this weight is by no means uncommon. The average length of a full-grown otter may be roughly estimated, when measured from the muzzle to the tip of the tail, at about forty inches, but there are many instances recorded of otters being captured whose length has been very greatly in excess of this measurement.

The word 'otter' is derived from the Anglo-Saxon *otter*, *otor*, or *oter*. The Latin word for otter—viz., *lutra*—is also not very dissimilar in sound. The strength of an otter is great; the bones large and short, and the muscular development of the neck remarkable. The tail, or 'pole,' as it is termed, is about fifteen inches in length, and gradually tapering ; it is thick and powerful. With the exception of man, the otter has no enemies which it has occasion to fear—at least, not in these islands. It was formerly supposed that the otters which inhabit our sea-coasts were a different variety to those found inland ; such a supposition has, however, been long since refuted by naturalists, both animals being now classified alike. Those found on the sea-coasts of Scotland and Ireland are said to be larger and darker in colour than the inland otters. This is probably due to the greater amount of food procurable by the former.

Although they can scarcely be included amongst those animals which may be termed 'dwellers in fields,' the present seems a suitable opportunity for making some short reference to the bats which are to be found in these islands. My own observations as to the habits of these creatures have been very scanty, and such information as I possess regarding them has been gleaned from the works of those naturalists who have devoted their attention to them.

All varieties of bats—at all events, those to be found in Britain—are insectivorous, and all are nocturnal in their habits. They make their appearance when the daylight is fading—some later than others—and seek their food amongst the myriads of insects which throng in the twilight, fluttering hither and thither, up and

down, right and left, never seeming to tire so
long as there is an insect to be captured. Thus
in their generations they perform the duties
allotted to them, and are worthy of our gratitude. We should fare ill without them, but they
are gruesome, ghostly little animals, and it is
not remarkable that, in the days of superstition,
they should have been regarded as spirits of evil
and creatures of ill omen.

There have been no fewer than fifteen varieties
of bats observed in Britain. Most of these are
rare.

The long-eared bat, the common bat, and the
great or noctule bat are most frequently met
with, the two first-named more especially; the
last is only found in certain localities. Jardine, in his work on Bats, mentions the fact of
nearly 250 of this variety having been captured
in two successive days under the eaves of King's
College, Cambridge. He states that it generally
flies in bands of about a dozen; is seldom to be
met with singly; that its flight is remarkably high
and rapid; that it comes abroad earlier in the
evening than any other species, adding that for
this latter reason the name 'noctule' is singularly inapplicable. The same author observes
that it is later in leaving its winter retreat than
other bats, and withdraws early in autumn. It
emits a shrill cry when on the wing. It inhabits
churches, buildings of various kinds, and hollow
trees. It is the largest but one of our British

THE GREATER HORSESHOE BAT

bats, that one exception being the mouse-coloured bat, which is exceedingly rare. I have myself frequently seen the great bat; indeed, I have, when a boy, occasionally shot it.

With the common bat everyone is more or less acquainted.

The greater horseshoe bat—so called from the peculiar shape of its nostrils, which, as viewed from in front, present the appearance of an inverted horseshoe—is, if not rare, at all events by no means common. It frequents buildings and caverns. There is a smaller variety of this bat—the smaller horseshoe bat—but it is rare, and restricted chiefly to some few places in the South of England. It is considerably smaller than the preceding variety, and differs in some respects, notably in colour, for whereas the fur of the greater horseshoe bat is reddish-gray above, and pale gray beneath, that of the smaller variety is grayish-brown above, the lower parts being pale gray tinged with yellow, the measurement across the wings being but eight and a half inches, as compared with fourteen inches.

The long-eared bat is one of the most common of our British varieties. It is easily distinguishable by the length of its ears, which are very large and curious. It is one of the most active and agile of the tribe. It is to be found distributed over the whole of Britain, and frequents steeples, towers, ruined buildings, and caverns. Like the common, or, as it is termed, the pipistrelle bat, it flies with a fluttering motion. Its fur is long, fine, and silky, of a dusky brownish-gray above and yellowish-gray beneath. Its voice is a low, chirping squeak.

These four are the only varieties which may be said to be common in Britain, viz. :

>The noctule or great bat.
>The greater horseshoe bat.
>The common or pipistrelle bat.
>The long-eared bat.

Those less common and rare are as follows, viz. :

>The smaller horseshoe bat (rare, local).
>The barbastelle bat (rare).
>The whiskered bat (rare).
>The reddish-gray bat (rare).
>Daubenton's bat (rare).
>The notch-eared bat (very rare).
>The mouse-coloured bat (very rare).
>Bechstein's bat (very rare).
>The serotine bat (rare, very local).
>The hairy-armed bat (excessively rare).
>The parti-coloured bat (excessively rare).

The following descriptions may suffice for the purpose of identification :

The barbastelle has been found in two or three parts of England—viz., in Devonshire, Northamptonshire, Cambridgeshire, and Kent. It is somewhat similar to the long-eared bat. The fur on the head and back is of a brownish-black, that on the hinder parts reddish-brown. The underneath parts are dark gray. The ears are about as long as the head, squarish in shape, and set obliquely forwards.

The whiskered bat may be recognised by its moustache and a row of hairs on its forehead. The upper parts are reddish-black, the lower ash-gray; the fur is long and woolly. It frequents houses, hollow trees, and caverns. It has been observed in Cambridgeshire, Northamptonshire, at Colchester in Essex, and at Chislehurst in Kent.

The reddish-gray bat has been found in Cambridgeshire, Colchester, Norwich, and Chislehurst. The colour of the fur is of a light reddish-gray above, and silver-gray beneath; the ears are of a yellowish-gray. Its general colour is said to be lighter than that of any other of our British bats. Of the specimens referred to (from Jardine's work), some were found in hollow trees, and some in the shaft of a chalk cavern, seventy feet below the surface.

Daubenton's bat, of which Jardine records four specimens as having been discovered in Britain, viz., in Northamptonshire, Islington, Fifeshire, and Dumfriesshire, is of a grayish-red above and ash-gray beneath; it measures nine inches across the wings.

The notch-eared bat, of which but a very few specimens have been discovered in this country, may be recognised by its beard and moustache.

Its colour is a light reddish-brown inclining to gray on the upper parts, and grayish-white tinged with brown on the lower. It measures some nine and a half inches across the wings.

The mouse-coloured bat, which Jardine states to have been found in one place only in Britain, viz., the gardens of the British Museum, is the largest of our bats, measuring fifteen inches across the wings. The upper parts of the body are of a reddish-brown, the lower of a dirty yellowish-white. From its rarity, and the position of the locality in which it was found, I should be inclined to suppose that it must have been brought to this country from abroad in some packing-cases or articles of a similar description, and so can hardly be considered as a British bat.

There is apparently but one recorded instance of Bechstein's bat having been found in Britain. Jardine thus describes it : 'The fur reddish-gray or yellowish-gray above, whitish-gray beneath, and eleven inches when measured across the wings.'

The serotine bat, a rare variety in Britain, has been found only in the neighbourhood of London. This bat has also been doubtless brought from the Continent, where it is stated to be common. This, the hairy-armed and the parti-coloured bat, is so exceedingly rare that I do not consider it within the scope of this work to refer to it, other than as being included in the list of British bats, because specimens have been discovered in this country. I am disposed to think that all three have been originally imported from abroad. Where specimens of rare bats have been found in the country inhabiting trees, caverns, etc., it may be assumed that they are truly British ; but in those instances in which but one or two specimens only have been observed, and those in the immediate vicinity of London or some large provincial seaport, it would appear that their presence is due to their having been brought from abroad. Several of the varieties to which I have above referred are so uncommon as to render it improbable that any of my readers would be likely to discover specimens of them. Nevertheless, I have extracted sufficient information respecting them to facilitate the determination of any doubtful specimen which may be procured—at all events, if not explicit enough to illustrate what it may be, sufficient to determine what it is not.

There are few summer evenings in which the common, the long-eared, or the great bat may not be observed, and but few localities in which they are not common. The districts in which insect life is most prolific are those most favoured by the bat tribe, or, as they are scientifically termed, the Cheiroptera (from the Greek χείρ, a hand, πτερον, a wing) or hand-winged family. On one occasion when fishing in Hampshire, in the course of half an hour I caught a swallow, a bat, and a good Test trout. Needless to remark, the first two catches were purely accidental, both bat and swallow mistaking my artificial fly, as I waved it in the air for the purpose of drying it, for the natural insect. Fortunately neither bat nor swallow was injured, their wings being merely entangled in the line.

It has occurred to me that the following table, which I have compiled from Jardine's work on Bats, may be found of use for the purposes of identification. I have selected this work in preference to many others at my disposal, believing it to be so thorough. Newer-fashioned treatises on natural history have made their appearance since it was first published, but, in my estimation, none of these are able to excel it. It has been much of a companion to me throughout my life. As a child its beautifully-executed plates filled me with delight and wonderment, and I have found its perusal a never-failing source of interest and information. It taught me to love natural history, and has helped me to understand much of the ways and habits of the animal creation.

DESCRIPTIVE TABLE OF BRITISH BATS, COMPILED FROM JARDINE'S WORK.

Name.	Colour, etc.	Where found.	Common or rare.	Occurrences.
1. Common or 'Pipistrelle.'	Deep reddish-brown above; light beneath; 8½ in. across the wings.	Everywhere.	Common.	
2. Great or 'Noctule.'	Reddish-brown; 14 in. across the wings.	In most places.	Fairly common.	
3. Greater Horseshoe.	Reddish-gray above; pale gray beneath; 14 in. across wings.	In many places.	Rather common.	
4. Smaller Horseshoe.	Grayish-brown above; pale yellowish-gray beneath; 8½ in. across the wings.	Wiltshire, and a few places in South of England.	Uncommon.	
5. 'Long-eared.'	Brownish-gray above; yellowish-gray beneath; 10 in. across wings.	Most places in Britain.	Common.	
6. 'Barbastelle.'	Brownish-black above; dark gray below; ears as long as head, and set obliquely forwards; 10¾ in. across wings.	Devon, Northamptonshire, Cambridgeshire, Kent.	Rare.	But few, comparatively.
7. 'Whiskered.'	Reddish-black above; ash-gray below; moustache, and row of hairs on forehead; 8½ in. across wings.	Hollow trees, caverns, houses, Cambridgeshire, Northamptonshire, Colchester, Kent.	Rare.	Few occurrences.
8. Reddish-gray.	Reddish-gray above; silver-gray beneath; ears yellowish-gray; 11 in. across wings.	Cambridgeshire, Colchester, Norwich, Kent, hollow trees, chalk caverns.	Rare.	Few occurrences.
9. 'Daubenton's.'	Grayish-red above; ash-gray beneath; 9 in. across wings.	Northamptonshire, Fifeshire, Islington, Dumfriesshire.	Rare.	Few occurrences.
10. 'Notch-eared.'	Light reddish-brown above; grayish-white tinged, with brown beneath; 9¾ in. across wings.	Hampshire, Kent.	Very rare.	Some two or three only.
11. 'Mouse-coloured.'	Reddish-brown above; yellowish-white below; 15 in. across wings.	Doubtful if inhabiting Britain. Probably imported.	Exceedingly rare.	One record.
12. 'Bechstein's.'	Reddish or yellowish gray above; whitish-gray beneath; 11 in. across wings.	Probably imported.	Exceedingly rare.	One record.
13. 'Serotine.'				
14. 'Hairy-armed.'	Too rare to be worth giving any description. Have most probably been imported.			
15. 'Parti-coloured.'				

DWELLERS IN NESTS.

PART I.

Wild Birds' Protection Act—Inefficiency of Protection Act—
Destruction of Birds and Nests by Boys—Act for the Preservation of Birds' Eggs—Caged Birds—The Bullfinch—
A Tame Bullfinch—Preference of Bullfinches for Dry
Situations—Two Varieties of British Bullfinch—Change of
Plumage of Caged Bullfinches—The Pine Grosbeak—The
Crossbill—Bird's-nesting at Harrow—Ned Powell—Siskins
and Redpoles—Bracing Birds—Training of Birds when
braced by Means of a Brace-board—A Tame Goldfinch—
Increase of Goldfinches in England—The Siskin—Summer
and Winter Migrants—Ring-Ouzel—Linnet and Redpole
compared—Large Flock of Linnets—Beauty of Linnets—
Beauty of Sparrow — The Tree-sparrow — Beauty of the
Nightingale—Nest of the Nightingale—Village Cats and
Village Birds — A Diving Cat — Home Surroundings —
Variety of Birds at Home—List of Rarer Birds noticed by
me at Home—Destruction of Useful Birds by Keepers and
Gardeners—Destruction of Sparrows and Starlings—Utility
of Blackbirds and Thrushes in Gardens—Destructiveness
of Rooks—Protection of Garden Produce from Birds—
Destruction of Hawks by Keepers—Bird Language—Warning Notes of Blackbirds—Destructiveness of Wild-ducks
and Herons in a Fishery—The Peewit—Plovers' Eggs—
Solicitude of Peewits for their Nests—Plovers and their
Flight—A Shower of Crystals—Plovers' Nests—The Stone

WILD BIRDS' PROTECTION ACT

Curlew—The Bustard—A *Rara Avis*—Extinction of Bustards in Britain—Flight of Bustards—Size of Bustards—Food-Supply of Birds—Birds affected by their Surroundings.

It is now several years since an Act was passed to ensure the protection of certain wild birds during the breeding season; penalties were provided for its infringement, and one of its clauses set forth that 'any persons found offending must furnish their names and addresses to anyone requesting them, or be liable to an additional penalty of ten shillings.'

It was hoped and supposed that, by means of the Act referred to, the wild birds mentioned in the schedule would escape molestation during the breeding-season, *i.e*, between March 15 and August 1. It has always appeared to me that the schedule is somewhat scanty, and that protection might very justly have been extended to several of our feathered friends whose names do not appear in its columns. Indeed, with the exception of some five or six varieties, it might have freely been accorded to all birds, seeing that they do more good than harm. I have seen it stated that the object of the Act was, principally, to afford protection to those birds which were in danger of becoming extinct. Allowing this to be reasonable and fitting, I fail to understand why the moor-hen should receive greater consideration than the water-rail, or the Dartford, reed, and sedge warblers than the marsh, garden, or grasshopper warblers. Is the honey buzzard so common or so harmful as to be necessarily left out in the cold ? What sins of commission are to be laid at the door of the shrike ? Care has been taken, and rightly so, too, to mention the spoonbill, which at one time used to breed on the southeastern portions of this country, but is now so rare a visitor that it can scarcely be called a British bird; but the golden oriole and the hoopoe are as carefully omitted. In addition to these, there are numerous other birds whose names have been passed over, and yet which should surely have been included. I cannot understand why so many should have been left unprotected, and amongst them those which, it might have been presumed, it would have been most desirable to guard from molestation, and by every means to encourage. Be this, however, as it may, the Act, despite the brevity of the lists of names in the schedule, would have been better than nothing had its due observance been more rigidly enforced. But, alas! like so many of its Parliamentary relations, it has been permitted to drop into disuse and abeyance, and so is infinitely worse than no Act at all, inasmuch as offenders, knowing that they can break it with impunity, scarcely hesitate to do so. When, may I ask, does the notification of a prosecution for offence against this Act appear in any of our local newspapers ? Our rural policemen are well aware that the Act is constantly infringed, and are often well aware of the names of the offenders; but they take no steps to bring them to justice. Of course, in the majority of instances, the culprits are boys, who, by means of catapults, stones, or other missiles—not infrequently a gun or an old horse-pistol—wilfully and wantonly slaughter every bird they see, and with just as little hesitation as if the Act did not exist. Last summer (1894) two boys, in the village in which I reside, coolly clambered up a lime-tree growing in front of my house and tore down the nest of a spotted fly-catcher. Having each abstracted one of the young birds, they threw the nest and the rest of the hapless brood over the railings into the adjoining field. I happened to be away from home at the time, but on my return I collected the little castaways, and, placing them in the disused nest of a thrush, inserted the latter amongst some ivy which grew on a wall close by, and had the satisfaction of knowing that at all events one of them survived, having doubtless been fed by the parent birds. The culprit in this instance was the son of our rural policeman. His father, to whom I stated the case, promised me that he would chastise him soundly, but I have good reason to doubt if the threatened castigation was ever administered, or, if so, if it was in any way remarkable for its severity, as I observed its supposed recipient swaggering down the village the next day, looking by no means the worse for wear, and with rather more assurance than usual.

It would be well if the use of the catapult were made illegal. Numberless birds are annually surreptitiously slaughtered or crippled by means of this detestable instrument. One of my garden pets is a poor robin (of all birds one which should receive all protection at our hands), which has been thus crippled. Its leg, which has been broken, is useless, and it is piteous to see the poor little creature trying to balance itself, with its broken limb outstretched behind, when it comes to the window to be fed. If the wind is ever so light, it is a matter of extreme difficulty for it to stand at all.

In the matter of birds'-nesting, we can all of us afford to be somewhat lenient, for what boy is able to resist the pleasure of making, or adding to, a collection of birds' eggs? It is rather the wholesale abstraction of the eggs out of a nest which should be strongly condemned, and very much might, and should, be done towards the prevention of this practice by the parents of the boys when cognizant of the fact. More frequently than not, when boys empty a nest they tear it down and cast it ruthlessly away. It is truly sad to see a newly-made nest thus lying on the ground—the snug little home, framed and completed with such marvellous skill, and with the expenditure of so many hours of labour, cast aside as a thing of naught; nay, well-nigh as if it were an offence.

The summary of the new Act for the protection

ACT FOR PRESERVATION OF BIRDS' EGGS

of certain birds' eggs during their nesting season has been forwarded to me by a friend. It appears to be a step in the right direction, but still hardly all that it might be, and, unless it is better enforced than its predecessor, utterly useless. I much doubt if, in any case, more than a very few individuals will take the trouble to apply for the protection which may be needed, and any action in the matter will necessarily rest very much with the farmers, a class of men who, with comparatively few exceptions, are strangely ignorant of the habits of birds, and, so long as their crops do not suffer, are absolutely indifferent as to whether any particular variety of bird requires protection or the reverse.

I feel it a duty to make known in the present instance, to any of my readers who may not be aware of its existence, that there is a society called the Society for the Protection of Birds, and that it is at the present time using every endeavour to promote the protection of our wild birds and their nests during the breeding season; the Duchess of Portland is the president, and the names of the vice-presidents, sixteen in number, are well known. The committee, also composed of sixteen individuals, are sufficient guarantee for its efficient working. The hon. secretary is Mr. F. E. Lemon, Hillcrest, Redhill. The subscription is so small as to be within the reach of the poorest.

Any person may become a member on paying

the sum of *twopence* as a registration fee, and agreeing to the objects of the society as stated in the rules.

Any member may become an associate on payment of not less than one shilling annually, or a life associate by a donation of a guinea.

All who desire to do so (and who would not?) may aid this praiseworthy society in the following ways, viz.:

1. By joining it, by inducing others to do so, and by forming local branches.

2. By inducing landowners to prevent bird-catching and nest-robbing.

3. By circulating the society's pamphlets.

4. By forbearing to wear the feathers of any birds (the ostrich excepted) not killed for food, and endeavouring to induce others to follow their example.

Can any sight be more painful to a lover of nature than that of a British bird in a cage? I am utterly at a loss to understand how anyone can derive the smallest degree of pleasure in keeping such birds in captivity. Such a proceeding ever seems to me to be indicative of ignorance or brutality. The poor, panting, fluttering, pining captive may sing, it is true—sing as if its heart were full of joy, and its owner deludes himself in the belief that such is the case. But listen to the song of a skylark in a cage, and then, when the burst of melody is finished, note the frantic efforts which the poor songster makes to burst its prison bars ; and should perchance the song of a caged bird receive answer from some more fortunate, unfettered songster of its kind, the efforts to escape are still more frantic and piteous to behold.

I never pass by the shop of a bird-fancier without experiencing a longing to purchase the entire stock of birds, if only for the infinite pleasure which it would afford me to open the prison doors, release the captives, and demolish the cages. The reflection that it would but too well encourage the trade has hitherto restrained me from so doing. Those people who keep British birds in cages cannot be lovers of Nature ; they cannot love bird, or beast, or flower, for were they capable of so doing they could never, for the sake of the selfish pleasure to be derived from its mere possession, deprive a living creature of its lawful liberty. I most heartily wish that the law prohibited the keeping of birds, other than falcons and hawks—which are permitted to soar, and so cannot justly be regarded in the same light—in a state of captivity.

There are but very few of our British birds which really do more harm than good. Indeed, I think I may say that the bullfinch is the only culprit, with which I am acquainted, which may be said to be a hopeless sinner in this respect. Yet it would be a sad day which saw its extinction. He can play the very mischief in a kitchen-garden, for he is not satisfied with abstracting the maggots from the diseased buds of the fruit-trees, but, with his powerful beak, twitches out buds which are perfectly sound, and so, wherever he abounds, war is waged against him ; but he is a beautiful bird, and easily tamed. It is but a few days ago that I saw a hen bullfinch flying about in a shop, the owner of which has tamed it in the most remarkable way. Though perfectly free to wander about the house at will, it has no wish to leave its mistress, to whom it is most devotedly attached. I think it is one of the tamest birds I ever saw, and apparently understands every word its mistress says to it. It has the greatest antipathy to men, and if a man approaches it, cranes out its neck, opens its mouth and makes a screaming kind of noise, showing its anger and aversion as strongly as it is capable of doing.

Bullfinches abound in the garden of a neighbour of mine, which is situated but a couple of hundred yards from my own gardens ; but, strange to say, I have never seen a single one on my premises, and this is the more peculiar because my neighbour's sons are for ever shooting them, whereas I myself, unless it may be when the snipe are in, never allow a gun to be fired off near the gardens, for fear of scaring the birds. I have been long puzzled as to the reason of this decided preference, and can only conclude that they prefer the higher, drier soil of my neighbour's grounds to my own, which are low-lying, and are surrounded by water. On the other hand, the goldfinches are very frequently to be seen in the lower grounds, and there are generally one or two pairs which breed in the vicinity of my house. Bullfinches are to be found in most parts of England, and many hundreds are trapped annually. It is asserted that two kinds of this bird are to be met with in this country, the one larger than the other, though the plumage of both is exactly similar. I am very much inclined to doubt the correctness of this. All birds vary in size more or less according to age, and I see no reason why bullfinches should be any exception to the rule. Even birds of the same year frequently differ in size.

Bewick asserts that, when in confinement, bullfinches are at times apt to change their plumage and become almost black, and that this is especially the case when they are fed on hemp-seed. Although the poet Thomson refers to the song of the bullfinch in the following line, 'The mellow bullfinch answers from the grove,' this bird is not by any means remarkable for its vocal powers when wild, although when kept in confinement it very readily learns to whistle, or 'pipe,' as it is termed, tunes. Its natural song has been correctly described as merely a plaintive whistle. The pine grosbeak is sometimes styled the 'pine bullfinch,' but it is so excessively rare a visitor to this country as to hardly deserve a place amongst British birds.

It is larger than the bullfinch, and very different in plumage. Most naturalists make mention of it, but Colonel Irby, in his 'Notes on British Birds,' states that there are only one or two instances in which it has been observed in Britain, and that, in his opinion, these were probably introduced.

The crossbill is a far less rare bird than is generally supposed. The late Mr. James Rawlence, of Wilton, to whose valuable collection of birds I shall doubtless have occasion to refer from time to time, informed me that large flocks of crossbills frequently visited his grounds for the purpose of feeding on the fir-cones, of which they are extremely fond. Wherever these trees are abundant, crossbills are likely to make their appearance. I have never had the good fortune to see one of these birds alive, but I believe that it is most interesting to watch them feeding on the fir-cones, the power of their beaks being extraordinary, and singularly adapted for the purpose of procuring their food. Mr. Rawlence showed me some beautifully mounted specimens of this bird which had been procured in his neighbourhood.

Bird-catching by means of clap-nets is, or used to be, very extensively carried on in the country round London, and when a schoolboy at Harrow I used at times to accompany one or other of the local bird-catchers on their expeditions. Goldfinches, linnets, redpoles, and siskins, were very plentiful. Most Harrow boys of thirty years ago will remember Ned Powell as a very decent, civil-spoken, and honest individual. He taught us not only how to catch birds, but also how to train them and manufacture all the appliances necessary for their capture, and these latter were multifarious. In addition to the nets, there were cage-birds, or, as they are termed, 'call-birds,' and braced birds. These last-named were birds which were, so to speak, harnessed with a strand of wool fastened round their bodies in front and behind the wings, and attached to a small swivel under the breast, by means of which they were fastened to the end of a short stick inserted in a peg of wood notched out to admit of the stick, when pulled by a string, playing up and down at will. When it was desired to attract a 'charm' of goldfinches or other birds, the string was pulled, and the braced bird was thus thrown up into the air, and on the flock settling the nets were pulled over, the captured birds transferred to a cage, in the top of which was a hole large enough to admit of a hand being inserted, the leg of a stocking being nailed round the hole and tied in a knot to prevent the birds escaping. In this manner a great many birds were caught in favourable weather, but it was cold work watching and waiting for their arrival, especially since these performances usually took place at an early hour in the winter mornings.

The siskins and redpoles were more easily trained than other birds, and these, as soon as they had got over their first shyness, were braced and fastened by a light chain to a cane hoop, which was fixed into a peculiar arrangement formed of two pieces of wood nailed together at right angles, resembling the back and bottom of a box, the back part being fixed against a wall on a nail, a hole being cut in the wood for the purpose of hanging it up. At the upper part of this was a small box with a lid, in which the seeds were placed, and immediately below it another smaller cane hoop was fixed. These two hoops served as perches for the bird. At the edge of the bottom board farthest away from the back was a small hole about an inch in diameter, across which was a light wire bar ; beneath this hole a broken wineglass was suspended by three strings about ten inches in length, and from the wire bar a small light bone thimble was hung by a single thread run through a hole bored on each side of the thimble. This thread was of such a length as to allow the thimble to rest on the bottom of the wineglass. At first the thimble was fastened close up to the wire, like a small bucket, and filled with water, and the box containing the seeds was propped open, the bucket being filled with water. By degrees the lid of the box was lowered, a little each day, and the thread of the bucket was also gradually lengthened. By these means the bird learned to open the box with its beak, and to draw up the bucket with its beak and foot, and when able to draw up the entire thread, the wine-glass was filled with water, and the bucket, falling into it, filled itself. It was curious to watch the bird drawing up the bucket. It took but a very short time for it to become perfect—if I remember rightly, about ten days or a fortnight from first to last. I cannot remember having tried to tame any goldfinches. I have no doubt, however, that it would have been a very easy matter, inasmuch as so many instances are recorded of the extraordinary tameness of these birds. Repentance comes with mature years, and I look back regretfully on the days when I aided and abetted a professional bird-catcher, an individual whose trade I would now most thankfully see abolished. The late Mr. Rowell, one of the curators of the Ashmolean Museum in Oxford, and a well-known naturalist, told me some few years ago of a goldfinch kept by his son-in-law, residing near London, which was allowed out of its cage daily, and was in the habit of roaming about at will throughout the day, but, summer and winter alike, it always returned about four o'clock in the afternoon to its cage. This had been going on for several years at the time he told me (1889), so it is hardly to be expected that the bird is yet alive.

Some few years ago goldfinches were becoming scarce in England. It is satisfactory to learn that their numbers have recently been increasing. They are of the greatest service to the farmer and gardener, as they feed principally on the seeds of thistles, where such are procurable. It may be said that wherever thistles are abundant, goldfinches may be found. Johns, in his work on British Birds, states that the French name for the goldfinch is *chardonneret*, *i.e.*, a "frequenter of thistles,' and that the ancient Greek and Latin name, *acanthis*, has a similar meaning. The true *acanthus* (the globe artichoke) is a thistle. The song of the goldfinch, if not remarkable for its variety, is sweet and lively. Its nest is one of the most beautiful of all birds.'

The siskin rarely breeds in England, though some few instances have been recorded, but it is said to do so regularly in Scotland and Ireland. Like the bullfinch and goldfinch, it congregates in flocks, and, like the latter bird, it feeds very much on the seeds of the thistle; but it loves those of the alder best, and wherever alder-trees are frequent the siskin may be looked for. It is a lively little bird, and clings to the branches in every conceivable attitude, after the manner of the tits; like the latter, as often back downwards as not, and ceaselessly jumping from one twig to another. The song of the siskin is by no means remarkable; but it is a bright, happy little bird, sociable in its habits and very easily tamed. The prevailing colour of its plumage is a yellowish-green. It is a smaller bird than the linnet. Although, as I have remarked, a certain number of these birds breed annually in Scotland and Ireland, the larger proportion leave us in the spring for the cooler climates of Russia and Scandinavia. When it is considered how apparently little difference exists between some of our winter and summer migrants as regards their covering, it is somewhat puzzling to account for the reason why one bird should prefer a cold climate to a warm and temperate one. The siskin is an instance of this. It is apparently not more warmly clad than the linnet or redpole, yet no sooner is the spring advanced than it leaves us for Russia. The bramble finch is another instance of this peculiarity; much the same may be observed of the redwing and fieldfare. Of course there is a reason why these birds should leave us at the approach of spring, and we may conclude that they elect to migrate at that period partly because the supply of food, such as the berries which are abundant during the winter months, has become exhausted. All the same, there are many seasons in which this description of food is scanty, and therefore more quickly consumed. I do not think that, when such is the case, the migration of these birds takes place at any earlier date than in those years in which it may be more plentiful.

The redwing, fieldfare, missel-thrush, and, indeed, all the thrushes save one, remain with us throughout the winter. This one exception is the ring-ouzel. Although during its residence in this country it is more especially an inhabitant of the mountain moorlands, as the time for its departure for a sunnier and warmer climate approaches, it ventures into the valleys, and may during the autumn months be frequently observed in the outlying copses in such localities, and, indeed, is not above visiting the fruit-orchards during the summer months. In size the ring-ouzel is rather larger than the blackbird, and very similar in shape. Its plumage is of a brownish-black, but with a conspicuous white crescent on the chest. It is by no means uncommon, and may be met with in nearly every county, except in those of the Midlands, which are, as a rule, too densely populated and low-lying. Neither in shape, size, nor in habits does it resemble the water-ouzel, or dipper, the latter being but seven inches in length, whereas the ring-ouzel measures eleven. There is, however, a similarity in plumage, both birds being dark-brown in colour, the water-ouzel having the throat and chest white. The nest, and also the eggs, of the ring-ouzel are somewhat like those of the blackbird; but the eggs are rather larger, the black spots on those of the blackbird being represented by reddish-brown.

A great similarity exists between the linnet and the common, or lesser, redpole. The prevailing colour of both is also somewhat similar, viz., brown, the head and breast in both birds being tinged with red; but a closer inspection reveals a very decided difference. The linnet is nearly an inch longer than the redpole, the red tinge on the head and breast of a brighter hue, and that on the breast is also more strongly marked and extends lower down, the tail is rather longer than that of the redpole. The general appearance of the redpole is also less sleek than that of the linnet, and the feathers on the crown partake somewhat of the character of a crest. The song of the linnet is peculiarly soft, sweet, and plaintive, though very simple; the note of the redpole is sharper and more decided. The linnet, moreover, prefers a dry situation, whereas the redpole, like the siskin, which it most resembles in habits and character, prefers such situations as are favourable to the growth of alder-trees, and on which, as does the siskin, it finds food to its liking. Both the linnet and redpole congregate in larger flocks than the siskin. When partridge-shooting last December (1894) an unusually large flock of linnets preceded the line of guns for a long distance, alternately settling and rising before us. This was, I think, the largest flock of these birds which I have ever seen.

On a warm and sunny afternoon in September, when walking along a rough hillside amongst the downs, a pair of linnets settled on a thistle close to me. Sitting down, I watched them through my field-glass. The afternoon sun was mellowing in the west, and shone full on the thistle and the birds. I had always thought linnets beautiful, but never till then had I known how beautiful they are. At that time of year their plumage is at its very best, and the effect of the sunlight falling on their crimson breasts is beyond my power to describe. They seemed all aglow with fire; every spike of thistledown glistened like the finest spun glass. It was a sight I shall never forget. I doubt if the plumage of some of our more soberly-dressed birds is not, after all, more truly beautiful than that of those of more brilliant hue. Even the sparrow is a really handsome bird, the male especially so, a fact of which I was never fully aware until, when a boy, the picture of a group of sparrows in the collection at Chatsworth attracted my attention. The plumage of the tree-sparrow is still more striking. To many people a sparrow is but a common, impertinent little brown bird, too common to be worthy of notice, and unworthy of notice just exactly because he *is* unnoticed; and yet he is a bird whose plumage is full of rich, warm colourings, in which russets, browns, ash, and pearl gray are exquisitely blended, these in the case of the tree-sparrow being still further heightened and relieved by white on the cheeks and ear-coverts, in the centre of which is a triangular black patch. He may at times be observed mingling in the society of his relations, the house-sparrows; but, unlike the latter, he ever prefers to make his nest in the trees and shrubs, to which he immediately betakes himself when alarmed.

There is, perhaps, no bird more graceful or beautiful in the quiet colour of its plumage than the nightingale. The Rev. Warde-Fowler gives so delightful a description of this bird, that I cannot refrain from quoting his words: 'It is of the ideal size for a bird . . . all its parts are in exquisite proportion. . . . Its plumage . . . is of three hues, all sober, but all possessing that reality of colour which is so satisfying to the eye on a sunny day. The uniform brown of the head, the wings, and the upper part of the back, is much like the brown of the robin . . . but either it is a little brighter or the larger surface gives it a richer tone. In both birds the brown is set off against a beautiful red; but this in the nightingale is only distinct when it flies or jerks the tail, the upper feathers of which, as well as the longer quills, and especially the innermost ones, are of that deep but bright russet that one associates with an autumn morning. And throat and breast are white, not pure white, but of the gentle tone of a cloud where the gray begins to meet the sunshine.' The above description is, to my mind, one of the most beautiful I have ever read. This author notices the similarity which exists, otherwise than in colouring, between the nightingale and the robin. There is also a certain similarity in form between the two birds; their habits are much alike, and they choose similar situations for building their nests. Both build on the ground as well as off it. Dixon, in his 'Rarer Birds,' states that 'the same anomaly exists between the nightingale and the robin as between the thrush and the redwing, although the robin and the thrush are residents, and the nightingale and redwing are migratory.' The nightingale is remarkable for the beauty of its song, and few of our birds can surpass the robin in that respect. In flight, general bearing, and carriage of their tails there is a strong resemblance between the two birds.

In the garden of a friend of mine, the vicar of a country parish in one of our Midland counties, and a sincere lover of birds, the nests of nightingales have been found on several occasions in the shrubberies, placed on the ground, and constructed of withered oak-leaves, the colour of the nest, eggs, and bird all harmonizing so perfectly with the surroundings as to easily escape observation. I have never as yet succeeded in finding the nest of a nightingale in my own gardens, though these birds pay me an annual visit, and during the earlier summer months sing to me in the wych-elms close to the house. I believe that they make their nests in these ivy-covered trees, where they are secure from the numerous cats which infest our village and scare away or destroy numberless birds.

I have been often tempted to shoot these

marauders, but do not like to do so, as they belong to the cottagers ; but it is very disappointing, after having watched some happy little brood day after day, to find them ruthlessly slaughtered by these poaching animals. I have every respect for really good cats, but when they take to killing birds they are rarely good mousers, and prefer feathers to fur. I once saw a cat dive off the bank of a deep river after a rat, which it captured and brought to land. It is the only instance I have known of a cat performing such a feat ; but I have had reason to suspect that a Persian tabby belonging to a friend of mine is in the habit of destroying fish, though I have as yet not been able to detect her in the act.

The character of the country in which my home is situated is peculiarly well adapted for the nesting and maintenance of a variety of birds. Large stretches of downland studded with gorse-bushes, plenty of woodlands and well-watered valleys, withy-beds and water-meadows, cultivated land and pastures, offer a combination of attraction not frequently to be met with. There are, besides these, plenty of strong hedgerows which are capable of affording food and shelter to those birds which affect such situations. And we are rich in bird-life. I myself have noticed nearly a hundred different kinds of birds, and there are also many others which I know to frequent the neighbourhood, but which I have not included in this number, either because I have not seen them myself, or have been uncertain as to their identity. I trust, however, ere long to be able to add them to my list, which, amongst those which may be termed our rarer birds, includes the stonechat, whinchat, wheatear, grasshopper warbler, sedge and reed warblers, gold-crested wren, marsh-tit, nut-hatch, tree-creeper, great gray shrike, goldfinch, brambling, siskin, bullfinch, gray wagtail, nightjar, green and spotted woodpeckers, wryneck, kingfisher (abundant), long and short-eared owls, hen-harrier, heron (abundant), wild-goose, turtle-dove, red-legged partridge, water-rail, stone curlew, gray Phalarope, green sandpiper, puffin, little grebe—a goodly list when taken in conjunction with the commoner kinds of land and water birds, and one which few districts can excel, or even equal. The moorhens and water-rails run about on the lawns, one or two pairs of kingfishers annually nest in the bank of the garden overhanging the river, and in the summer months all the commoner kinds of warblers may be found within a hundred yards of my house, to say nothing of flycatchers, wagtails, ring-doves, turtle-doves, jack-daws, starlings, meadow-pipits, and such-like. The golden-crested wren builds in a large cedar, the woodpecker, wryneck, and tree-creeper occasionally make their appearance, and I have also noticed the great, blue, cole, marsh, and long-tailed tits. The bearded tit has been also found in the neighbourhood, though I have never been fortunate enough to come across it. The corn and yellow buntings are common enough. Each and all of these birds may be encountered at one time or another within a stone's-throw of my home. A pair of turtle-doves generally make their nest in the wych-elms near the house, and last summer one of these birds rarely failed to come down and mingle with my poultry at feeding-time. I am looking forward to its return this spring. The summer snipe pays me a short visit at the period of its migration, and in frosty weather numbers of common snipe frequent my kitchen garden and the surrounding osier-beds. The jack snipe also puts in an appearance when working his passage to and fro on migration.

Keepers and gardeners will not be convinced that, by slaughtering birds which do more good than harm, they must of necessity do harm to their own interests. Sparrows *must* be kept within reasonable limits, and much the same may be said with regard to the starlings, though I grieve to be forced to make the admission; but these birds have increased so enormously in numbers of recent years as to necessitate some drastic measures being employed against them. But that should not be considered a sufficient reason for their wholesale destruction, and were this to be carried out, we should suffer very greatly as a natural consequence, for a reasonable supply of starlings is essential to the well-being of a farm or garden. Blackbirds and thrushes may trouble a gardener sadly at times, but their good qualities should not be forgotten.

Rooks, especially in a dry season, are by no means the farmer's best friends, but Parson Rook holds a sort of clerical dispensation, I suppose, and he is also too cute to be easily caught or permanently scared, and will enjoy himself to the full under the very shadow of the scarecrow, the hat and coat of which he is well acquainted with, and equally well aware is he that old Dobbs, to whom they formerly belonged, never stuffed himself with straw like that; and he thus reasons with himself: 'If it were old Dobbs himself it would not matter, for he never could hit anything with his gun, and is even more frightened of it than we are. As often as not it won't go off, and when it does it nearly knocks him backwards. No, it's not old Dobbs, so here goes for the potatoes.'

After all, it entails but little trouble or expense to protect the contents of kitchen-gardens from the depredations of birds. Black cotton is very cheap, and when it is well placed there are few birds which will face it. Where this remedy is ineffectual, netting can easily be substituted, and this is now so inexpensive as to be within the means of everyone who can afford to keep a gardener.

Time was when keepers were the bitterest foes of sparrow-hawks and kestrels, and I fear the prejudice against these birds is still very general; but there are some few who are able to recognise the fact that the slaughter of hawks and owls is a mistake. By all means let the keeper's tree be garnished with stoats, weasels, magpies, jays, crows, and such-like hopeless sinners; they are altogether beyond the pale, and crafty to boot. I cannot find it in me to extend the hand of mercy to stoat or weasel, but though I invariably empty a barrel at a magpie, jay, or crow, I do so with a certain amount of regret.

I think it must be allowed that birds have a language of their own. One warning note from the sentinel rook, and he and his sable brethren are up and away in a second. Should the cause of alarm be a man with a gun, they contrive to keep just out of gunshot; if, however, the gun be exchanged for a walking-stick, the hurry is less apparent.

Blackbirds use different warning-notes for different objects. Thus, if the object be a man, a dog, a stoat, or a cat, the note is varied. A young and very intelligent keeper, at one time in the employ of a friend of mine, was so conversant with these as to be able to pronounce with certainty what the object was which had occasioned the alarm. My friend told me that he had repeatedly proved the correctness of his assertions by having seen him go in quest of the animal and shoot it while he waited.

Wild-ducks, where they are plentiful, play

havoc with a fishery by eating the fish-spawn, but tame ducks are infinitely more destructive in this respect, and should be discouraged on any streams where it is desired to preserve the fish; they may be reckoned amongst the worst enemies to fishing. Much the same may also be said regarding herons, where these birds are numerous, as in the case of a heronry situated within easy reach of a river, but only when their numbers are excessive. In all other cases they should be spared. There are no fewer than three heronries whose occupants are within visiting distance of our river, and very grievous is the damage which the trout sustain from their society when the season is dry and the water low. It is extraordinary what large fish they are capable of extracting. I have known several instances in which trout considerably exceeding a pound in weight have fallen victims to the unerring stroke of their powerful beaks.

Of all our British birds, the peewit may be reckoned as the farmer's best friend, and, strange to say, farmers are, as a rule, well aware of the fact. It is much to be regretted that there are so many people who are able to esteem plovers' eggs a delicacy. Their appearance, when served in the shells and garnished with fresh green moss, is certainly very tempting, for the egg is very beautifully marked. It seems positively sinful that the sale of plovers' eggs should be so extensively carried on, and especially so when the beauty and utility of the birds are taken into

PEEWITS AND THEIR NESTS

consideration. I can hardly dare to hope that plovers will, to any great extent, derive any benefit from the recent Act. Considering the number of men who, for several weeks in every season, are busily employed searching for plovers' eggs, it is much to be wondered that this bird has not been altogether exterminated by reason of the demands of a senseless and selfish fashion—one which I hope my readers, be they many or few, will do their utmost to discourage.

Poor little birds! they may well evince such solicitude regarding the safety of their nests, when so many eager hands are outstretched to rob them. It is at times almost painful to witness the intense anxiety which a pair of plovers will display if anyone chances to wander near their nesting-place, as they fly round and round, making the most frantic endeavours to entice the intruder away from the spot, uttering the most plaintive cries, wheeling round and round, almost beating him with their wings, and never relaxing their efforts until they consider all danger is at an end. I have frequently been quite annoyed by these birds when fishing. On such occasions one's progress is but slow, and so long as I have remained within a couple of hundred yards of the nest I have had to endure this ceaseless screaming and flapping of wings around my head, until I have felt tempted to throw a stone at the birds, if only to get rid of them for a time.

It is a saying amongst the country-folk that

when the plovers flock high in the air it is a
sign of bad weather coming, and I have never
found it fail. I shall never forget the effect of
a flock of plovers against a mass of dark clouds
upon which the afternoon sun was shining. At
one time they were almost invisible, then, as
they wheeled, their dark bodies appeared like a
number of black spots fluttering against the cloud,
and as they turned again, exposing their white
wings and breasts to the sunlight, the appearance
presented was that of a shower of the most
brilliant crystals. I have often seen a somewhat similar display, but never one to equal it.
Where peewits elect to make their nests in a
ploughed field, as is frequently the case, they
invariably do so on the ridges, and never in the
furrows. In our down district the stone-curlew,
or, as it is sometimes termed, the great plover
or 'thick-knee,' frequently nests in the same field
with the peewit. They remain in the neighbourhood till quite late in September, sometimes even
later. Large, ungainly, untidy-looking birds they
are, too, and very shy and wary; and yet they
can hardly be termed ugly, for, despite their
shape, their plumage is a beautiful mixture of
gray, relieved by the pale-yellow colour of their
bills and legs. The iris of the eye is also of a
similar colour, but of a more decided yellow.
Their bodies are covered with a thick layer of
oily fat. Although I have skinned them, I have
never attempted to eat them. I am inclined to

the belief that their flesh would be the reverse of palatable. Their food consists principally of the worms, snails and beetles which they find under the stones, hence, perhaps, the name of stone-curlew, and their preference for those localities where stones are plentiful, and of a size which they can turn over, such as may be found in the cultivated portions of our chalky downlands. The stone-curlew will, at times, also kill frogs, lizards, and field-mice. A bird whose dietary consists of these creatures can hardly be expected to be suitable for food. The ordinary plover lays four eggs, the stone-curlew two only, of a dirty-white ground colour, spotted and streaked with gray and brown shades. These markings vary considerably, some of the eggs being entirely without blotches, and covered with streaks only. They are far more difficult to find than the eggs of the peewit, as their colour partakes very much of that of their surroundings. This bird is sometimes called the bustard plover, and, indeed, it is by no means unlike a bustard in some respects, not only in its habits and appearance, but in the fact of its laying but two eggs, whereas all the plover tribe lay four. It is also essentially a land-bird.

Once upon a time the great bustard was no rarity on our Southern downs. Some few years ago, when fishing in a stream at the foot of the Wiltshire downs, in a part of the country to which I was a stranger, I heard a bird calling in a field behind me. There was something in the note which seemed familiar to me, but I was puzzled as to what kind of bird it could possibly be. Sticking my rod in the ground, I walked in the direction whence the sound proceeded, and could just discern by the fading light a large bird, craning its neck and uttering the most peculiar call, much like that of a peacock, but less grating and powerful. On seeing me it rose and flew away in a straight line very close to the ground, across the river, and disappeared in the darkness. There were no houses or cottages near, and I was more perplexed than ever. I racked my brains to try and imagine what bird it could be, and concluded it must be either a peacock or a bustard. In size it more resembled the latter, yet in such a district it was quite as unlikely to be the one as the other. I was troubled in mind and not a little vexed that I could not come to any definite conclusion.

Some few days later I chanced to meet an acquaintance who lived in the neighbourhood, and on my mentioning the circumstance to him, he solved the mystery by explaining that one of the cottagers, who lived further down the valley, possessed a young peahen which was in the habit of straying far away from home. This, then, was my *rara avis*. The district was a wild one, and I, of course, never thought it probable or possible that such a bird should be roaming about, especially so late in the evening.

It was fortunate that I had not communicated my experiences to any of the sporting papers, and so made myself appear ridiculous.

It is much to be regretted that both the great and the little bustard have ceased to reside with us, and, moreover, no longer visit this country. Aplin, in his 'Birds of Oxfordshire,' states that a lesser bustard was shot in a wood near Oxford in 1859. I also have, amongst my own notes on birds, the account given me by a relative of one which was shot in Tubney Wood, in Berkshire, some six or seven miles from Oxford, by a friend of his about that date, probably the same bird. There have been, unless I am much mistaken, a few instances recorded of both the great and lesser bustards having been shot still more recently in different parts of this country.* It is commonly believed that the flight of bustards is too weak to admit of their extending their migrations. This is, however, an erroneous impression, and has doubtless originated from the fact that the weight of a bustard is not only very great, but that it is more prone to run than to get on the wing. Bustards, on the contrary, are able to fly with remarkable power. Colonel Campbell, in his letters from the Crimea, written

---

* A considerable number of great bustards arrived in the Orkneys in the winter of 1870; a smaller migration was noticed in England during the winter 1879-80.

Two of the smaller bustards were obtained in Ireland in December, 1887.—*Vide* Saunders' 'British Birds.'

during the war between England and Russia, makes special mention of their power of flight as follows : 'An immense flight of bustards passed over here about two days ago, going south. I was not out shooting that day, but a great many were killed near the Highland Division. I heard of one that weighed thirty pounds. I had no idea that their powers of flight were so great. They appear to fly quite as well as wild-geese, which they much resemble on the wing.'

Baldwin, in his 'African Hunting,' mentions having killed a bustard weighing, at the lowest estimate, fifty-four pounds. It was the large-crested bustard. Referring to the lesser bustard, he says : 'They are the most delicious birds, from three to five pounds in weight, and real game in their habits. . . . They are very difficult birds to put up ; they run like land-rails. . . . These bustards will often run more than half a mile.' He also speaks of a medium-sized bustard, probably the variety which were formerly to be found in England, as weighing from fifteen to thirty pounds.

If bustards possess great powers of flight, as may be concluded from the fact of their ever reaching this country, it seems strange that they should so rarely be seen in this country nowadays. That this is so may, perhaps, be due to the increased cultivation of the land, these birds preferring to reside in wild, uncultivated districts. Even in India they are less common than formerly.

The oubara and florican, lesser varieties of the bustard, are now somewhat rare.

Climate, and the supply of such food as is necessary for their maintenance, have, of course, everything to do with the variety of birds in a district. The greater the variety of bird-food, the greater will be the variety of birds which visit or reside in the locality, always provided that there are conveniences for their nesting, such as are afforded by hedgerows, woods, trees, gorse-coverts, and lastly, but by no means least, a plentiful supply of water. Where all these conditions are present, and the climate is moderate, bird-life will be varied and plentiful. It may be interesting to quote an instance of how birds are affected by their surroundings. I have the statement on the most reliable authority. 'In the neighbourhood of Wilton Park, in Wiltshire, the seat of the Earl of Pembroke, nightingales are by no means infrequent visitors; but in the park itself, of all places perhaps the one apparently most suitable for such birds, it is stated that no nightingale is ever seen or heard.'

DWELLERS IN NESTS.

PART II.

Garden Birds—Severe Winter of 1894-95—Mortality amongst Kingfishers from Prolonged Frost—An Enemy to Kingfishers—Extract from Jackson's *Oxford Journal*—Indian and British Kingfishers—Kingfisher's Feathers used for Salmon-flies — Anecdotes respecting Kingfishers — Kingfishers—Protection of Owls' Eggs in Oxfordshire under the New Act—The Law of Retaliation—Birds and Caterpillars —Woodpeckers—Varieties of British Woodpeckers— Great Green Woodpecker—Quotation from C. Kingsley's Poems—Woodpeckers in Devonshire—Greater Spotted and Lesser Barred Woodpeckers—The Wryneck—Cure for Gapes in Poultry, Pheasants, etc.—Observations on Woodpeckers and Wrynecks—Difficulty in detecting Song of Birds—Wrynecks in my own Garden—Name of Cuckoo's Mate—Plumage of Wryneck—Eggs of Wryneck—Peculiar Structure of Neck of Wryneck—Name of Snake-bird— Migration of Cuckoos—The Cuckoo—Instance of Cuckoo rearing its Young—Peculiar Formation of Back of Young Cuckoo—Deposition of Egg by Cuckoo—Varying Colour of Eggs—The Note of the Cuckoo—Too many Nightingales—Rearing of Young Cuckoos—Nests utilized by Cuckoo for depositing its Egg—Instance of a Thrush feeding a Young Cuckoo—Birds feeding Young Cuckoos —Disproportionate Sizes of Birds and their Eggs— The Mound Bird and the Cuckoo—Preference of Cuckoo

GARDEN BIRDS

for Pipit's Nest—Slaughter of Larks—'Hedge Potterers' —Woodlark and Skylark—Larks and Pipits—Varieties of Pipits—The Tree-pipit—The Meadow-pipit—French Lines on the Lark, and Translation—Reference to other Varieties of British Birds—The Buntings—The Cirl Bunting and the Yellow-hammer—The Corn Bunting —Songs of Buntings—The Reed and Black-headed Bunting—The Snow Bunting—Peculiarity in Change of Plumage of Bunting.

As I previously remarked, a certain number of birds are essential to the well-being of a garden, inasmuch as the good they do in the way of destroying slugs, caterpillars, and such-like enemies to vegetation, is incalculable, whereas any malpractices which may be laid to their charge in the matter of fruit-stealing, etc., are infinitely more than compensated for by the former. But besides all this, a garden would be but dreary and pleasureless if denuded of its bird-life. Such a state of affairs would be most depressing. What should we do without our blackbirds and thrushes? I would far sooner keep a garden stocked for the sole purpose of attracting birds, than be forced to kill the latter in order that I might the better enjoy the products of the garden. But it is a difficult matter to induce a gardener to believe such a statement. An old man who used to do work for me at times could not understand why I was so persistent in my prohibiting the destruction of birds, and never failed to tell me of his discovery of some new nest, requesting permission to destroy it, adding, that the damage to the peas or the strawberries would be dreadful if I did not allow him to have his way. But my answer was invariably the same : ' Never mind the peas. I can buy them if I want them ; but I cannot buy birds, and I prefer them to the peas.' I fear he cherished feelings of dire hatred towards my poor birds, but I am bound to say he never attempted to make away with a single nest. He was perfectly right in his opinion, and they did play havoc with the peas ; but, all the same, I had plenty for my own consumption, and managed to retain my birds also.

A relation of a friend of mine, who lived in the neighbourhood of London, and who was passionately fond of birds, yet dreadfully afraid of his gardener, used to remove the netting from the strawberry-beds on Sunday when the gardener was absent, in order to let the birds feast on the fruit.

I fear that the prolonged and severe weather which prevails at the time I write must cause the death of numbers of our birds from hunger, thirst, and cold. In the towns and the suburbs they fare better than in the country, as most people nowadays remember the birds, and food is plentifully bestowed ; but I dread to think what must have been the fate of many of our country birds. The kingfishers must have been nearly decimated, and numbers of them will, I fear, be found dead in the streams when the thaw comes.

And these are birds which we can but ill afford to lose. In the neighbourhood of my home they are plentiful, and I have no anxiety regarding their welfare, as our little river never freezes, and they are thus able to support themselves. It is rather in the larger and more sluggish streams of the Midland counties that these birds will, I fear, suffer most severely.

I cannot forbear quoting the following article, which appears in the *Oxford Journal* of yesterday's date (February 16, 1895):

'We regret very much to learn that in some parts of this county a war of extermination is being waged against the kingfisher, the most beautiful, without exception, of any of our birds. A very short time ago a well-known Fellow of Oriel had two live kingfishers offered him for sale; they had been caught in nets in the Ottmoor district, and the story was that an Oxford bird-stuffer would give eighteenpence apiece for them. One of the children of the Oriel Fellow insisted on her father buying the birds as a birthday present for herself, in order that she might have the happiness of releasing them. But we have a much sadder story of the kingfishers to tell than that, for we fear it is too true that in the neighbourhood of Adderbury scores have been ruthlessly killed under the ridiculous pretext of preserving a trout stream. We have it on very good authority that a so-called sportsman, or his keeper, has destroyed this season no fewer than eighty-five kingfishers. The few trout fry that the kingfisher may possibly eat would never be missed, for Nature in her bounty has taken care to provide abundance for other fish, for birds, for otters even, and for man, the most selfish too often of all the animal race. Those who know that beautiful little trout-stream, the Dorne, which, rising near Little Tew, meanders on to Blenheim Lake and the Evenlode, know a stream which, for its size, can never be surpassed as a trout-stream, yet you may often see the heron on its banks, and note the jewelled form of the kingfisher flash by you. The stream is stocked with fish such as perch, and even has pike in its waters, while crayfish, a supposed deadly enemy to spawn, are found there in abundance, yet there is no finer trout-stream anywhere in the Midlands. If our words can reach the kingfisher's enemy, we would implore him to spare this beautiful bird, which feeds principally on sticklebacks and minnows. He will not catch one trout the less, and his sport will surely be the sweeter when he knows it has not been associated with the destruction of one of the most lovely of the Creator's works.'

There are times when the feeling of righteous wrath is too strong to find expression in words. I therefore forbear to comment on the above, further than to add that previous to its appearance in print I had been informed of the facts of the case, and have but too sufficient reason to believe

INDIAN AND BRITISH KINGFISHERS 127

them to be absolutely true. For the rest, I leave the reader to think and say what he pleases. There is but little one can say when one's feelings are so grievously outraged. I can only feel too thankful that there are no such bird-murderers in the county in which I reside. I rarely fail to see two or three kingfishers during my walks by the side of the river, for scarcely an hour passes without one or other of these birds showing itself as it wings its way up and down the stream.

Our British variety, though small, is perhaps as beautiful as any of the tribe. When snipe-shooting in India, I observed two different species, one exactly similar to our own, and a larger gray-spotted kind. I have also seen them in large numbers fishing together in some of the streams which surround the djheels. Very beautiful they were, with the sunlight falling on their brilliant plumage as they hovered in the air. I shot some two or three on different occasions in order to examine them more closely. The gray variety is not remarkable for any beauty of form or colouring—indeed, may be described as a plain bird; but those which resemble our British bird are slightly larger, and I do not think quite as brilliant. The vivid colours of the kingfisher's plumage fades very rapidly after death, almost as quickly as those of a freshly-caught mackerel. The bright blue feathers are much used in the manufacture of certain salmon-flies;

but, as all salmon fishermen are aware, they are very soon spoiled, and after being used a few times the colour disappears. For this reason I always prefer to substitute the feathers of the chatterer jay or the blue-enamelled thrush, which, though possessing less lustre, are more permanent.

Last summer (1894) a man fishing in the canal at Kidlington, near Oxford, noticed a dead kingfisher floating on the surface of the water. On bringing it to land, he discovered that its death had resulted from suffocation, a ruffe (a small fish with a large back fin armed with sharp spines) being fixed in its gullet. A cousin of mine, when fishing in the same neighbourhood, observed a kingfisher strike at a small fish and miss it; immediately afterwards it settled on the top of his rod, and there remained for several seconds preening its feathers.

On another occasion a kingfisher darted through the bars of the scullery window in the house of another relation of mine in Lincolnshire, and, coming in contact with the lid of a saucepan or some such article hanging on the wall opposite, was killed. The bird doubtless thought that the bright shining metal indicated a hole in the wall. In this there was, perhaps, nothing very remarkable, but it was worthy of note, inasmuch as kingfishers are uncommon in that immediate district; and although there is a large pond within a couple of hundred yards of the house, it is situated on the side farthest away from that occupied by the servants' offices.

That kingfishers are capable of destroying fish is indisputable, but they should be surely free of every stream in Britain. No true English sportsman would ever think of harming them. The man that can do so ought to be ostracised from the society of all decent Englishmen.

Since commencing this portion of the present work, I am delighted to be able to inform my readers that I have received information that in Oxfordshire steps are being taken to procure protection for the eggs of the owls in that county during the nesting season, and I trust ere long to have the opportunity of examining the list. It is sincerely to be hoped that other counties, if they have not already done so, may follow this example. Should this happen, the new Act will be indeed welcomed by all lovers of birds, by none more so than myself; but it will be necessary for those in authority to see that the notices are properly posted in every village; that they are protected from injury; and that a penalty is *not only threatened, but enforced* in every instance in which they are defaced. At present the annual notice of the former Act, which relates to the protection of wild-birds, is not always properly posted in our villages, in some not at all.

As I have endeavoured to show, the majority

of birds—indeed, with one or two exceptions, I may say *all* of them—do more good than harm. They serve to rid us of innumerable pests in the shape of slugs, snails, wire-worms, maggots, and insects of all kinds; it is, I believe, a well-ascertained fact that, in those districts in which indiscriminate war has been waged against birds which were supposed to have weakened the crops, the law of retaliation has exacted a heavy penalty, other and worse pests having increased and multiplied in proportion. A district which has been denuded of birds can be neither thriving nor desirable to live in; the demolition of trees and hedgerows for the purpose of depriving the birds of their harbourage must as surely ruin a neighbourhood as mar its beauty.

The damage which caterpillars, grubs, *et hoc genus*, are capable of inflicting on garden and field produce is, as all are aware, very considerable. I do not think that it is going too far to assert that, but for the birds, there would be but few crops, and vegetation generally would suffer to an equal extent. Gilbert White, in his 'Natural History of Selborne,' mentions an instance of the oak-trees in the neighbourhood of Selborne being stripped of their leaves, and the fact of a flight of swifts being busily engaged in hawking after the moth of the caterpillar which had occasioned the damage. Markwick, in a note referring to White's statement, describes a similar occurrence, but corrects White's specification as to the variety of caterpillar, the latter supposing it to be the *Phalæna quercus*, whereas Markwick declares it to be the *Phalæna viridana*. In the early part of last summer (June, 1894), I noticed several acres of young oak-trees, in Tubney Warren, in Berkshire, completely denuded of their leaves, and on making inquiry as to the cause, was told that it was the work of a kind of grub. I do not mention this as being by any means a rare occurrence, but merely to illustrate how serious would be the depredations of the progeny of such caterpillars were it not for the aid afforded us by the birds in killing the parent moths.

Woodpeckers are most foully accused by the more ignorant of causing the destruction of trees, and woodmen and keepers accordingly seize every opportunity which offers for slaughtering them. Now, such an accusation is most unwarrantable; these birds are in reality the woodman's stanchest allies, for not only do they destroy the insects which ruin the trees, but by their presence indicate those which require his attention. It never occurs to these people to ask themselves in what way the woodpecker is in the habit of damaging trees, or why he labours so indefatigably with his bill. They have been told that the bird does harm, and that is sufficient for them to warrant its destruction. I suppose they conclude that it lives on wood. Were they but to take the trouble to open the crop of one of their victims, they would be very much surprised, and might in future be persuaded to spare the life of one of our most beautiful and interesting birds.

There are three varieties of woodpeckers in Britain—viz., the green, the great spotted, and the lesser spotted, or, as it is sometimes termed, the barred—and these three birds differ considerably in size and plumage. The green woodpecker is by far the largest, measuring from thirteen to fourteen inches in length. The general colour of the body is a greenish-yellow, and in all three varieties the crown of the head is scarlet.

The flight of the woodpecker is peculiar, consisting of a series of undulations; that of the wryneck is also somewhat similar, though the undulatory motion is not, perhaps, so clearly defined. The green woodpecker is in some districts called the yaffil. I am inclined to think this name may have originated from the curious cry of the bird, which has by some naturalists been described as sounding like a laugh. The country people assert, and truly, that when the woodpecker laughs loudly rain may be expected. Kingsley, in one of his poems, refers to this well-known peculiarity in the following verses, evidently written when he was longing for the rain to fall, in order that he might enjoy a day's fishing, porbably in the lake known as the Fleet Pond, near Aldershot:

'O blessed drums of Aldershot!
O blest South-Western train!
O blessed, blessed speaker's clock!
All prophesying rain.

'O blessed *yaffil* laughing loud!
O blessed falling grass!
O blessed fan of cold gray cloud!
O blessed smelling grass!

'O blest South Wind which toots his horn
Through every hole and crack!
I'm off at eight to-morrow morn
To bring such fishes back!'

When shooting in Devonshire some four or five years ago, I was much struck with the large number of green woodpeckers in the district in which I was staying. The country was well wooded, as is, indeed, nearly the whole of that county; but there was in addition a long stretch of rough, sandy fields, extending for nearly a mile between two large woodlands, evidently a clearing, and this ground was covered with mole-hills, affording a plentiful supply of ants, which are the woodpecker's favourite food, for, as I have before remarked, these insects may be found in any old mole-hill.

But few really good fishing-days fall to the lot of the angler during the season; before rain neither salmon or trout are ever in the humour, and on such occasions the woodpecker is apt to be especially noisy. There is, on a well-known salmon-river in one of our Southern counties, an old water-keeper for whom I entertain the greatest regard, and his views on most subjects are especially amusing and original. If there is one thing he cordially hates it is a woodpecker, and when sport has failed he invariably attributes it to the influence of the 'yaffil,' as he calls it. ' There! I might ha' know'd we shouldn't catch no fish to-day; I heard that blessed yaffil again last night.' It is, however, not a little remarkable that the 'blessed yaffil' is not mentioned until the close of the day, when all efforts to secure a fish have proved utterly futile, and so, as ' there are more fish in the river than ever come out of it,' that 'blessed yaffil' is pretty freely anathematized.

The greater spotted woodpecker is between nine and ten inches in length, the lesser variety under six inches. Both birds are, with the exception of the scarlet crown on their heads, black and white. The back and wings of the former bird are black with white spots, and the vent scarlet, whereas in the latter the middle of the back is marked with very distinct bars of black and white. The difference between these birds is thus very clearly defined, and they cannot well be mistaken. The greater and lesser spotted are far less common than the green variety. I am inclined to believe that these two birds are in the habit of seeking their food under the bark of the trees rather than by boring into the wood, as is the habit of the green woodpecker, which,

CURE FOR GAPES IN POULTRY, ETC.

its strength being greater, is better able to work through the harder portions of wood which frequently cover those limbs of a tree that are internally decayed; but all three birds construct their nests—if nests they can be called—by boring a hole through the rotten wood and laying their eggs in the hollow of the trunk, when, as is often the case, a suitable hole is at hand ready-made. The tails of woodpeckers are stiff and pointed, enabling them to support themselves when clinging to the bark of trees in their search for food. The tail of the wryneck, which bird very closely resembles that of the woodpecker in shape and habits, is not furnished with these stiff feathers, nor does it procure its food in precisely the same manner. The woodpecker inserts its beak into the crevices of the bark and extracts the insects with its tongue, which is sharp, horny, and well adapted for the purpose; whereas the wryneck projects its tongue beyond its beak. The tongue of both birds is covered with a glutinous substance which enables them to extract the insects upon which they feed. The tongue of the woodpecker is frequently used by keepers for the purpose of extracting the worms which, congregating in the throats of chickens and young pheasants, are the cause of the disease known as 'gapes,' and to which these birds are very subject in wet seasons. Apropos of which, I may as well mention that I have found that a drop or two of camphorated oil is an effectual remedy for this disease. The best method of applying it is to take an ordinary feather—a pigeon's or partridge's wing-feather is as suitable as any—pull off all the fibres, except those at the extreme tip, dip it in the camphorated oil, and thrust it down the throat, giving it a twist between the finger and thumb. It was a remedy which I discovered quite by accident, and one which I have never known to fail.

I have on one or two occasions noticed the green woodpecker in the neighbourhood of our village, and last summer one of the large spotted variety paid me a visit. The lesser barred woodpecker I have never had the good fortune to see, though when living in Hampshire I heard of an occasional specimen being procured, and they are doubtless more common than is supposed; but they are difficult birds to catch sight of, and I am not sufficiently conversant with their note to recognize it, especially when other birds are in full song at the time. I know nothing more difficult than to be able to detect the songs of different birds when there are several singing at once, and I often regret my inability to do so. Some people are so fortunately constituted as to be able to distinguish every variety of bird under such circumstances; it is a great advantage to a lover of birds. Although I have often tried to acquire the power my ear gets confused.

I have observed the wryneck on one or two

occasions in my garden, but it is by no means a frequent or a regular visitor to our district. On one occasion I am almost certain that I saw a wryneck fly out of a large ash-tree, and, strange to say, immediately after a cuckoo had flown out of it. Although this bird is frequently called the cuckoo's mate, it is not in the habit of associating with the cuckoo, the name being derived merely from the fact of its making its appearance about the same time as the cuckoo. The wryneck is one of the most beautiful of our more soberly-clad birds, its plumage consisting of the most exquisite combination of browns and grays, arranged in a series of broken bars, somewhat similar to that of the goatsucker, or, as I prefer to call it, the nightjar. Like the woodpecker, it makes its nest in the holes of trees, etc., and its eggs are very similar to those of that bird, being of a shining white.

During the present summer (1895) some wrynecks, which have, I believe, made their nest in an elm-tree in a neighbouring meadow, have paid frequent visits to my garden. At times they were very clamorous, though, needless to add, by no means equal to the sedge-warblers, which are here very abundant, one or other of which was sure to instantly mimic the notes of the wryneck, and an exceedingly clever imitation it was. The wryneck possesses the power of moving its head in every direction, as if the neck were provided with a ball and socket joint, hence its name. The barred markings of its plumage, coupled with the peculiar hissing noise which this bird makes if its nest is approached, have earned for it the sobriquet of 'the snake bird' in some districts. Unlike the woodpeckers, which are residents, the wryneck* only remains in this country for a few weeks after the adult cuckoos have taken their departure in August, the younger cuckoos remaining with us till October.

The cuckoo is, perhaps, of all our birds the most interesting and peculiar in its habits. Everyone knows that the cuckoo is in the habit of placing its eggs in the nests of other birds, and that very much to the detriment of the occupants of the nests selected, which sooner or later are discarded by their parents, who bestow all their attention on the usurper. From these facts several theories have arisen, one being that the cuckoo never rears its own young (and certainly in this country there is no record of its having done so), and therefore, so far as our acquaintance with this bird extends, it appears never likely to do so. It was, then, not a little startling to ornithologists to receive the news that in Germany a cuckoo had been known to bring up its young. This incident is referred to by the Rev. Warde Fowler, as having been recorded in

* Since writing the above, a wryneck has been hanging about my garden for several days, and calling incessantly, an impertinent sedge-warbler frequently imitating it.

VARYING COLOUR OF CUCKOO'S EGGS

the *Ibis* of April, 1889. What has once taken place may happen again.

In the back of the young cuckoo there is a curious depression, and scientists have asserted that this is a provision of Nature to enable the young bird to eject the other eggs which are in the nest, a theory which I find it difficult to accept, though unable to suggest any other reason for this conformation. It is commonly believed that the cuckoo actually lays its egg in the nest which it may select for the purpose. Now, when the size of the bird is compared with that of the nests in which it is known to deposit its egg, and also when the shape of some of these nests is considered, it will be seen at once how impracticable such a performance must be. The egg is without doubt *placed* in the nest, the bird carrying it in its bill for the purpose, an operation for which the latter is peculiarly well adapted.

An acquaintance of mine living in Hampshire, a student of ornithology, stated in the *Field* some few years ago the names of the different birds in whose nests he had from time to time discovered the eggs of the cuckoo. The list was a long one, thereby proving his research, but what seemed most worthy of note was his assertion that he had observed that the colour of the egg invariably partook very much of that of the other eggs in the nest; for instance, if the egg was found in that of a robin, its general tone was reddish; if in that of a hedge-sparrow, it was of a bluish tinge, etc. I have never myself made any observation either in proof or disproof of this statement. If it is correct, and I have no reason to doubt that it is so, it is, to say the least, one of the most remarkable things in natural history.

We annually look forward to the arrival of the cuckoo as the harbinger of spring. For the first few days its note is but little heard, but after a time there are few hours in the twenty-four in which it is silent. I have heard it as late as between eleven and twelve o'clock at night. Cuckoos are very abundant in the neighbourhood of my home, and, I am almost ashamed to confess, there are times when I could wish them silent. Fond as I am of all birds, it is quite possible to have too much of a good thing. I may be thought a heretic, but I am forced to admit that I have positively been bored to death with the songs of nightingales. I was staying on a visit with a friend residing in Surrey; the window of my bedroom looked out upon a part of the garden thickly planted with tall shrubs, and in these the nightingales assembled every evening. Neither before nor since have I ever heard such a chorus of these birds. At first I was enchanted, but when, night after night, their music prevented my sleeping, I found myself heartily wishing they would take their departure. My room was small, and the weather too hot to admit of my closing the window. There are not many people, I take it,

REARING OF YOUNG CUCKOOS

who have ever been able to make a similar complaint.

It is strange how entirely those birds, in whose nest a cuckoo's egg has been deposited, neglect their own offspring for the non-paying guest which has been foisted upon them. All their energies are devoted to the feeding and rearing of the young giant. One by one their own chicks are turned out of the nest, and the poor deluded parents are kept incessantly at work to provide food for the newcomer.* The amount of food a young cuckoo can consume in the twenty-four hours is simply appalling, and his growth is proportionate. At last he becomes too big for the nest, and so props himself up outside it ; not infrequently he tumbles out of it altogether, a hideous, piteous monster for ever squalling for more food. Like the daughters of the horse-leech, his cry is ever, 'Give, give'; and he gets it, too, for should his foster parents fail to feed him, other birds will do so. One of these stray ogres, which had tumbled out of the nest, was seen to be fed by a thrush, and yet the thrush is one of those birds in whose nest the egg of the cuckoo is never found. The hedge-sparrow, robin, redstart, whitethroat, willow and sedge warblers, wagtail, pipit, skylark, yellow-hammer, chaffinch, green-

* Saunders, in his work on British birds, states that Mr. Hancock saw the nestling cuckoo begin to eject the young of the hedge-sparrow when the former had only been hatched about thirty hours.

finch, linnet, wren, and blackbird, are all subject to be imposed upon more or less frequently, the pipit being more often made use of than the rest; but the thrush seems to be exempt. So it is all the more remarkable that a bird of this species should have elected to feed a cuckoo. But all the birds seem to go mad on the subject of young cuckoos, and if one presents a deaf ear to the pleadings for food, another is ever ready to undertake the heavy responsibility of supplying the larder. A friend of mine, in whose garden a young cuckoo was being brought up by some small birds (I forget what description of birds they were), told me that it was almost piteous to observe the frantic endeavours the poor little creatures made to supply their adopted infant with food.

It is curious how very disproportionate some eggs are to the size of the bird. Thus, the mound bird, a native of Australia, lays the largest egg of any bird in proportion to its size. The measurement which I have procured of this bird is as follows: from the tip of the bill to the end of the body, eleven inches. The size of the egg is three and three-eighths inches by two and one-eighth inches. The egg of the cuckoo is perhaps the smaller in proportion to the size of the bird; in both instances the dispensation of Providence is apparent. Were the egg of the cuckoo proportionate to the size of the bird, it would be too large for the purpose of incubation in the nests of those birds which are most suitable for rearing the young cuckoo. The egg of the cuckoo is about the size of that of the pipit; it is for this reason, perhaps, that the nest of the latter is so frequently selected. The ground colour of the eggs of the two birds is, moreover, somewhat similar.

The wholesale slaughter of larks which takes place annually is a disgrace. Still more so is it that there should be so great a demand for these birds for table purposes. So long as there exist people whose consciences are so dulled as to admit of their eating them, so long they will continue to be slaughtered. Englishmen hold the name of Vitellius in detestation quite as much because he feasted on the tongues of nightingales as for any other of his numerous vices. Yet it seems to me to be quite as disgusting to eat a skylark as a nightingale. Tens of thousands of these birds are exposed for sale in the markets during the winter *as food!* I often wonder, if those people who purchase them were to be told that these are the birds which carol high in the air over the April corn, whether they could find it in their hearts to condemn such joyous little minstrels to death. I cannot but suppose that when they purchase them they are under the impression that they are a different kind of bird to the skylark, of which poets have sung, and of the beauty of whose melody they themselves can talk so glibly and rapturously.

Were it otherwise, I feel sure they could never encourage its destruction, for the love of birds is too strongly implanted in most of the English people to sacrifice so sweet a songster to satisfy so disgusting a vice as gluttony. Many a pipit and many a woodlark is doubtless included in the bag of the hedge-potterer, who, prowling about with his gun, shoots at anything and everything which presents itself. Last winter I encountered one of these loafers proudly carrying a large bundle of skylarks, which he was doubtless taking to the nearest poulterer's shop.

The song of the woodlark equals, if it does not excel, that of the skylark, although it is a considerably smaller bird, being nearly an inch shorter.* It may be distinguished from the skylark by its habit of perching on trees, as also by its flight when it soars. The skylark flies straight up into the air or waves to and fro, whereas the woodlark mounts in circles. The skylark never perches, for the best of all reasons, viz., that it cannot, its hinder toe being too straight to admit of its so doing.

The pipits and larks are so similar in plumage as to be frequently mistaken. It may be of service to some of my readers if I briefly explain how they may be readily distinguished.

Referring to Colonel Irby's list of British birds, I find that there are no less than seven varieties of pipits included. Of this number, two, viz., the

* At times it also sings by night.

tree and meadow pipits, are common; one, the rock pipit (chiefly a resident on the sea-coast and mud-flats in the winter), is local, and therefore more or less uncommon. The rest, viz., the red-throated, water, tawny, and Richard's pipits, are too rare and seldom met with to come within the scope of this work. I therefore think that it is unnecessary to refer to more than the two first-named varieties, *i.e.*, the tree and the meadow pipits. Of these, the former is the longer. It is a migratory bird, coming in the spring and leaving in the autumn. Its hinder claw is *curved*. Its entire length is six inches and a half. Its habits are peculiarly distinct from those of the meadow pipit. Yarrell thus describes it: 'He generally sings while perched on the top of a bush, or one of the upper branches of an elm-tree standing in a hedgerow . . . he will be seen to ascend about as high again as the tree; then, stretching out his wings and expanding his tail, he descends slowly by a half-circle, singing the whole time, to the same branch from which he started, or to the top of the nearest other tree. . . . Its descent to the ground is generally performed in the same manner.' All the pipits move their tails very much after the fashion of the wagtails, and this habit serves to distinguish them from the larks, which they so strongly resemble in some other respects.

Unlike the tree-pipit, the meadow-pipit does not perch on trees, its hinder claw being too straight to permit of its doing so. It is therefore always to be observed on the ground. It *has* been seen to rest on a bough, but merely for a second or two, in the course of its descent. This pipit is not migratory, and so remains with us throughout the year. Its length is given at five inches and a half, being thus smaller by an inch than the tree-pipit. Its song is not remarkable for its variety or melody, being short and simple.

The Rev. C. A. Johns, in his 'British Birds,' quotes the following very beautiful French lines on the skylark, which a friend of mine has translated. I give both the original and the translation :

> 'La gentille alouette, avec son tirelire,
> Tirelire, relire et tirelirant tire
> Vers la voute du ciel ; puis son vol en ce lieu
> Vire, et semble nous dire : Adieu, adieu, adieu.'

TRANSLATION.
> 'The skylark, with his roundelay,
> Trills, trills, and trilling, mounts his way
> To heaven's blue vault ; then soars from view,
> And seems to bid us : Adieu, adieu.'

The lines necessarily lose somewhat of their value in the translation, but the author of the latter has, I think, very gracefully rendered their exact meaning.

There are some three or four families of our British birds to which I have not as yet referred, and which are apt to be somewhat confusing to a person not sufficiently acquainted with their appearance. I propose, therefore, to endeavour to explain as simply as possible how they may readily be distinguished. Amongst these are the buntings, warblers, tits, hawks, and owls.

Were the present work intended to be one on natural history, I should have placed the various animals and birds in their proper order ; but, as I have remarked in my preface, although I am anxious to avoid posing as a naturalist, I am no less desirous to attract the attention of the reader to a few of our commoner British animals, birds, etc., so that he may, if unacquainted with them, learn to recognize them in the course of his daily walks, and also, I trust, learn to love them. Any stereotyped plan of arrangement would savour too much of an ordinary work on natural history ; I have therefore, in order to excite additional interest, broken up the subject as much as possible.

As regards the buntings, no fewer than eleven varieties are included in the list of British birds, viz. :

- The black-headed bunting (three occurrences only).
- The corn bunting (resident).
- The yellow bunting, or yellow-hammer (resident).
- The cirl bunting (resident in the South of England).
- Brandt's Siberian bunting (one occurrence).

The ortolan bunting (straggler on migration).
The rustic bunting (three occurrences).
The little bunting (one record).
The reed bunting (resident).
The snow bunting (rare, chiefly North of Scotland).
The Lapland bunting (irregular straggler).

By the above, taken from Colonel Irby's list, it will be observed that only four of these birds—viz., the common or corn bunting, the yellow bunting (or yellow-hammer), the cirl bunting, and the reed bunting—are resident. The cirl bunting is also a somewhat rare bird, but as it is, perhaps, less so than those which I have set aside, and is resident, I think it as well to devote some few words to its appearance, character, and habits. Since this bird resembles the yellow-hammer, or yellow bunting, I think it as well to take the two together, in order that I may the better explain how they may be distinguished. Of the two, the yellow-hammer is the larger by about half an inch, the cirl bunting measuring but six inches in length, whereas the yellow-hammer varies in length from six and a half to seven inches.*
The chin and the throat of the cirl bunting

---

* These measurements are Colonel Irby's. Saunders gives the length of both birds as equal, viz., six and a half inches.

are black; whereas in the case of the yellow-hammer the entire head is of a lemon-yellow colour. There are various other differences in the plumage, but this one peculiarity is quite sufficient to distinguish them. The yellow-hammer may be met with in all parts of the country; the cirl bunting, preferring warmth to cold, confines itself to the southern counties. The yellow-hammer is also more fearless than the cirl bunting, which is an excessively shy bird, and prefers to frequent the tops of trees; whereas the yellow-hammer is most generally to be observed amongst the hedgerows and such-like places. The latter generally builds its nest on the ground; the cirl bunting very rarely does so. Dixon, referring to the song of the cirl bunting, says: ' It is, however, a most industrious musician, and its song proclaims its presence to him who is conversant with the notes of birds. This resembles very closely the yellow-hammer's love-song, but wants the long-drawn note which usually terminates that bird's refrain.'*

The common or corn bunting is about the size of the yellow-hammer—viz., seven inches in length. Its general colour is a grayish-brown, with dark-brown streaks. The tail, which is brown, is edged and tipped with yellowish-white. All the buntings present a somewhat rough and untidy appearance, as if their feathers had been

* The Rev. C. A. Johns states that the name yellow-hammer is derived from the German word *Ammer* = a bunting.

brushed up by machinery. The Rev. C. A. Johns describes the song of this bird as 'harsh and unmelodious.' The Rev. W. Fowler, in comparing its song with that of the yellow-hammer, and referring to the latter, says : ' This song (if, indeed, it can be called one) is a much better one than that of the corn bunting, and is occasionally even a little varied.' In another place he remarks of the buntings in general that they are 'melancholy birds,' and, 'I have just been looking through a series of plates and descriptions of all the buntings of Europe, and in almost every one of them I see the same deflected tail and listless attitude, and read of the same monotonous and continually-repeated note. . . . Look at the common corn bunting as he sits on the wires or the hedge-top ; he is lumpy, loose-feathered, spiritless, and flies off with his legs hanging down, and without a trace of agility or vivacity. He is a dull bird, and seems to know it ; even his voice is half-hearted.'

The characteristics of the reed bunting are much the same as those of the other three to which I have referred ; but he is generally to be found in the vicinity of water, perched upon the bough of an alder, a withy, or amongst the reeds. He is by no means an uncommon bird, though, I fancy, somewhat local.* The Rev. C. A. Johns

---

* They are common in the neighbourhood of my home, and are frequently to be seen perched on the top of some reed by the riverside.

describes this bird as the black-headed bunting. The latter is a full inch longer than the reed bunting, and is an exceedingly rare bird, only three occurrences having been noted, and those, according to Colonel Irby, females and young birds. These three specimens were observed as follows—viz.: Sussex, 1868; Notts, 1884; and Scotland, 1887. Colonel Irby thus describes the plumage of the two birds:

The black-headed; head and ear-coverts black; back and rump chestnut; chin and under parts bright yellow.

The reed bunting (male, in spring): head and throat black; cheeks white; eye-stripe white; white collar from bill round nape; rump bluish-gray; lesser wing-coverts chestnut. In autumn the black is hidden by rufous edgings, and the white by sandy-brown edgings.

The females of these birds vary considerably from the males, the hens of both being much alike. In both the black parts about the head are replaced by brown striped with black. In the female of the black-headed bunting, the back and under parts are very similar to those of the male. The breast and flanks of the female reed bunting are white streaked with blackish markings, and the outside web of the second tail-feather is white.

The reed bunting, or, as it is sometimes termed, the reed sparrow, is a resident. The black-headed bunting is migratory. Another authority praises the song of this bird, and states that, like the nightingale, it sings during the night. This is altogether wrong, for the bird has no song to speak of, and what it possesses is by no means remarkable for its melodious qualities, nor does it sing during the night. Altogether, I am inclined to think that some ornithologists are not very clear in their ideas respecting this bird, and yet it is quite common enough to afford plenty of opportunity to those who care to observe it for acquiring information as to its peculiarities. All the buntings build their nests either on or close to the ground.

The snow bunting I have never seen alive; I was recently shown a preserved specimen which had been shot in my own neighbourhood some years ago ; I should, however, imagine that there are but few of our counties in which it has not at some time or other been observed. It rarely makes its appearance save in exceptionally severe winters. It is a migratory bird, though Colonel Irby states that a few pairs breed on the mountains in the North of Scotland. I have made mention of this bird very much on account of the peculiarity of its plumage. The majority of birds which change from their ordinary plumage to white, such as the ptarmigan, etc., do so in the winter. In Colonel Irby's description he states that the plumage of the snow bunting varies as follows : In summer the head, neck, and under surface white ; above black ; wing-coverts white ; bill black. In winter, crown reddish-brown ; feathers on upper parts broadly edged with reddish-brown ; bill yellowish, with dark tip. Length, six and a half to seven inches.

A friend of mine informs me that the snow bunting is by no means infrequently to be seen in the London parks.

DWELLERS IN NESTS

PART III.

British Warblers—Common British Warblers—Difficulty in distinguishing Certain Warblers—Making Observations on Birds—Classification of the Commoner Warblers—The Rev. W. Fowler's 'Year with the Birds'—Classification of the Commoner British Warblers—The Whitethroats—The Garden Warbler—The Blackcap—The Chiffchaff—The Willow Warbler—The Reed and Sedge Warblers—An Idle Hour with the Birds—A Favoured Spot—'Among the Golden Reed-beds'—The Spotted and Pied Flycatchers—The Wagtails—White and Pied Wagtails—Gray and Yellow Wagtails—Bird-stuffers and Taxidermists—A Specimen of Provincial Taxidermy—Taxidermists and Naturalists—Messrs. Butt and Ward—The Tit Family—The Long-tailed Tit—The Great Tit—The Blue Tit—Marsh and Coal Tits—Feeding Tits in Winter—The Bearded Tit.

THE British warblers, or Sylviinæ, as they are more scientifically called, comprise a large number of birds, no less than twenty different varieties having at one time and another been observed in these islands. I think it as well to give the list *in extenso*, although many of them are exceedingly rare, and only one of them, the Dartford warbler, can be called a resident, all the others being migratory. The Dartford warbler is only found in the gorse districts south of the Thames. The list which Colonel Irby gives is as follows :

1. The whitethroat (common).
2. The lesser whitethroat (common).
3. The garden warbler (common).
4. The blackcap (common).
5. The western orphean warbler (very rare, two records only).
6. The barred warbler (scarce straggler on migration).
7. The Dartford or furze warbler (local in gorse districts only).
8. The western rufous warbler (three occurrences only).
9. The great reed warbler (very rare straggler).
10. The reed warbler (common).
11. The marsh warbler (uncommon, local).
12. The sedge warbler (common).
13. The aquatic warbler (three occurrences only).
14. The grasshopper warbler (fairly common).
15. Savi's warbler (rare, local).
16. The yellow tree warbler (very rare straggler).
17. The yellow-browed warbler (rare straggler on migration).
18. The chiffchaff warbler (common).
19. The willow warbler (common).
20. The wood warbler (not common).

It will be seen that out of these eight only can be regarded as really common in Britain, these being :

    1. The whitethroat.
    2. The lesser whitethroat.
    3. The garden warbler.
    4. The blackcap.
  10. The reed warbler.
  12. The sedge warbler.
  18. The chiffchaff.
  19. The willow wren.

No. 7, the Dartford or furze warbler, though resident, is local. The remaining eleven varieties are mostly too rare or uncommon for me to refer to.

It is exceedingly difficult for any but a skilled naturalist to distinguish at first sight the differences which exist between some of even these more common of our warblers. I refer, of course, to the *living* birds. I do not think that they are more shy than other birds, but their movements are so quick that before it is possible to examine them, even with the assistance of a field-glass, they have disappeared from view; and so, unless the gun is brought into requisition, no little practice and patience are necessary to enable an inexperienced observer to pronounce with certainty as to the description of bird which may be before him. But what true lover of birds can find it in his heart to take the life of such bright-eyed, joyous little creatures? Let them live, by all means. Other opportunities for making a more satisfactory inspection will doubtless offer themselves, and the very difficulty of obtaining a good view of some particular bird adds to the interest which surrounds it. It is better to remain in ignorance than to gaze on the limp and lifeless body of some poor tiny creature whose life we have taken, yet which was so full of activity and happiness until our curiosity condemned it to death.

When making observations on birds—and be it remembered the best time for so doing is while the trees are yet leafless—a good field-glass is a necessity. If provided with shades, so much the better, as the sunlight falling on the glass is apt to be annoying. A long walking-stick is very useful, not only for walking with, but also for the purpose of steadying the hand and preserving the bearing of the glass when making notes. Where it is practicable, all notes should be entered in a book kept for the purpose, *and on the spot.* A light campstool is a luxury much to be appreciated when, as is so frequently the case, it may be necessary to watch and wait for a long time for the approach of some special bird. One other article remains to be mentioned: this is a gun. I would suggest that it should always be left behind on such occasions.

The Rev. Warde Fowler, in his delightful book, 'A Year with the Birds,' has done much to simplify the difficulties which existed amongst amateurs in recognizing the eight warblers which

I have mentioned as being those most common in the list above referred to. I would strongly advise the reader to peruse the work in question ; if he is not already acquainted with the appearance and habits of those birds to which it has reference, he will find it full of interest and information.

He divides these eight birds into three groups, *i.e.*, under the genera to which they severally belong, viz., the Sylviinæ, or birds of the woodlands ; the Phylloscopinæ, or leaf-searching birds ; and the Acrocephalinæ, or birds belonging to a group many of the members of which have the front of the head narrow and depressed.

To the Sylviinæ belong, amongst others, the following, viz. :

>The whitethroat.
>The lesser whitethroat.
>The blackcap.
>The garden warbler.

The nests of these birds are rarely, if ever, built upon the ground, but some two or three feet above it. Those of the whitethroats are constructed of grass, dry stems, willow-down, wool, and horsehair, and are cup-shaped; they are also frequently placed amongst nettles, a habit which has earned for them the sobriquet of 'nettle-creeper.' The nests of the blackcap and garden warbler are very similar ; they are also cup-shaped, made of dry grass, and lined with fibrous roots and hair.

To the Phylloscopinæ belong :
The chiffchaff.
The willow wren or willow warbler.

These two birds build upon the ground; their nests are domed, and lined with feathers.

To the Acrocephalinæ belong :
The reed warbler.
The sedge warbler.

These prefer to build in the reeds by the waterside. Their nests are cup-shaped, that of the reed warbler being built firmly into the reeds and lined with horsehair only; whereas that of the sedge warbler is in a measure suspended from the reeds rather than built into them, and is lined with feathers.

Though called the greater and lesser whitethroats, there is little, if any, difference in the size of these birds—a quarter of an inch at the most. Colonel Irby gives their length as being five and a half and five and a quarter inches respectively. As their names imply, the throats of both birds are pure white. This of itself serves to distinguish them from the chiffchaff and garden warbler. which they much resemble in other respects. The back of the whitethroat is *reddish-brown*, the legs of a *pale brown*. The *head* and *back* of the lesser whitethroat are of a *bluish-gray with a brownish tinge*, the *legs lead-coloured*. The songs of the two birds are also different. The Rev. Warde Fowler describes the song of the greater whitethroat as follows: 'As we walk along, a rough, grating sound, something like the noise of a diminutive corn-crake, is heard on the other side of the hedge, stopping when we stop, and sounding ahead of us as we walk on. This is the teasing way of the greater whitethroat. . . . If you give him time, however, he will show himself, flirting up to the top of the hedge, crooning, craking, and popping into it again; then flying out a little way, cheerily singing a soft and truly warbling song, with fluttering wings and roughened feathers, and then perhaps perching on a twig to repeat it.'

Of the lesser whitethroat he says: 'The larger bird warbles, but the lesser one, after a little preliminary soliloquy in an undertone, bursts out into a succession of high notes, all of exactly the same pitch.'

With reference to the larger of these birds, the Rev. C. A. Johns states that, 'though not naturally a nocturnal musician, it does not, like most other birds when disturbed at night, quietly steal away to another place of shelter, but bursts into repeated snatches of song, though this song is rarely heard except in the months of May and June.' I have frequently heard birds twittering at night when disturbed, and there are some one or two birds which may justly be termed 'nocturnal musicians'; but I have no recollection of anything which could be termed a song proceeding from the whitethroat under such circumstances. Aplin describes the song of the greater whitethroat as 'rather harsh and chattering,' the bird 'often mounting in the air to deliver it on the wing'; that of the lesser whitethroat as 'curious,' consisting 'of a preliminary subdued warble, followed by a succession of high-pitched notes all in the same pitch.'

Although these birds cannot be called shy, it is often a difficult matter to procure a good view of them by reason of their restlessness and habit of keeping to the hedgerows always a little in advance of their would-be observer, with whom they appear to invite a game of hide-and-seek, reserving all the hiding part of the performance to themselves. They are happy, unobtrusive little birds, amusing themselves and enjoying life in their own quiet way, neither courting nor, when the trees and hedgerows are bare of leaves, shunning observation. The whitethroat, like many other birds, raises the feathers of its head when singing, thereby presenting the appearance of a crest. It is, as I have observed, migratory, arriving here about the end of April or the beginning of May, and remaining with us until September.

The garden warbler is somewhat larger than the greater whitethroat, viz., slightly under six inches in length. At first sight the plumage of this bird gives the impression of being brown above and pale gray below, but a nearer inspection reveals a strong tinge of olive pervading the brown, the pale gray extending throughout the under parts from the bill. In the distance, this lighter colour might readily pass for white, and the bird be mistaken for one of the whitethroats. If, however, the two are compared, the pure white of the whitethroat becomes a very marked characteristic of that bird. Moreover, not only is the garden-warbler the larger, but its general bearing is altogether different, and the head less shapely and graceful than that of the whitethroat. It is a less showy bird, but this lack of smartness is more than compensated for by the sweetness of its song, which is very real and melodious. The whitethroat may be met with anywhere and everywhere, but the garden warbler is none too common. Its song is not unlike that of the blackcap; but there is a difference, which the Rev. W. Fowler thus aptly describes : ' The strain of the blackcap is shorter, forming, in fact, one lengthened phrase, "in sweetness long drawn out," while the garden warbler will go on almost continuously for many minutes together ; and secondly, the blackcap's music is played upon a mellower instrument.'

The blackcap can hardly be mistaken for any other bird, although I have heard it stated that a great similarity exists between it and the coal tit. Its manner and demeanour, to say nothing of its exquisite song, are very different from those of the last-named. It is also larger, and destitute of the white markings on the wing, nape, and cheeks which characterize the coal tit. The tits are not a particularly musical family; but the blackcap is one of our sweetest songsters, and has been declared to be little inferior in this respect to the nightingale, an assertion which—though a great admirer of the vocal powers of the blackcap—I cannot fully endorse. The blackcap is a veritable garden bird, and loves to perch on the standard rose-trees, to which it does good service by ridding them of caterpillars, and is a true friend to the gardener, who, after the manner of his kind, doubtless often shoots it, in the belief that he is ridding the garden of 'one of them blessed tits.'

Of the two members of the Phylloscopinæ, viz., the chiffchaff and the willow warbler, the chiffchaff is the earliest of all our migratory birds in making its appearance, and, I may also add, the last to leave us in the autumn; and for this reason, if for no other, it is entitled to our affection and sympathy. Long before the buds of the daffodils have begun to swell and turn yellow, the brave little creature returns to make its home with us, and we may readily suppose that he would all too gladly remain throughout the year if it were possible—indeed, instances are recorded of his having done so. Mr. Aplin states that a chiffchaff remained in this country, at Bodicote, in Oxon, throughout the whole of the winter of 1881-82. It was heard in December, and seen early in

January, 'when it was still in song.' He also observed 'a chiffchaff in song on February 26 and 27, 1887,' evidence that the bird had not migrated, though the season had been very severe.

The chiffchaff derives its name from its song, or, rather, from the two notes which constitute what, by a stretch of imagination, may be termed its song. These two notes are repeated, and are better represented by the word when spelt chuff-chuff, and may be readily recognized, even when all the other birds are trying to sing each other down. It is a little bird, being no more than four inches and three-quarters in length. The colour of its upper parts is a yellowish olive-green, that of the under parts a yellowish-white. *Above the eyes there is a narrow, pale, yellowish-white streak, and its feet are dark brown.* I have italicized the foregoing in order to aid distinction between this bird and the willow warbler, which it much resembles, as a novice might be very easily misled, for not only are they very similar in plumage, but their habits are also alike. The chiffchaff is, however, the smaller.

Last summer (1894) two of these birds built a nest just inside some hurdles which had been placed round one of the plantations in the University parks in Oxford, at the edge of the cricket-ground, where many hundreds of spectators daily assembled to watch the matches, and not a few of them were standing close to the spinny, within a couple of yards of the ribes bush at the foot of which the nest was situated. Yet, notwithstanding their presence, the parent birds never ceased to feed their young ones, going and returning every few minutes with some fresh dainty. I watched the performance for some three days, but, alas! on the fourth I discovered that the entire nest had been ruthlessly abstracted —doubtless by some youths whom, at my request, the park-keeper had ejected for having attempted to shoot the birds with a catapult. These parks are rich in birds, but it is much to be regretted that the generosity of the University authorities in throwing them open to the public should be so shamefully abused. On one occasion I flushed a woodcock in these grounds at the time when a football-match between the University and Cooper's Hill was being played within a hundred yards of the spot, and there must have been many hundreds of people watching the progress of the game.

The willow warbler is, as I have remarked, somewhat larger than the chiffchaff, measuring five inches in length. This bird is also called the willow wren, though why it has earned the sobriquet of 'willow' it is difficult to understand, since it is not to be found more frequently in the vicinity of those trees than that of others. It does not arrive in this country much before the middle of April, and leaves us in September. It is one of the commonest of all our warblers. Its general colour is very similar to that of the chiffchaff, but it is of a brighter olive-green. The streak, which, like that of the chiffchaff, *is above the eyes, is yellower, and perhaps more clearly defined; its legs are light brown.* This bird is also called the hay-bird, from its being so frequently observed in the vicinity of hay-fields, and from its habit of utilizing the bents in the construction of its nest; this name would appear to be the most suitable.

Despite the similarity in plumage which exists between the chiffchaff and the willow warbler, there is no comparison between the songs of the two birds, that of the former being conspicuous by its absence, that of the latter being varied and peculiar, commencing with a full high-pitched note, then gradually falling and fading in regular intervals, as if the whole performance had to be completed in one single exhalation; and this peculiarity serves to distinguish it very clearly from the chiffchaff.

Of the two birds belonging to the Acrocephalinæ, the reed and sedge warblers, the former is the larger. The measurements given by Colonel Irby are as follows: The reed warbler five inches and a half in length, the sedge warbler from four inches and three-quarters to five inches. In order to observe these birds, it is necessary to go to the riverside, where they make their nests amongst the reeds, which they prefer for

REED AND SEDGE WARBLERS

the purpose, though at times they select other situations, even those at some little distance from the riverside. I have on several occasions found the nest of the reed warbler built into the branched stems of the 'cow-parsley,' although an unlimited supply of reeds was close at hand. I found five such nests recently (1895), and within twenty yards of a very thick bed of reeds, the latter in close proximity to the river, and equally sheltered and secluded as the spots selected. The plumage of the reed warbler is of an olive-brown above, below pale buff, a reddish tinge pervading both the upper and lower parts. That of the sedge warbler is brown in the upper parts, but *each feather is marked with a dark centre; the crown is blackish-brown, streaked with lighter brown.* A still more marked characteristic serves to distinguish the two birds, viz., the stripe above the eyes of the reed warbler is narrow, and of a pale buff colour; that similarly situated in the sedge warbler is broad, and of a yellowish white. The reed warbler is far less common than the sedge warbler, though it cannot be termed rare or even uncommon, for wherever there is water, and plenty of reeds surrounding it, it is pretty sure to be found. At first sight the reed-bed may appear destitute of bird-life, but the instant the reeds are disturbed the birds appear as if by magic.

The reed warbler not only prefers to make its nest by the waterside, but is not often to be seen at any great distance from the vicinity of the stream, whereas it is by no means infrequent to find the sedge warbler disporting itself in fields far away from the river. The songs of the two birds are dissimilar. The sedge warbler cackles and clicks incessantly, and is a notorious mimic, copying the notes of other birds; nor is it silent when the daylight is past, as it may be frequently heard at all hours of the summer night. The Rev. W. Fowler thus compares the two birds. 'The reed warbler, on the other hand, is quieter and gentler, and utters, by way of song, a long crooning soliloquy, in accents not sweet, but much less harsh and declamatory than those of his cousin . . . but the sedge warbler . . . like a fidgety and ill-trained child, is never in one place, or in the same vein of song, for more than a minute at a time. . . . The sedge-bird rattling along in a state of the intensest excitement, pitching up his voice into a series of loud squeaks, and then dropping it into a long-drawn grating noise . . . while the reed warbler . . . takes his own line in a continued prattle of gentle content and self-sufficiency.'

To those who care for such things, there is endless amusement to be derived by studying the habits of birds; many an idle hour may be profitably and pleasurably passed in so doing; and there should be no lack of occupation for a summer's day in any quiet neighbourhood where birds are plentiful.

AN IDLE HOUR WITH THE BIRDS

The country around London, especially in the direction of Harrow, Pinner, Watford, etc., is rich in bird-life, and many of our rarer varieties frequent this district. The Essex marshes are by no means as barren as they may appear to a casual observer, and a walk along the eastern bank of the river below Tilbury Fort, even on a winter's day, should not be unattended with success, for at times, especially in hard frosty weather, there is, or used to be, no lack of water-birds of various kinds, each creek and ditch producing something worthy of notice.

But, in my opinion, no spot is so suitable for the study of bird-life as by the edge of some withy-bed, situated on a quiet backwater, for such spots are frequently well stocked with birds. But the would-be observer must keep quiet and well concealed. After a time a moorhen, or it may be a coot, emerges from the fringe of water-plants which line the river banks, at first peering cautiously around, and then, waxing bolder, with a low chuckle, swims out into mid-stream. A slight rustling sound amongst the rushes, and a water-rail may be seen threading its way, with outstretched bill and crouching body, between the roots and boles of the willow-sets, the bright little eye taking in everything at a glance, and ready to beat a hasty retreat at the least unusual sight or sound. A kingfisher flashes down the very centre of the stream, a lovely vision of emerald green and sapphire, gone all too soon, and yet no sooner missed than it has come and gone again.

On the extreme top of a small alder-bush a little brownish-coloured bird sits swinging to and fro in the light summer breeze; now and again it flies off, quivers for an instant in the air, and, before the eye can take it all in, is back again at its post. If its flight is observed, it will be seen to dart off at some passing insect, repeating the performance until its mouth is crammed with flies. As it turns its body the spots on its breast become visible, and proclaim it to be the spotted flycatcher.

A clicking, cackling kind of chirp amongst the willows, and a sedge warbler appears on the scene, darting about amongst the willow-rods, its body poised obliquely to the branch on which it rests, now and again flitting into the deeper cover, to reappear in the same spot, but in such constant motion as to render observation difficult.

The flycatcher is now busily occupied making quick and continuous darts at the water-flies which, hatching out in numbers, are spinning up from the surface of the stream; but ere they have had time to make the briefest survey of the world around them, they are snapped up by the swallows and martins which have assembled to the feast, and are sweeping up and down on wings which never seem to tire. Now a swallow skims past, the purple tint on its back gleaming in the sunlight, followed by a whole posse of housemartins, the latter conspicuous by the white on their backs, and amongst them, here and there, a sand-martin in gray coat and white shirt-front. The stream is now fairly teeming with life, yet half an hour ago not a bird was visible. The widening circles on the surface of the water show that the trout are beginning to rouse themselves from their afternoon slumbers, and so, for the best part of the next hour, birds and fish are alike busily employed in waging war on the hapless duns, but few of which survive the onslaught. By degrees the swallows and martins lessen in numbers, till but one or two of the more indefatigable of the party are left, and they too at last take their departure. The flycatcher, finding that business is getting somewhat slack, makes off also. The surface of the water is now no longer dimpled by the rising fish, and save where the sunlight marks the passage of a water-vole as he crosses to the farther bank, or the hoarse croak of the moor-hen as she collects her family for their evening meal is heard in the reed-beds, all is still as before.

Nor is a withy-bed without its attractions in the winter evenings, when, in the glow of the setting sun, the leafless branches appear like rods of fiery gold. It is there, while waiting for wild-duck or snipe, that the birds which come in to roost can be better observed than when the willow-rods are in full leaf. It may be damp and cold, but it is all very beautiful as long as it lasts, and what with the starlings, tits, wrens, and other birds which are constantly dropping into the reeds, there is no lack of life and interest for those who care to observe. The one thing needful is to remain perfectly quiet, regardless of chilled fingers and numbing feet. Watching and waiting may be repaid, but a restless hanging about mars all hopes of sport. Just when the light is fading, and further waiting seems hopeless, a faint quacking, speedily followed by a rush of wings, betokens the arrival of a flight of ducks, which come into view, checking their flight as they prepare to settle down in the stream. Quickly as the gun has been brought up to the shoulder, they have seen it, and hurry off; two reports, followed by a swishing sound as one bird falls lifeless in the reeds, a splash as a second strikes the water, and but three out of the five are left to wing their way down the valley to other feeding-grounds. A few minutes later and the small birds, which were startled out of their wits, are again settling down for the night.

I previously made reference to the spotted flycatcher, one of the most common of our migratory birds. Arriving here in the spring, it stays with us until the first frosts of autumn warn it that it is time to take its departure to sunnier lands than ours. It is a cheery little bird, and by no means shy, frequently building its nest in the vicinity of houses. As Mr. Johns says of these birds : 'They have neither song to recommend them, nor brilliancy of colouring ; yet the absence of these qualities is more than compensated by the confidence they repose in the innocent intentions of the human beings whose protection they claim by their strong local attachments, and by their unceasing activity in the pursuit of flying insects.'

It may be said that wherever there are plenty of flies there are sure to be flycatchers; but these birds are so unobtrusive in their plumage and vocal powers as to frequently escape notice. One hears a weak little chirping, and on turning round to ascertain whence it proceeds, a small brown bird, with a pale-gray breast faintly spotted with darker gray, may be observed perched on some post or railing, apparently doing and thinking of nothing ; but its quick eye has detected some unlucky insect, which, all unconscious of danger, is winging its way into the very jaws of death. A dart, a flutter of wings, and the bird is back again at its post, as still as if it had never left it, but the insect is no more. And thus it passes the daylight hours, from time to time disgorging its collection of flies into the widely-opened mouths of its young ones in their nest in some neighbouring bush or bough.

Three varieties of flycatchers are included amongst our British birds, viz., the spotted, pied, and red-breasted. The last-named is, however, too rare to claim notice here, and the pied is by no means common. Its manner of procuring its food is similar to that of the spotted flycatcher, but it prefers to make its home away from houses, and is very local in its choice of habitations. Dixon speaks of it as being common in the wooded hill-districts of Yorkshire, and loving the birch-copses near mountain streams, especially where old and decaying timber is abundant. Of its vocal powers he says : 'Unlike the spotted flycatcher, which sings but rarely, the pied flycatcher is a fairly good musician, and warbles incessantly, especially in early summer.' The two birds vary in size, the length of the spotted flycatcher being five inches and a half, that of the pied half an inch less. The plumage of the latter is thus described by Colonel Irby : ' Above black, except white forehead and white wing-bar . . . under parts white ; the tail also black, except the lower part of the outer web of the three outer feathers on each side, which is white.' This description should suffice for the ready identification of this bird, especially when its habit of always returning to the same spot after each raid upon the flies is remembered. All three varieties of the flycatcher are migratory.

Everyone is acquainted with one or more of the six varieties of wagtails which visit us annually, and which are comprised in the following list :

THE WAGTAILS

1. The white wagtail.
2. The pied wagtail.
3. The gray wagtail.
4. The blue-headed yellow wagtail.
5. The gray-headed yellow wagtail.
6. The yellow wagtail.

Of these six birds, three only—*i.e.*, the pied, the gray, and the yellow—are common. The white and the pied are so very similar as to be often mistaken for each other; the white is, however, the far less common of the two. Both are with us from the spring to the autumn, the pied frequently remaining throughout the entire year. The chief distinction between these two varieties consists in the colour of the back, which in the pied wagtail is black, whereas in the white it is of an ash-coloured gray. The back of the female of the pied in spring is also of an ashy gray, but mingled with a few blackish feathers.

For some years past one or two pairs of pied wagtails have bred in my garden, and reared their young ones with more or less success. Last summer I was distressed at finding a whole brood of them had been destroyed by one of our village cats. The bereaved parents had been indefatigable in their efforts to supply their offspring with food, and it was a great pleasure to me to watch them popping about the lawn. After this catastrophe they disappeared for a time, but erelong returned again. Every now and then during the winter months they put in an appearance in mild weather, but when severe frost prevails they take their departure; where they go to at these times is somewhat of a mystery to me, for their absence is not sufficiently prolonged to admit of their migrating to any very great distance.

Some considerable similarity exists between the yellow and gray wagtails, but it may be here observed that whereas the yellow wagtail is a summer visitant, the gray leaves us in the spring, and remains with us only during the autumn and winter months. Of the two birds, the gray is the larger by nearly an inch. The back of the latter is of a bluish-gray, the eye-stripe being white. The back of the former is of an olive-green, the eye-stripe bright yellow. The head, and, indeed, the entire plumage, of the yellow variety is of a more decided yellow. The gray wagtail is more frequently to be observed in the vicinity of streams; it is a more hardy bird than the yellow, and prefers the Northern counties, though it is pretty generally distributed throughout the country.

The blue-headed yellow wagtail is also a summer visitor. In size it is similar to the yellow variety. Its plumage is, however, less yellow, and its throat is white. The stripe over the eye, which extends from the bill to the nape of the neck, is broad and white. The gray-headed yellow

PRESERVED AND MOUNTED

wagtail is a very rare visitor to England. It is very like the former, but has no stripe over the eye. The chin only is white.

Referring to the gray wagtail, the Rev. W. Fowler says that it is misnamed, and should be called the long-tailed wagtail, by reason of its tail being an inch longer than that of any other species, or the brook wagtail, from its predilection for the neighbourhood of rocky streams and brooks. He very justly adds that no stuffed specimen or picture can convey the slightest impression of what a bird is like 'whose most remarkable feature is never still.'* Birds, when well preserved and mounted, are very pleasing ornaments to a house, and are useful and desirable in a museum for purposes of identification; but their plumage is very liable to fade even under the most favourable conditions, and this is especially the case with those specimens in which the colouring consists of the more sober, delicate shades of brown and gray. So liable are they to change and fade, that it is at times extremely difficult to identify them, especially if the specimen has not been very carefully preserved from contact with the air, or was not in perfect plumage at the time of its acquirement. The more modern school

* While looking over the proof-sheets of the present work, a gray wagtail and a nuthatch are disporting themselves on the lawn close to my window. The former is the first which I have observed this season (1895). It is, surely, the most graceful of all our British birds!

of scientists set their faces strongly against mounted specimens of birds, advocating merely the preservation of the skins, which are kept in drawers or cases, and labelled according to their genera. This system, however, does not appear to fulfil all requirements. It may suffice for purely scientific purposes, but it does not convey an idea of the shape, bearing, or general demeanour of the bird. Judging from the terribly grotesque and unnatural specimens so often encountered, it would appear that, whereas there are any number of professional taxidermists in England, but comparatively few of them are really entitled to the name. They are not naturalists, but bird-stuffers in the most literal acceptation of the term. They profess their ability to preserve and mount any specimen which may be placed in their hands for the purpose. Such prowess, however, is far too frequently profession, and no more. They cram the bird, beast, or whatever it may be, as tightly as the skin will bear, and then proceed to place it in position according to their fancy, or from an ill-drawn design in some execrably-illustrated work on natural history. They themselves have, in all probability, never seen the creature in a state of nature, and, knowing nothing regarding its habits, is it to be wondered at that the result is so often a failure painful to witness? Many a good specimen is thus hopelessly ruined. Where accessories, such as dyed grasses, ferns, and lichens, are made use of, they are often selected in the most reckless manner, and without the slightest regard to their suitability, so long as the case is made to look smart. Not long ago a friend of mine asked my opinion regarding a large trout of some nine or ten pounds weight which had been preserved and mounted by a provincial bird-stuffer, who had, moreover, charged between two and three guineas for his work. I had seen many of his productions, all of them being remarkable for their unnatural and vulgar appearance; but this effort crowned them all. Not only was the fish literally *stuffed* well-nigh to bursting-point, but the tow used for the purpose almost protruded from its open mouth. Large splashes of light-red paint had been literally smeared over the entire body from head to tail, and, to complete the illusion, a profusion of dyed *upland* grasses were artistically arranged in various parts of the case, amongst them what is known as quaking-grass being especially conspicuous. What could I say? I thought it better to be truthful, and so suggested to my friend that the sooner he sent it to a more competent artist the better, adding that in the meantime it might with advantage be turned with its face towards the wall.

There are, of course, some really good taxidermists in our country towns, men whose work can vie with the best in the trade. Amongst these, few are able to compete with Mr. Cullingford, curator of the Durham University Museum, who is also employed by the authorities of the Museum at Cambridge. His work is most excellent, he is a thorough naturalist, and his charges are moderate. His heart is in his labour, which is one of love, and the specimens mounted by him require no tricking up in the way of accessories. The latter are not only needless, but would, in my opinion, mar the beauty of his work.

The best specimens of stuffed fish which I have seen have been from the workshop of Mr. Butt, of Wigmore Street, at one time, I believe, foreman to Mr. Rowland Ward, in Oxford Street, whose name is sufficiently well known. It is, perhaps, more difficult to procure a really well preserved and mounted specimen of a fish than of most other creatures, inasmuch as it is necessary to have recourse to the use of paint and varnish to a great extent, the natural colours being so soon liable to fade—indeed, they lose very much of their lustre directly the fish is dead—and this colouring requires, to be carried out successfully, the hand of a master in the art.

Unless birds are well mounted, and posed with a due regard to the attitudes which they assume when alive, it is far better to keep their skins unmounted until a suitable opportunity for having them well set up presents itself; the skins are very easily softened by an experienced taxidermist.

I fear, however, that I have somewhat strayed

from my subject, following the train of ideas which presented themselves when quoting from Mr. W. Fowler's remarks, and I have been discussing the subject of taxidermists instead of tomtits, as I had intended.

Of the well-known family of tits, there are six or seven varieties commonly included in the list of British birds, as follows :

> The long-tailed or bottle tit.
> The great tit.
> The blue tit.
> The coal tit.
> The marsh tit.
> The crested tit.
> The bearded tit.

Of these seven varieties, the last-named, the bearded, cannot be truly described as belonging to the family, being a kind of remote cousin, and more correctly styled the bearded *reedling*.

The crested tit is rare, and found only in the pine-forests of Central Scotland. Now and again a specimen is recorded as being procured in England, even in the Southern counties, but such occurrences are very infrequent. It is an extremely beautiful and lively little bird, of about four and a half inches in length, of a grayish-brown, the feathers being edged and tipped with white, the throat and crown of the head black, and with a very conspicuous crest. I have seen some specimens of this bird, which were shot in

Wiltshire, but it has never been my fortune to view a living specimen.

The first five varieties I have enumerated are more or less common throughout the country. The long-tailed, or bottle tit as it is sometimes called, has the smallest body and the longest tail of all the family. Unlike the other tits, it is rarely to be seen in the neighbourhood of houses, though it frequents the gardens and orchards, and drives the gardeners well-nigh frantic when the green peas are forming in the pods. It is a rough, woolly-looking little bird, with a white head, the rest of its plumage being a mixture of blue and fluffy-looking yellow feathers. The colour of the tail feathers is of the most beautiful blue tint, an almost indescribable shade. These are the only feathers which are suitable for the wings of the artificial trout-fly known to fishermen as the 'iron blue,' and they are exceedingly difficult to manipulate by reason of the extreme delicacy of their fibres. The nest is a marvel of beauty and neatness, and too well known to need description. It is generally situated in the deepest recesses of some dense, thorny bush, and so, fortunately, not easily procurable.

Whereas the long-tailed tit is the smallest of the tit family, the great tit is considerably the largest—a strong, powerful and pugnacious little bird, easily distinguishable by the black stripe down the centre of its breast and belly, and with a bluish-black crown and white cheeks, the under parts being, with the exception of the black stripe, of a greenish-yellow colour.

The blue tit is, by an inch and a half, smaller than the great tit, being about four and a half inches in length. The under parts of this bird are also of a yellowish-green, but the crown and wing-coverts are of a brilliant azure blue. It is, in my opinion, the most beautiful of the family.

Seen in a dull light, the coal and the marsh tit may be easily mistaken for each other, and they are much the same in size. Under more favourable conditions, however, the difference is very apparent, for although the heads of both birds are black, the nape and cheeks of the coal tit are white; there are also two very decided white bars on its wings, and the back is of a blue-gray colour. The marsh tit has no white about it, and its back is of a gray-brown hue. The name of marsh tit must not lead to the inference that this bird is only to be found in marshy places, though it is, perhaps, more common in well-watered districts than elsewhere.

To a lover of birds, it is well worth the trouble of hanging up a greasy bone or a lump of fat to the bough of a tree, well within sight of the house, during the winter months. Every tit in the neighbourhood will be sure to visit it, and it is most amusing to watch them, as they hang in every conceivable position, pecking and tearing away as if their lives depended on the rapidity of their labours. Now and again a great tit will make his appearance, and drive off all other intruders. I find it the better plan to hang out three or four such inducements, in order that all comers may participate. Poor little birds! they are often sore pressed for food in hard weather, and must find it a difficult matter to exist at times, though they contrive to endure the cold and scarcity of food better than many other birds.

It may be as well to here remark, for the benefit of the reader, that whereas the long-tailed tit makes its nest in the centre of a thicket or some thorny bush, the blue tit lays its eggs in almost any place where there is a hole suitable for the purpose. It is especially fond of utilizing the holes in walls and buildings. Last summer (1894) I saw some five or six of these birds, which had taken up their quarters in as many holes in an old garden wall, and all within a few feet of each other, in a row.

The coal tit prefers to build in some decayed stump or hole of a tree, the marsh tit selecting, when practicable, a hollow willow, or some similar tree in the vicinity of water, and where the ground is wet and low-lying.

All the several varieties of British tits are resident.

The bearded tit, or bearded reedling, is very easily distinguished from the ordinary tits, not only by its colour, which is a kind of buff-cinnamon, but also by its curious long black moustache. Its length is equal to that of the great tit, viz., six inches. It is found only among reed-beds, and is very local—indeed, it may be considered a rare bird. The female is paler in colour, and has no moustache.

DWELLERS IN NESTS.

PART IV.

The Golden-crested Wren—The Fire-crested Wren—The Crow Tribe—The Chough—The Raven—Crows, Rooks, and Jackdaws—The Crow—The Rook—The Jackdaw—The Crow Family—An Indian Crow—An Indian Hot Season—Rooks washing—Rooks fishing—A Rook Court-martial—Jays and Magpies—The Nuthatch and Tree-creeper—The Stonechat, Winchat, and Wheatear—The Nightjar—Owls—Sight of Owls—Ear of Owls—White or Barn Owl—Tawny Owl—Long-eared Owl—Short-eared Owl—Similarity between Hawks and Owls—British Harriers—The Marsh Harrier—The Hen Harrier—Montagu's Harrier—The Buzzards—The Common Buzzard—The Rough-legged Buzzard—The Honey Buzzard—Protection needed for Buzzards—Bird-collectors.

ANY work relating to our British birds would be very incomplete without some reference to the golden-crested wren, the smallest and daintiest of them all. Wherever there is a cedar-tree of any size, there is almost sure to be found one or more nests of these little birds, carefully concealed amongst the wide-spreading, fan-like foliage. Delicately formed though they are, these tiny creatures remain with us, more or less, throughout the year. If they disappear for a time, they cannot be considered as regular migrants, as they merely shift their quarters to the more southern and warmer parts of the country. I have heard it stated that at certain periods of the year they brave the Channel passage and cross over to Ireland, and that their lifeless bodies are at times found in considerable numbers on the coasts of that island, having been driven thither by heavy gales. I myself have had no such experience of them, and so can but quote the statement. Nearly every year one or two pairs of these birds build in my garden in a large cedar-tree. When the young ones first leave the nest, and are still weak on the wing, they are the funniest little objects. I have often caught them and put them back into their nest; but in a few minutes they flutter out again. So delicately formed are they that it seems almost impossible to handle them without injuring them. Their note is a curious, weak, jarring chirp; Johns describes it as resembling the noise made by rubbing a damp finger lightly along a pane of glass. They are more abundant, or, rather, visible in greater numbers, during the winter months, if the weather keeps mild and open, and, apparently, congregate in small flocks. In the summer, when the foliage is thick, it is an exceedingly difficult matter to see them at all, even though their note may be audible.

There is also another variety, the fire-crested wren, but I do not remember having ever seen it alive. Colonel Irby describes it as a scarce straggler to this country. The crest of this bird is flame-coloured, and there is a whitish streak over the eye. It is longer than the gold crest by half an inch, the latter measuring but three inches and a half.

If the golden-crested wren is the smallest of our British birds. the crow is one of the largest. Of this family—the Corvidæ—there are nine varieties, viz. :

    1. The chough.
    2. The nutcracker.
    3. The jay.
    4. The magpie.
    5. The jackdaw.
    6. The raven.
    7. The carrion crow.
    8. The hooded crow.
    9. The rook.

Of these, the first two (the chough and nutcracker) are rare, the latter especially so. The chough, which is very local, is found only on rocky coasts, such as those of Devon and Cornwall. It is easily identified by its red bill, feet, and legs.

With the jay and magpie everyone is well acquainted; and very beautiful birds they are, though both of them are most terrible poachers.

The raven, it is to be regretted, is all but extinct. Now and again a tame specimen may be encountered; but these birds are now so rare in this country as to hardly own a position in our British avifauna. A year or two ago some gipsies brought me some young kestrels, which they had been told I wished for, and they also had with them a tame raven. A raven is always a more or less uncanny bird, but this one was surpassingly so. No sooner was it inside the gates than it paid a visit to every hole and corner of the establishment, hopping about and croaking. Not caring to risk the lives of some bantam chickens, I told the owner to catch it, which he eventually succeeded in doing, but not before he also had inspected the premises more closely than I liked. I asked them if they wished to part with it, but they refused to do so, considering, I imagine, that it would bring them ill-luck.

I believe that there are so many people unable to discriminate between a jackdaw, a rook, and a crow, that I think it may perhaps be of service to some of my readers if I here explain how they may be distinguished.

As may be seen from the above list of the Corvidæ, there are two varieties of crows in Britain, viz.: the carrion and the hooded. Both are of the same size, but whereas the former is wholly black, and has bristly feathers on its nostrils, the latter is conspicuous by the colour of its back, which is of a dull leaden gray.

The rook is also black, but its whole plumage is lustrous with a purplish-blue sheen.

The jackdaw is the smallest of the four, measuring but fourteen inches; the other three are from eighteen to twenty inches in length. The head of the jackdaw is of the same colour as the back of the hooded crow, *i.e.*, a gray, leaden hue.

The crow family generally are all rascals and terrible thieves, though very amusing in their ways; but for downright consummate impudence the Indian crow is far in advance of his English relations. No one who has not had experience of these birds could possibly credit all which they can dare and do. The native servants never carry an uncovered dish from the cookhouse without taking the precautions of waving a hand or a stick quickly to and fro over it, for as surely as they omit to do so, so surely will a crow or a kite swoop down and steal the contents.

An Indian crow can be most truly irritating by disturbing the sleep and rest which are so sorely needed during the hot Indian day after a hard morning's work. It is at such times as these that one of them will elect to perch on the topmost bough of the nearest tree, or, worse still, on the top of the chimney, and croak unceasingly. It is all very well to drive it away: it speedily returns, and renders sleep hopeless. Were it an ordinary crow, it might be possible to encompass its destruction; but there is no getting a chance at the wretch, and before the gun can be taken in hand it is off.

Oh! those hot days in the Indian plains, worst of all when, during the rainy season, everything is steaming, and the air so heavy and loaded that suffocation seems inevitable; the nights bringing neither relief nor rest; the knowledge that thousands of miles intervene between the vaporous atmosphere and the green meadows of England, through which the well-remembered and well-loved streams are gliding beneath the shade of the willows, where the air is fragrant with the sweetly-scented water-mint, whose leaves are gently bruised as the river flows on; the grass so fresh and cool; the willow wrens twittering in the osier-beds; and all the sights and sounds which, ever dear to us, we never love so well as when gasping for breath under the flapping curtain of a punkah pulled by a somnolent coolie, and a sable demon is croaking overhead.

I am not one of those persons who think it the correct thing to abuse India and Indian ways. On the contrary, I consider it a paradise for a poor man who is fond of sport; but it has its drawbacks, and the intense heat and consequent feeling of want of rest are dreadfully trying to any but the strongest constitutions. It is well, perhaps, to have had some such experiences, if only the better to realize how true it is that 'there *is* no place like home.'

During the nesting-season, the rooks which

build in the elm-trees near my house afford me infinite amusement. Every morning they cross the river to bathe in the ditches of the water-meadows in front of my windows. Such a tumbling about and sousing takes place! I suppose their object is to rid their bodies of the vermin which infest them, more especially at this time of year. When their ablutions are completed, they hop about in the meadow to dry themselves. A wet rook is a truly pitiable-looking object, but when the feathers have been well preened and the toilet is completed, the blue-black plumage is very beautiful in the sunlight.

Many years ago I remember to have seen a number of rooks fishing for dace in the river Cherwell with as great dexterity as gannets, though not diving after the fish, as is the habit of those birds. Hovering over the centre of the stream, they made periodical descents on the shoals of small fish which lay near the surface of the water on the shallows.

A friend of mine recently told me that he had been an eye-witness of a rook parliament on the Wiltshire downs. The rooks were arranged in a kind of circle, one of their number, evidently a defaulter, being in the midst. After some considerable confabulation and chattering, they set upon the wretched culprit and pecked him to death. I have heard that rooks are in the habit of thus holding a kind of court-martial on some offending member of their community, but I have never myself had the opportunity of witnessing such a performance.

Volumes might be written regarding the knavery and craftiness of the crow tribe. The misdeeds of the magpie are many. Nor is the jay more sinned against than sinning, for both birds, despite the beauty of their plumage, are hopeless sinners, and are, with no little reason, detested by keepers; for, as I have elsewhere observed, they are terribly addicted to pilfering the eggs of game, and not averse to waging war on the young chicks. For the matter of that, a rook is by no means immaculate in these respects. Both the jay and magpie exhibit a wonderful talent for keeping out of gunshot distance, and it is a difficult matter to stalk them. They invariably contrive to break away on the safe side of the hedgerow or covert. Ireland is prolific in magpies; why this should be I know not, but there are certainly at least twenty magpies in that country for every one in this. It may be that game preservation is not as strictly carried out there as in England. Since it is a country of superstitions, perhaps the magpies are preserved in preference to the game.

There are two birds which are so often mistaken for each other by those persons who are not able to distinguish between them, that I may as well make some reference to them. These are the nuthatch and the tree-creeper. The former is slightly larger than the latter, its length being five inches and a half, as against five inches. Both are resident, and both are in the habit of frequenting trees. Their plumage is, however, very different. The back of the nuthatch is of a blue, slate colour, the throat nearly white and the under parts of a reddish-buff, whereas the back of the tree-creeper is brown, with lighter brown spots, the under parts being white, and the tail-feathers furnished with stiff points. The habits of both birds are apparently similar, and both possess the power of clinging to the bark of the trees. The tree-creeper, however, utilizes the sharp points of its tail-feathers in climbing a tree, in a similar manner to the woodpecker, in its search for insect food, and nearly always moves in an upward or horizontal course. The nuthatch, on the contrary, though unprovided with the same sharp-pointed tail-feathers, is able not only to ascend trees with equal facility, but also to descend them, and if the two birds were alike in plumage, this peculiarity would alone suffice to distinguish them. But apart from these differences, there are others which also suffice for their identification. The one, the tree-creeper, feeds almost exclusively on insects, and its bill is slender and pointed, and has a downward curve; whereas that of the nuthatch is short, strong, and pointed. Its use is apparent to anyone who examines the rough bark of any trees, such as the elm or oak, near to which hazels or filbert-trees may be grow-

THE NUTHATCH

ing. The shells of nuts, each with a hole drilled in it, will be found edged in between the crevices of the bark, which the bird utilizes as a vice to hold the nuts, which it pierces with its beak. The power possessed by so small a bird is extraordinary. I have often examined these empty shells, many of them being of great thickness, and bearing witness to the marvellous strength of the little workman which had pierced them, and the shape and temper of the tool it had used for the purpose. Although the vocal powers of the nuthatch are by no means considerable, still, at times, more especially in the spring and summer, it is able to offer something in the way of a song, by no means unmelodious, though rather partaking of the monotony of a Gregorian chant. The musical powers and talent of the creeper are, however, conspicuous by their absence.

The names of birds are often confusing and misleading to the uninitiated. Thus, the stonechat is at times confounded with the whinchat or furzechat. It would have been far better if the name of stone-clink, sometimes applied to the former bird, were generally adopted, and it is also a more suitable name, its note being very similar to the sound produced by striking two flint stones together. The two birds are not, except as regards their size, in any respects alike, though both frequent those districts where gorse-bushes are abundant. There is, however, some similarity between the whinchat and the wheatear, though the wheatear is considerably larger than the whinchat. The measurements of the three birds are as follows :

Stonechat (resident), $5\frac{1}{4}$ inches.
Whinchat (spring to autumn), 5 inches.
Wheatear (resident), $6\frac{1}{2}$ inches.

It is rather at a distance that the whinchat and the wheatear present a similar appearance, the rump of the latter bird and the under part of the tail of the whinchat being white, favouring the possibility of mistake. Seen more closely, the difference in size and plumage is more apparent, though in both birds there is a white stripe over the eye.

The wheatear is a resident, but the whinchat remains with us only from spring to autumn. As regards their plumage, the upper parts of the wheatear are of a pale slate-colour, the under parts white, and the ears—or, rather, I should say, the ear-coverts—are black. The plumage of the whinchat is of a dull brown above, the throat and sides of the neck white, the neck and breast yellowish-red, and a large white spot on each wing; the base of the tail is also white. The head, chin, and throat of the stonechat are black, the lower part of the sides of the neck and rump white, and the wings are also marked with two short white bars; the breast is of a bright sorrel colour; near the tail, the under parts are of a yellowish-white; the back, wings, and tail are black. The shape of this bird is different to that of the whinchat and wheatear, being rounder and fuller, and its general bearing is more pretentious. It is also specially addicted to perching itself on the topmost branches of the furze-bushes.

Both the whinchat and the wheatear are considered equally good for the table—the latter especially so—and numbers are sold annually in the markets for that purpose. On the Sussex and other downs, where they are plentiful, great numbers are caught in traps, made by cutting out a sod of turf, in shape and size like a brick, and putting it across the trench formed by the excavation, with a horsehair noose attached to the under part of the sod. The wheatear is in the habit of running under any covert which may be at hand when it is scared, and in this manner the birds are snared. I have seen these traps in considerable numbers on the downs near Brighton, the birds being sold in the streets by hawkers.

From its nocturnal habits the nightjar, though by no means uncommon, is perhaps less well known than many other of our summer visitants which are less numerous. In the dusk of the summer and early autumn evenings there are few localities in which it may not be heard or seen. It is a very beautiful and interesting bird. I know no bird whose plumage is more delicate in colour, soft grays and rich browns blending together in the most exquisite combination, the feathers being exceedingly soft and downy in texture. As I write these lines, a very beautifully-preserved specimen of this bird hangs on the wall in front of me. I am bound to admit that I always regard it with feelings of self-reproach, though its destruction was most purely unintentional on my part. I had been rabbit-shooting one evening in early September, and just as I was about to cross a fence, a bird flashed past me in the dusk, and, without a thought, I fired, and discovered to my sorrow that I had killed a goatsucker; regrets were unavailing, so, as it was an exceptionally good specimen, I sent it to my friend Mr. Cullingford, of the Durham Museum, who stuffed and mounted it for me, and it has hung on the wall of my room ever since, silently rebuking me for my thoughtlessness in having slain it.

Of all the various names by which this bird is known; that of nightjar, or, as it is more correctly termed, night-churr, is perhaps the most suitable, whereas that of goatsucker is the least so. 'To give a dog a bad name is to hang him.' If there is one creature in Britain more inoffensive than another, it is the nightjar, yet ignorance and superstition have credited it with the performance of a feat of which no bird which ever lived could be capable, viz., sucking the udders of goats. At this present time I have not the slightest doubt that there are hundreds of people who believe most implicitly that such is the habit of this bird, and who would not hesitate to destroy it if oppor-

THE NIGHTJAR

tunity occurred for so doing, in the belief that they would be performing a duty to the public. How such a superstition ever originated it is difficult to imagine, and much the same may be said regarding most superstitions. It is but a few days ago that a friend of mine had occasion to question an old man who works in his garden as to the disappearance of some yellow crocuses, and was informed that they were *there*. 'Where are they, then?' asked my friend; 'I can see plenty of snowdrops, but the crocuses have vanished.' 'Oh, they have changed into snowdrops, I suppose,' was the reply. 'Changed into snowdrops! What on earth do you mean?' 'Oh, they often does that; I've knowed them do it many a time.' And this the old man adhered to and most fully believed, nor could he be convinced to the contrary. I strongly suspect that the rooks could have easily explained all about the crocuses.

The name of nightjar, or night-churr, very well describes the note of the bird, which is of a burring or whizzing character, as it hawks after such insects as are abroad in the summer evenings. Nor is the appellation of 'dor-hawk' less appropriate, since the word 'dor' has reference to the dor-beetle, or cockchafer, which insect the bird preys upon.

The chief peculiarities in the conformation of the nightjar are its enormous mouth, exceedingly short and tender beak, short legs, and great length of wing. Its flight is noiseless and rapid, and not unlike that of the bat. Its eggs are singularly beautiful, being of a very pale gray, marked with large splotches of deep, rich brown and ash colour. These are laid on the bare ground on some wild waste place between the patches of heath or bracken, and are but two in number. Although a visitant, the nightjar is rarely seen in this country before the middle of May, but it remains with us until the end of September, and, in very mild seasons, for some weeks later still. Two other varieties of this bird have been noticed in this country, and so are included in the list of British birds, viz., the rufous-naped and the isabelline ; but, according to Colonel Irby, only one occurrence of each has been recorded, so their title to rank as British birds is somewhat slender.

From the nightjar we may well turn to the owl tribe, and here again there are no fewer than ten varieties which find a place amongst the birds of this country. They are as follows :

1. The white or barn owl (resident).
2. The long-eared owl (resident).
3. The short-eared owl (autumn to spring).
4. The tawny or brown owl (resident).
5. Tengmalm's owl (very rare wanderer).
6. The snowy owl (rare wanderer).
7. The hawk owl (very rare wanderer).*

---

* I have been given to understand that the only specimen of the *European* hawk owl which has been obtained in this

8. The scops owl (rare on migration).*
9. The eagle owl (very rare wanderer).
10. The little owl (rare straggler).

Thus, but four out of the ten are sufficiently common to claim our attention. Of these, the tawny or brown owl is by far the largest, measuring from eighteen to nineteen inches in length. Next in size to this comes the short-eared owl, which measures from fourteen to over sixteen inches, the long-eared and the white or barn owls measuring alike fourteen inches.

It is commonly believed that all owls are equally helpless in the daytime. Such is, however, not the case, for some of the family are able to see, if not as well in the day as the night, at all events well enough for all practical purposes; and I have known the short-eared owl, otherwise termed the woodcock owl, by reason of its arriving in this country about the same time as the woodcock, make a flight of considerable length in bright sunlight. On one occasion, when snipe-shooting in a bog in Anglesea, I flushed some five or six of these owls, and they flew nearly as well

---

country is one which was found near Amesbury, in Wiltshire. This bird is in the collection of the late Mr. James Rawlence, of Wilton, who when living kindly showed it to me. He procured it from the father of a lady with whom I am well acquainted.

* Two scops owls—male and female—have recently been observed in Wilton Park (October, 1895).

and strongly as any ordinary bird. Although they are reckoned as migratory birds, some few of them remain to breed in this country, in the moors and marshy grounds.

The sense of hearing possessed by owls must be extremely acute. If the ear of an owl is examined, its structure will be observed to be very peculiar. The face of an owl is, generally speaking, nearly circular, and is termed the disc, the feathers radiating outwards. The outer edges of this disc are capable of being raised or depressed at will; and if lifted up, they will be seen to be two large pocket-shaped ear-flaps, affording very efficient protection to the ear when closed, but when opened acting as ear-trumpets. They are lined with a tough membranous skin, and are destitute of feathers. In writing of the short-eared owl, the Rev. C. A. Johns, in his work on British birds, remarks: 'The short-eared owl affords a beautiful illustration of a fact not generally known—that the nocturnal birds of prey have the right and left ear differently formed, one ear being so made as to hear sounds from above, and the other from below. The opening into the channel for conveying sound is in the *right* ear placed *beneath* the transverse fold, and directed *upwards*, while in the *left* ear the same opening is placed *above* the channel for conveying sound, and is directed *downwards*.'

For the purpose of the present work, reference

to the four commoner varieties of British owls will suffice, being those with which the reader is more likely to have the opportunity of becoming acquainted. As I have stated, the white or barn owl, the tawny owl, and the long-eared owl are all residents, the short-eared or woodcock owl being migratory.

There are few localities in England in which the white or barn owl is not more or less common, and a most excellent friend this owl is to the community in general, by reason of its predilection for mice and other similar vermin. This bird is sometimes called the yellow owl, for though when seen in the dusk of a summer's evening its general appearance is white, there is in reality nearly as much yellow as white in its plumage. Wherever there are old buildings or hollow trees this owl is almost sure to take up its abode, always provided that the neighbourhood is one capable of supplying it with suitable food. Colonel Irby, in his list of British birds, remarks : ' This owl, most useful to man, can be preserved and increased by fixing an old cask (about eighteen-gallon size) in a tree. The barrel should be placed on its side, and have a hole cut in the upper part of the head, for the owls to enter. Care must be taken that jackdaws do not take possession.' These owl-casks may frequently be seen thus utilized for the benefit of the owls by those people who are able to appreciate the good they do in killing mice, etc. A piece of a large hollow tree, boarded at the ends, is less unsightly than a cask, and answers the purpose equally well, only it must be large enough. This arrangement is also less likely to attract the attention of passers-by, if. the tree selected for the purpose is perilously near a village or public road. Waterton states that the number of mice which these owls destroy is incredible. The owls generally are handsome birds, but I am inclined to think that the white owl excels them all in this respect. It is, too, a bird which merits all our care and preservation, making its home close to our dwellings, as if trusting to us for the protection which is its due in return for the good service it renders to us. The person who is capable of destroying one of these birds is truly deserving of social excommunication. I have been familiar with these owls from my childhood. Adjoining the stables at my home there is an old tower which, until it was repaired some few years ago, was the favourite resort of these birds. In the summer evenings they were to be seen hawking about after mice and other similar dainties, and at other times their snorings were so loud as to be distinctly audible in the nursery, the windows of which were but a very short distance from the tower, and on a level with the battlements. I have, therefore, every reason to feel affection for these owls, if only because of their connection with my very earliest recollection and the happy days of childhood.

The tawny owl, the largest of the four more

common of our British birds, unlike the white owl, prefers to make its home in the less frequented woodlands, where, in the hollow of some old pollard tree, it constructs its nest, if nest it can be called. It is said to be a bit of a poacher, but I am somewhat disinclined to admit the allegation. There may be truth in the statement, but I have never had any reason to believe the charge to be well founded, and, I may add, I have no desire to do so, for I would far sooner aid in its protection than its extermination, and it is nowadays not nearly as common as it was formerly. The plumage is of a reddish-yellow, with dark-brown stripes and spots, mingled here and there with black and gray markings, the general tone being of that colour from which it derives its name.

Last autumn (1894) a friend of mine sent me a specimen of a long-eared owl, which one of his labourers had picked up in an exhausted condition. Various remedies had been tried to restore it, but without success, and the poor bird died very soon after it had been found. I could not ascertain any marks of violence, and it appeared to be in perfectly good health, though thin. I skinned and mounted it, and, as it was in particularly good plumage and a success, I put it in a case and returned it to my friend, who very fully appreciated the compliment. In the majority of instances an owl is by no means easy to skin, as it is difficult to avoid losing a great many feathers during the operation. In this instance, however, I experienced no trouble, and was fortunate enough to complete the job with the loss of but a very few feathers, and those of little or no consequence I am therefore inclined to the supposition that the feathers of some varieties of the owl tribe are more firmly rooted than others. Both this and the short-eared owl are able to see equally well in the daytime as at night. This bird is not so common as the white, the tawny, or the short-eared owl—at all events, not in this country, though the Rev. C. A. Johns states that it is very common in France, and that it is held in detestation by all other birds, which take every opportunity of mobbing and molesting it, by reason of its thievish propensities. My acquaintance with this variety of owl has been but slight, and I have had no opportunity of witnessing these attacks, though I can readily imagine that, if the character it bears is deserved, it would, like other birds given to cause annoyance to the weaker members of the feathered community, be subjected to no small degree of co-operative molestation, in like manner as are hawks, crows, and such-like pirates, when the opportunity offers itself for retaliation.

When 'the leaves are paling yellow or kindling into red,' the short-eared owl, the companion of the woodcock, makes its appearance in this country, and in some districts, and at times, in considerable numbers. On first rising, especially if out of the branches, its flight and appearance are by no means unlike that of the woodcock, and it has been often mistaken for that bird. Inversely, it may be remarked that many a woodcock, when first flushed, has been mistaken for this owl; the appellation of woodcock owl is, however, derived from the periods of its annual visitation and departure coinciding with that of the woodcock. The colour of the plumage of this bird is of a somewhat lighter and yellower shade than that of the long-eared owl, and it frequents localities different to those preferred by the latter, being more generally to be found in marshes, boglands, or even turnip-fields; and it is, moreover, generally to be seen in company with others of its kind. They are said to be addicted to destroying game, but I have myself never been able as yet to prove the assertion, though they are powerful birds, and somewhat hawk-like in their flight when well on the wing; nor is their diet restricted to mice alone, since they are capable of striking at the largest of the tribe of small birds. Nevertheless, although I have repeatedly seen them when shooting, I have never discovered any evidence of their deserving the reputation of being destructive to game.

In many respects hawks and owls resemble each other, and the link between the two families is met with in the harriers, which possess, in a measure, the same peculiar arrangement of feathers on the face, forming a kind of disc, though the latter is less clearly defined than in the case of the owl. Again, the hawk owl is in its bearing and shape so very like a hawk that it might at first sight be mistaken for a member of that order. There are three varieties of British harriers, viz., the marsh harrier, the hen harrier, and Montagu's harrier. Of these three birds, the measurements are as follows :

> Marsh harrier, 21 to 23 inches.
> Hen harrier, $21\frac{1}{2}$ inches.
> Montagu's harrier, 18 to 19 inches.

It will be observed that the marsh harrier is the largest of the three. It was formerly by no means infrequent in England and Ireland, but, sad to say, it has been nearly exterminated. It is at times to be met with in the Eastern counties, though very rarely nowadays. All three varieties of the harrier may be recognized by their peculiar manner of, as it were, beating the ground over which they are hunting, backward and forward, as a setter would beat a turnip-field. The prevailing colour of the plumage of the marsh harrier is a dark red-brown, the head, chin, and throat varying in colour from a chocolate-brown to a creamy-white, with blackish-brown streaks. The wings and tail are long, the legs short and slender.

The hen harrier is by no means uncommon in certain districts. I have noticed it occasionally on the Wiltshire downs, and some two or three specimens have to my knowledge been shot in the neighbourhood of my home. The colour of the upper parts and the breast of this bird is of a pale slate-gray, the under parts white, and the wings black. It is also a resident, though I am inclined to the belief that it shifts its quarters from one part of the country to another, according to the season and weather. In some districts it is known as the partridge hawk, being said to kill partridges. Whether this is the case or not I am unable to state, as I have never caught it red-handed; but I should think that it is perfectly capable of so doing, as its flight is very rapid and powerful. When on the wing hunting, its motions are singularly graceful, turning up at the end of its beat like a swallow, and yet without any decrease of speed.

Montagu's harrier, so called after a well-known naturalist of that name, is a migrant, arriving in this country in the spring, and leaving in the autumn. In plumage the mature male bird very much resembles the hen harrier, but the under parts, though white, are marked with reddish streaks, and when the wings are closed a black band is observable across the secondary feathers. Its inferiority in size also serves to distinguish it from the marsh and hen harriers. A friend of mine shot one of these harriers in a wood adjoining a covert of my own a year or two ago.

Although included amongst the Falconidæ, and similar in appearance to the other members of that tribe, the buzzards, of which there are three varieties in Britain, are wanting in the finer qualities which are so markedly characteristic of the falcon and hawks. They are, compared with these, lazy, non-aggressive birds, doing no harm, despite the assertions of some naturalists to the contrary, and feeding on mice, frogs, anything which they can procure without much exertion, and, it is asserted, by no means averse to carrion if it comes in their way. The three kinds of British buzzards are:

> The common buzzard, 20 to 23 inches in length.
> The rough-legged buzzard, 23 to 26 inches in length.
> The honey buzzard, 22 to 25 inches in length.

The common buzzard, though resident, is but scarce nowadays. As regards the plumage of this bird, Colonel Irby (whose measurements I have given in preference to other authorities) states that it varies so much as to defy description. The legs and toes are short, and bare of feathers, the former being only about three inches in length, very old birds being sometimes of a very dark bluish-black above, and with only a few light markings on the breast, the tail of the adult bird being brown, barred with twelve or thirteen bands of darker brown.

The rough-legged buzzard is a winter visitor to Britain, and it has never bred in this country.

THE BUZZARDS

Its plumage varies as greatly as that of the common buzzard. It may be recognised by the front of its legs being feathered as are those of the eagle. The crown of the head is of a buffish-white, with brown patches on each feather; the upper parts are dark brown, with white and reddish markings, the basal half of the tail being white, the rest brown and a broad black band tipped with white.

It is many years ago since I have seen either the rough-legged or the common buzzard. I fear they are both very scarce at the present time. The last time I saw the common buzzard was on the sides of Skiddaw.

The honey buzzard, which is also a migrant, though, unlike the rough-legged buzzard, it makes its appearance in the spring, remaining until early in the autumn, is more generally distributed over the country than either of the two other varieties, and has been known to breed from the New Forest as far North as Aberdeenshire, in Scotland. It is essentially a denizen of the woodlands, where it feeds on wasp-grubs, beetles, lizards, mice, frogs, and such-like creatures. The spaces between the eyes and bill of this bird, which are termed the lores, are covered with feathers. The upper parts are brown, the under parts white, the chest being barred and spotted with brown, the colour of the head of an ash-gray. It is, indeed, much to be hoped for and desired that in future greater protection may be afforded to the buzzards than has hitherto been the case. As I have observed, they are birds which are not only absolutely inoffensive, but render us good service in destroying an immense amount of vermin, such as mice, etc., and they are also handsome and interesting. Every living thing is nowadays sacrificed to the peripatetic collector, despite the facilities afforded to all classes for the examination of objects of natural history in the many museums which are open for that purpose free of charge; it is surely more interesting to study the habits of the living creature. I make it a rule never to take the life of any bird or beast unless it may be in the way of legitimate sport, or for the purpose of destroying them as vermin. There are some people who, so long as they have a gun in hand, cannot refrain from shooting at every bird which comes within their reach, and not infrequently they are those for whom there is the least excuse to be made.

DWELLERS IN NESTS.

PART V.

British Falconidæ—The Eagles—The Golden Eagle—The White-tailed Eagle—The Goshawk—The Old Hawking Club—The Sparrow-hawk—The Kestrel—The Red Kite—Greenland, Iceland, and Gyr Falcons—The Peregrine Falcon—The Hobby—The Merlin—The Red-footed Falcon and Lesser Kestrel—The Black Kite—The Osprey—The Wearing of Osprey Plumes, etc.

THE list of those birds which are included in the category of British Falconidæ is very considerable, and, therefore, admits of my referring to those only which are most commonly to be met with. As it may interest the reader to know the several varieties which have, at one time or other, been observed in Britain, and so claim the title to be considered British birds, I append their names, the asterisks denoting those of greater or less rarity.

Including the harriers and buzzards, references to which have already been made, there are no fewer than twenty-three varieties which come under the head of British Falconidæ, viz. :

1. Marsh harrier.*
2. Hen harrier.

3. Montagu's harrier.
4. Common buzzard.*
5. Rough-legged buzzard.
6. Honey buzzard.
7. Spotted eagle.**
8. Golden eagle.*
9. White-tailed or sea eagle.*
10. Goshawk.*
11. Sparrow hawk.
12. Red kite.**
13. Black kite.***
14. Greenland falcon.*
15. Iceland falcon.**
16. Gyr falcon.***
17. Peregrine falcon.
18. Hobby.*
19. Merlin.
20. Red-footed falcon.**
21. Kestrel.
22. Lesser kestrel.***
23. Osprey.

Of the eagles, the white-tailed or sea eagle is less rare than the golden eagle, which latter, though now well-nigh extinct, was formerly resident in Scotland and Ireland. Now and again some misguided bird makes its appearance in a district; scores of gunners immediately seek to slaughter it, and, grievous to add, generally succeed in their endeavours, unless it is wise enough to take the hint and its departure. Both this bird and the spotted eagle have the front portion of their legs, down to the toes, covered with feathers, whereas the legs of the sea eagle are bare. The spotted eagle is excessively rare. It is smaller than the other two birds, measuring some twenty-six inches. The prevailing colour of its plumage is dark red-brown.

The golden eagle, which is the largest of the three, measures from thirty-two to thirty-six inches in length. Its colour is somewhat similar to that of the spotted eagle, save in the plumage of its head and neck, which are of a light brown shade. Dixon, in 'Our Rarer Birds'—a work to which I have before referred—thus charmingly describes this bird: 'The morning sun glances on the yellow feathers of his head and neck, making them glow like burnished gold, and his dark plumage shows almost black against the blue water.' One can as vividly picture the scene, as if surveyed from the top of some wild sea-cliff, such as are frequent on the Northumbrian and Highland coasts: the bird sailing majestically past, and the morning sunlight gilding the light brown feathers, making them appear golden indeed; while, hundreds of feet below, the waves are plashing against the claret-coloured rocks, and the swinging seaweeds rise and fall in the waters of the ebb-tide.

When a boy, I remember to have seen a specimen of the golden eagle at the hotel at Ulleswater; the poor bird was fettered to prevent its escape. What terrible degradation for the noblest of all the feathered tribe! How heart-broken it must have been, and how it must have longed to expand its wings and soar away over the surrounding hills! Better far to run the gauntlet of every gunner in the countryside than be daily bullied and poked at by the sticks and parasols of every fresh batch of visitors.

Notices of the white-tailed eagle having been observed are far from uncommon, and are from time to time recorded in some one or other of the sporting papers. Not long ago, a case containing two very beautiful specimens of this eagle was offered to me for a very moderate sum by a friend of mine; I was sorely tempted to purchase it, and have since regretted that I did not do so, since the birds were admirably preserved and mounted. In colour of plumage this bird is of a dark rich brown, the tail being white. Its length varies from twenty-eight to thirty-four inches.

The goshawk, which but rarely visits this country, is one of the largest of what may be termed the hawks proper. As is generally the case with the Falconidæ, the female is considerably larger than the male, the former measuring nearly two feet in length, whereas the latter averages some nineteen or twenty inches only. The upper parts of its plumage are of an ashy-brown, the under parts white with ashy-brown bars, the tail brown, marked with bands of darker brown, a thin white line being noticeable above the ear-coverts. Some few of these hawks are brought over to this country annually, being used for hawking purposes. It is said to be one of the hawks most easily reclaimed. I may, perhaps, as well here remark, for the benefit of any of my readers who are unfamiliar with this term, that in falconry a hawk is said to be reclaimed when it has been captured, and not brought up as an eyas, or nestling. Reclaimed birds are more valuable than eyasses. The time required for reclamation varies very considerably. Some kinds of hawks are very readily tamed, whilst others demand the exercise of great patience, perseverance, and constant watching day and night, in order to keep them from sleeping; this system, accompanied with starvation and gentleness, rarely failing to subdue the wildest haggard, a term which, in falconry parlance, signifies a freshly-caught mature hawk.

There are many people who are under the impression that hawking, as a sport, is obsolete. Such, however, is, I am glad to say, far from the case. The Old Hawking Club can muster pretty strong, and there are, besides its members, many individuals who still keep hawks for sport, and within the last few days the above-named association has held a meeting within twenty miles of my home.

I have in my possession a drawing, given me by her owner, F. H. Salwin, Esq., of a well-known goshawk. This bird was a female, named Gosette, and, from the accounts I have heard and read of her performances, must have been a truly marvellous hawk. At one time the goshawk used to breed in Britain, though nowadays it has ceased to do so. It is a beautiful bird, and powerful enough to kill rabbits, or even hares. Many of those which are brought to this country are procured from the Valkenswaard, in Holland, where they are captured when migrating. The male bird is not often used for hawking purposes, being less powerful than the female. The goshawk, from all accounts, appears to be an extremely intelligent and hard-working hawk when well trained, and is therefore of considerable value for sporting purposes. It is very much to be regretted that it has ceased to make its home with us as formerly.

The plumage of the goshawk is ashy-brown above, with a light band passing over the eye; the under parts are white barred with ashy-brown, and the tail ashy-brown barred with dark brown. The length of the male bird is but nineteen inches, that of the female from twenty-three to twenty-four inches.

Of our British hawks, the sparrow hawk and kestrel are the most common, and both may be said to be resident in this country. A short time ago a friend of mine, who is devoted to the study of birds, remarked to me that he considered the sparrow hawk, in appearance and general bearing, to be, for its size, by far the gamest-looking of the tribe, an opinion which I think many people will readily endorse. As my friend observed to me, 'a sparrow hawk does look such a fighting bird.' The sparrow hawk and the goshawk are what are termed short-winged hawks, and are the only two of this description. In the training of hawks for sport, it is, of course, necessary to exercise them, in order to strengthen them and mature their powers. This process is termed 'hacking,' and consists in allowing the birds, when they have been trained to come to whistle or call, to fly at large. With the sparrow hawk and goshawk this is rendered less necessary, inasmuch as they get their power of flight at once. All the other hawks, being long-winged, require to be hacked, unless they have been reclaimed.

Mr. Corballis, in his work 'Forty-five Years of Sport,' declares the sparrow hawk to be the boldest of all hawks, and states that he has killed as many as twenty couple of quail in one day with one female sparrow hawk, the bird in question having been reclaimed and trained by him, with the assistance of a Syrian falconer, in the short space of a fortnight.

Some few years ago, when shooting on the Hampshire downs, I observed a sparrow hawk busily engaged in devouring a bird which it had killed. Not wishing to walk over the ground which lay in front of me, I fired two or three barrels at it, at long range, too far to injure it, though the shot must have struck it. It was not, however, until I had fired the third barrel that it could be induced to leave its prey. Although, generally speaking, it is a shy, wary bird, I have frequently noticed that on such occasions it will stick to its prey in the most recklessly-persistent manner, and so often falls a victim to its temerity. The length of the male bird is about twelve inches, that of the female some three inches longer, the plumage of the former being of a slaty-blue above, the under parts white with reddish-brown bars, the back of the head being mottled with white. The breast of the female bird is barred with grayish-brown.

As I have elsewhere remarked, sparrow hawks, and hawks generally, do more good than harm. Keepers, in their ignorance, shoot them whenever they get the opportunity, thus ill-requiting the good service they receive from these birds by killing vermin which are destructive to game. Moreover, if the killing of game can be laid to their charge, it should be remembered that it is, generally speaking, such birds only as are weakly or diseased, and so are better destroyed.

Of all inhuman devices for the destruction of hawks, etc., the pole-trap is the most cruel. So much has been said against it of recent years that its use seems to have been well-nigh abandoned, and it is very sincerely to be hoped that it may never again be resumed.

Bold as the sparrow hawk undoubtedly is, it not infrequently gets considerably bullied by the very birds on which it preys. At times I have seen it only too glad to escape from its antagonists, which, making common cause against their enemy, compel it to take refuge in some copse or tall tree-top, but not before they have administered many a buffet, recalling to memory the reply of Prince Geraint to the armourer in 'The Idylls of the King':

> ' A thousand pips eat up your sparrow hawk ;
> Tits, wrens, and all wing'd nothings peck him dead !'

If there is any one of the Falconidæ deserving of our protection more than another, it is the kestrel. It is a pity that keepers cannot be brought to understand and believe that this is so. To them a hawk is a hawk, and must therefore be slaughtered, and no amount of reasoning or argument will convince them that such birds are their friends rather than their foes. The poor kestrel is a most harmless and inoffensive bird, feeding almost entirely on grubs, beetles, and such-like creatures, and it must be hard pressed for food to wage war on another bird. Indeed, there is nothing larger than a quail which it would be likely to attack, and young game-birds, whether partridges or pheasants, it leaves unmolested.

The kestrel may be readily distinguished from the sparrow hawk not only by its colour, but also by its peculiar habit of hovering in the air, something after the manner of a skylark, and from which it is at times termed the windhover. Its size is much the same as the sparrow hawk, viz., from thirteen to fifteen inches in length. The male and the female are very similar as regards their proportions. In the male kestrel the head, neck, lower part of the back, and tail, are of a lead-coloured gray, the tail being barred with a broad black band tipped with white. The upper part of the back is of a light chestnut colour with small black spots.

The plumage of the female bird is entirely of a reddish-brown with black bars; the tail, which is similar in colour and markings, is tipped with a broad black band.

It has never been my good fortune to see a kite in this country. For many years past this bird has been getting more and more scarce, and is now well-nigh exterminated. In colour it much resembles the kestrel in size—it measures some two feet. On my first arrival in India, I remember that the number of kites which clustered round the vessel attracted my attention infinitely more than any of the other novelties which greeted me on first going on deck in the morning. I little thought how much I was destined to see of these birds during my sojourn in that country, or how useful they are in devouring the offal and refuse which, but for them, would only engender disease by rapidly becoming putrid. Were it not for the kites, jackals, and pariah dogs, India would be a very hot-bed of disease, whereas it is, despite the heat of the climate and other drawbacks, probably one of the healthiest of all countries. I often endeavoured to catch one of these birds by means of a long fishing-line with a large hook and a piece of meat thrown to a distance ; but although the bait was often seized, as soon as the line was pulled the meat was adroitly dropped. It was, perhaps, as well that I was not successful, for, as I have before remarked, an Indian kite is a most foul feeder, and I should have had good reason to regret a capture.

If the English kites were as daring as those of India, it is perhaps as well that they are no longer plentiful in this country, for their depredations on game and poultry would be deplorable. Now and again a kite is observed in some one or other of the more Northern counties, less rarely, perhaps, in Scotland ; such occurrences are, however, but seldom, and erelong will doubtless altogether cease.

Both the Greenland and Iceland falcons are rare in this country, and the gyr falcon is even still rarer, all three birds being far too uncommon for any further reference in the present instance.

The peregrine falcon was nearly exterminated some years ago, but, owing to the efforts which have been made to preserve it in this country, it is, I am glad to say, now more frequently seen amongst us. As is well known, a pair of these birds have more than once been known to take up their quarters in St. Paul's Cathedral, and similar situations appear to offer attraction to peregrines, Salisbury Cathedral, and doubtless many other such structures, being selected by them. Dixon, to whom I have so frequently referred, says: 'I have known many instances of this bird taking up his quarters in some tower in a noisy town.'

The peregrine is a bold and beautiful bird, and for hawking purposes most valuable. It is, however, amongst the high, rocky cliffs which overhang the sea that it is more frequently to be met with, for not only are such localities most free from intrusion, but they are generally the home of numerous wild-fowl, which supply these birds with abundant food. The power of this bird is very great, and its flight is very rapid. The speed with which it hurls itself at its quarry is terrific, though, should it miss the latter, it will not always again stoop at it. It is, perhaps, of all hawks the most valuable for sport, and has been from time immemorial held in the highest repute for hawking purposes, for, apart from its power and speed, it is singularly intelligent, and easily trained.

Mr. Corballis, in the work previously referred to, makes mention of his having used peregrine falcons when grouse-shooting, in order to induce the grouse, which in the later part of the season are apt to become wild, to lie. His plan was to fly a cast of falcon over the ground on which he was shooting, and he apparently found it answered the

THE PEREGRINE FALCON

desired purpose, and was preferable to the use of an artificial kite. I imagine that there are few sportsmen who would not endorse this opinion. I have never been able to reconcile myself to the use of the artificial kite. There ever appears to be an unsportsmanlike element about the whole thing, though I am well aware that in exceptionally dry seasons, when birds are generally plentiful and covert scarce, it may with some reason be argued a necessity to adopt some such measures in order to thin too heavy a stock of game. The artificial kite is, however, difficult to manage well; even in practised hands affairs do not always run as smoothly as might be desired, and when it is possible to use really well-trained falcons, as suggested by Mr. Corballis, such a system would doubtless add to the interest of the proceedings; but the training necessary to permit the use of falcons under such circumstances must be of a very high order. In a later chapter I shall have occasion to refer to an interesting anecdote of an encounter between a peregrine falcon and a heron, of which a friend of mine, who narrated the occurrence to me, was an eye-witness. The latter part of the account serves to substantiate the assertion that these falcons, unless trained and actually flown at a quarry, are not always persistent in their attacks, though at other times they will fight to the death.

By far the greater number of peregrine falcons

used for sport are taken from the nest as eyasses. The taking of the young birds is an operation by no means unaccompanied with danger, as it frequently necessitates the use of a long rope, held from above, by means of which the person engaged in taking them is lowered to the nest. The middle of June is the period usually selected for the operation, when the young birds are in a most suitable condition. There may, indeed, be said to be almost one day on which the occupants of each nest are most fit to take, viz., just before they are able to fly. In order to ascertain this time, it is necessary to watch the nest carefully day by day. The stronger the birds are, the better, of course; yet, if left too long, they would fly, or, at all events, flutter about, and so considerably increase the difficulty of their capture, or injure themselves in falling.

In length the peregrine falcon varies from fifteen to twenty inches, the female being larger than the male. In colour its eggs are very similar to those of the kestrel, being of a dull light red, spotted with dark red blotches. I may also here remark that the eggs of the merlin, kestrel and peregrine are very much alike. Those of the hobby are also spotted with reddish-brown, but the under colour is of a yellowish-green tinge. The plumage of the peregrine is of a bluish-gray on the back; the crown of the head, cheeks and ears are nearly black. The under parts are of a yellowish-white, with dark spots on the throat and breast, the lower portion of the latter being marked with black-brown bars.

The hobby, which is more generally a denizen of the woodlands, is a summer visitor to this country, and rarely found in Scotland or Ireland. Dixon describes it as being a miniature peregrine in its appearance, and much resembling that bird in its habits, being, in fact, the peregrine of the woodlands. It is one of the most beautiful of the British falcons, but it is unfortunately somewhat rare in England, though, perhaps, less so of recent years. Its length of wing is peculiar, and its flight very rapid. Falconers used them for the taking of small birds, such as larks, etc. It is very easily trained. In length it varies from twelve to fourteen inches, the width across its wings being some twenty-four inches, the latter, when closed, extending beyond the tail. The upper part of its plumage is of a bluish-black, underneath of a yellowish-red colour, striped with brown, the stripes running lengthwise—black moustache. In the female the colouring is less distinct, and the stripes are broader. The Rev. C. A. Johns states that the periods of migration of the hobby take place at the same time as those of the swallow, both in coming to and leaving this country and the Continent. He also observes that its utility for purposes of falconry is impaired by reason of its being prone to pine if kept in captivity after its period for departure.

The merlin, which is another of our smaller

hawks, is a resident in this country, breeding on the moorlands, chiefly from Derbyshire northwards. In length the female measures some twelve inches, as compared with twenty-four inches across the wings. The colour of its plumage is slaty-blue above, the throat white; the under parts reddish, with blackish-brown streaks; the tail also bluish-gray, with broad black bars, and tipped with white. The male bird is two inches shorter than the female. Colonel Irby states that the female very rarely lives to acquire the same plumage as the adult male.

It is stated that the merlin clutches its victim by the throat until it is quite dead; the falcon breaks the neck or opens the jugular-vein; while the short-winged hawks (the goshawk and the sparrow hawk) kill with the foot, being provided by nature with long, sharp talons and a powerful foot for the purpose. I may remark, for the benefit of the reader, that the falcons or long-winged hawks differ from the short-winged or true hawks in the following respects: The British falcons possess a kind of tooth on the upper mandible, and the second primary feather is the longest, or is equal in length to the third. The iris of the eye of the falcon is dark, whereas that of the short-winged hawk is yellow.

The merlin, if unmolested, is apparently in the habit of making its nest in the same place annually. There is, in the Ashmolean Museum at Oxford, a merlin's nest which, from having been added to year after year, measures some four feet across —a truly gigantic nest for so small a bird. I regret to add that the parent birds and their eggs also accompany this nest in the above-named collection. Merlins were at one time trained for taking larks; but the female, by reason of her greater size and strength, is capable of killing pigeons, being formerly, and still when kept at the present time, used for that purpose. It is a graceful, charming little bird, but I have been given to understand that it is particularly subject to being infested with vermin. Hence, in captivity, it requires extra care and cleanliness, though both of these are absolutely essential to the maintenance of all tame falcons and hawks in proper health and condition. Great numbers of these birds are captured annually in the wild-fowlers' nets in Norfolk during the autumnal equinoctial gales. These are doubtless visitors on passage from Scotland and the Northern counties.

Of the red-footed falcon and the lesser kestrel, both of which birds I named in the list of British Falconidæ at the beginning of the present chapter, there is but little to be said, inasmuch as they are especially rare. Indeed, of the latter but four occurrences have been recorded in this country, the last three or four years ago. In plumage it is very similar to the common kestrel, but shorter in length by two or three inches.

The red-footed falcon is mentioned as a rare wanderer to England when on migration. Its length is from eleven to twelve inches. The general tone of its plumage is of a leaden gray in the male bird, the legs and feet being red. The plumage of the female is of an ash-gray colour barred with bluish-black, the head and under parts of a reddish tinge. Any further reference to these birds would, I consider, be unnecessary in the present instance.

For the same reason I have purposely omitted any allusion to the black kite, which lays claim to be included in the list of British birds solely from the fact of its having been but once noticed in this country, and that some eight-and-twenty years ago.

The osprey, or fish hawk, though the last on our list, is by no means the least worthy member of the family to which it belongs. It is also stated to have been named the ossifrage, from the fact of fragments of large bones having been found in its stomach. It is principally a native of the colder European countries. At one time it is said to have bred in Scotland; but it is now so nearly exterminated in Great Britain that only a very few pairs elect to do so, and these frequent the wildest and most secluded parts of the Highlands of Scotland. It is a bold and beautiful bird, its shape and plumage being singularly adapted to its mode of life. Its length measures some two feet, its wings being four feet six inches and upwards from tip to tip. The head and neck are white, save where a band of brown passes from the beak down the sides of the neck. The upper parts are brown; the breast is marked with brown, the under parts being white. It feeds solely upon fish, hovering over the shoals at a great height, and dropping on them with incredible velocity. I once, when at sea off the coast of Scotland, had my attention attracted to some birds fishing in this manner, and on my inquiring what description of birds they were, was informed that they were ospreys. They were some two or three miles distant from the vessel; but as the sea was unusually calm—literally as smooth as glass—I could discern, even at that distance, the splash of the water as they dived after their prey. My informant assured me that they were ospreys, but, from their numbers, I concluded that they must have been gannets, ospreys being far too uncommon on our coasts to be seen in such quantity.

It is much to be regretted that the fashion of wearing the plumes of the osprey, the egrets, and those of the smaller herons should obtain favour. It is probably not generally known how few of the feathers used as aigrettes are obtainable from a single bird, and those only during the breeding season. If the parent birds are thus ruthlessly slaughtered at this period, what must be the fate of their young ones, which are thus deprived of their parents at a time when they are unable to feed themselves?

DWELLERS IN NESTS.

PART VI.

British Doves—The Ring-dove and Stock-dove—The Rock-dove—The Turtle-dove—British Game-birds—Shooting or taking of Woodcock and Snipe—The Capercailzie—The Blackcock—The Grouse—Measurements of the Capercailzie, Blackcock, and Grouse—The Ptarmigan—The Pheasant—The Partridge—The French Partridge—The Quail—The Land-rail—The Spotted and Little Crakes—The Water-rail—In the Moonlight—Destruction of Kingfishers, Herons, and Moor-hens in Fisheries—The Moor-hen—Moor-hen shooting—The Coot.

FOUR varieties of the dove inhabit this country, viz., the ring-dove, or, as it is more commonly called, the wood-pigeon ; the stock-dove ; the rock-dove ; and the turtle-dove. Of these four, the three first-named are resident ; the last (the turtle-dove) remains with us from the spring to the autumn.

The ring-dove, otherwise called the wood-pigeon, cushat-dove, quest, is the largest of the four, measuring from sixteen to seventeen inches in length, the stock-dove being smaller, and measuring thirteen inches only. These two birds,

THE RING-DOVE AND STOCK-DOVE

though differing in size and plumage, are so frequently confounded with each other by those who are not well acquainted with them, that I think it may be as well to explain how they may readily be distinguished.

The ring-dove takes its name from the ring of white feathers which nearly surrounds its neck, and when the wings are expanded in flight the white on its wing-coverts is very apparent. The stock-dove is not only considerably the smaller bird of the two, but has no white in its plumage. The necks of both birds are remarkable for the exquisite metallic bronze-green colour of the feathers. The ring-dove generally prefers to make its nest in trees. The stock-dove seems to select various kinds of nesting-places, one time in an old ivy bush, at another, and by no means infrequently, in a rabbit-hole, or it may be in the stump of a tree. Its flight is also more rapid than that of the ring-dove. Our various breeds of tame pigeons are all said to derive their origin from the stock-dove, and it has been stated that its name has been given to it from this fact. As is well known, many of our commoner tame pigeons singularly resemble the stock-dove. It may not, however, have been as generally observed that, even in some of the pure white varieties, the iridescent colours which add so much to the beauty of those resembling the stock-dove are, under certain conditions of light, discernible. For many years past I have kept a considerable number of white fantail pigeons; as they are remarkably tame, I have had full opportunity for noticing any peculiarities regarding them, and I have frequently been struck with this iridescence which at times pervades their snowy feathers, more especially when they are in full plumage. This is no mere fancy on my part, for I have pointed it out to other people, who have also been able to distinguish it, and this peculiarity is perhaps even more apparent on a dull day than when the sun is shining brightly.

Although the ring-dove is a resident in this country, our stock of these birds is very greatly augmented from time to time by the appearance of large flocks which visit us, much to the regret of the farmers, whose crops sustain very material damage by their depredations. Some eight or ten years ago one of these huge flocks visited the part of Hampshire in which I was then residing, and for a time they were little short of a plague to the farmers. At night they roosted in a large neighbouring woodland. I happened to pass through this wood on one occasion during that period, and close to one of their roosting-places. The bushes were covered with their feathers, and the branches torn and broken away with the weight of the birds, which had evidently crowded together for the sake of protection. On another occasion I saw them as they were winging their way to roost, and I should be afraid to state my opinion either as to their number, or even as to the distance covered by the flock from front to rear, lest I should be accused of exaggeration; but there must have been, to put it mildly, very *many* thousands in the flock. Some of my readers may know that part of the country, and if so, they will recognize the names of the places to which I am about to refer. A friend of mine stated to me that he noticed the head of the flock entering the wood on Toot Hill when the rear of it was crossing the river Test at that part of it which flows below the well-known summer-house in the shrubbery, named after Lord Palmerston, the former owner of the property. Nor was this a mere lengthened straggling stream of birds, but a broad, dense flock.

There is an individual who, travelling about Wiltshire, earns his livelihood by undertaking to destroy the pigeons for the farmers at certain times of the year, and a very good thing he makes out of it, I believe, though the system which he adopts necessitates some days of careful preparation in order to attract a sufficient number of birds.

The note of the wood-pigeon calling to its mate is one of our most pleasing woodland sounds. It may, perhaps, be best described as Cŏo-cōo, cōo, cŏo-cŏo, often repeated, and generally ending with a cŏoc.

There are few birds which test the skill of the gunner more than a wood-pigeon in full swing rattling through the tree-tops, and if an attempt is made to stalk one of these pigeons, the chances are ten to one that it elects to dart off on the far-side of the tree. Where it is necessary to destroy them, the better plan is to wait for them when coming home to roost. Few birds are better eating than a well-fed wood-pigeon at the proper season.

The stock-dove, though perhaps somewhat less common than the ring-dove, is, nevertheless, pretty generally distributed throughout the length of Great Britain, making its home in the woodlands, and not infrequently in the sea-cliffs, from which circumstance it is often mistaken for the rock-dove, the much-persecuted blue-rock. In size these two birds are similar, nor is their plumage very unlike, though two marked characteristics serve to distinguish the rock-dove, the rump of the latter bird being white and its wings doubly barred with black. The rock-dove, as its name implies, makes its home amongst the rocks and caves on the sea-coast; those inhabiting this country are found more especially in the Northern parts.

The turtle-dove is fairly common in our Midland and Southern counties. For some years past one or two pairs have bred in my garden. One of these birds was so fearless and tame that it was in the habit of coming down to feed with the poultry, waiting on the bough of a neighbouring tree until the evening meal of grain was served out to them. It is the smallest of the British doves, being only eleven and a half inches in length. Its plumage is very different to that of the other three varieties. The head, neck, and lower part of the back and sides are of a bluish ash colour, the centre part of the back cinnamon-coloured, the breast of a paler hue, the under parts white, tail-feathers tipped with white, and a collarette of black feathers, also tipped with white, on either side of the neck. Its note is a soft, gentle, broken 'coo.' It arrives in this country in May, remaining with us until September, when it takes its departure for the more congenial climates of Africa and Egypt.

The following constitute our British game-birds :

Capercailzie, or cock of the woods.
Black grouse, or blackcock.
Red or common grouse.
Pheasant.
Partridge.
Quail.

In addition to these we have the three-toed or Pallas's sand grouse, the ptarmigan, and the red-legged partridge, otherwise called the French partridge.

As I have frequently heard doubts expressed as to whether woodcock and snipe are game, it may possibly be of use to some of my readers to here remark that the law concerning them is somewhat peculiar, requiring a game-license if a gun is used for their destruction, though no such license is necessary if their capture is effected by means of nets or springes, such methods of fowling being specially exempted from game duties (by Act 52 Geo. III., c. 93).

In point of size the capercailzie is by far the largest of British game-birds. Though formerly it is said to have bred in Britain and Ireland, it became extinct, and it is now nearly sixty years since its reintroduction to Scotland, where it has since thriven fairly well. Some fifteen years ago a relation of mine shot eleven of these birds in one season, and unless my memory is at fault, I think that they were all shot by him in the same day. This took place in Stirlingshire, in which county they have done remarkably well. It is stated that the stray females of the capercailzie at times interbreed with the blackcock, the result being a very handsome hybrid, with a tail somewhat similar to that of the blackcock. The capercailzie would doubtless breed in other parts of the United Kingdom if introduced into those districts suitable for its reception. It is possible that some of the larger fir-woods in Kent, or in the neighbourhood of Woolmer Forest, might prove to be favourable, more especially the latter, since there are numerous small streams which intersect the forest, and it is a wild and thinly populated district. The New Forest would also appear to be well adapted for the purpose.

Efforts have been made for several years past to induce the blackcock to breed in the New Forest. To a certain extent the attempt has succeeded, since a few broods are annually hatched and reared, but they do not appear to have increased to any very appreciable extent. Why this is so it is difficult to understand, for the conditions seem to be most favourable for their well-doing, and no care has been spared to ensure their protection.

But the blackcock, although it is most common in Scotland, is fairly well distributed over this country. On some of the Devonshire moors they are to be found in considerable numbers. Indeed, these birds are to be found more or less wherever there are wild heaths, and in almost all the Northern counties.

A blackcock in the springtime, when his 'fancy lightly turns to thoughts of love,' is capable of making himself the very biggest fool in the whole of the bird creation. At such times his antics and vanities are incredibly ludicrous. He is also a remarkably pugnacious bird, and during the pairing season will fight all day, and every day, until he has secured a partner. Sad to say, he is as faithless as he is pugnacious and vain, and soon tires of the society of his wife, whom he quietly deserts, and leaves to manage the housekeeping as best she can, while he goes off to enjoy himself in the company of his male acquaintances, all of whom have treated their spouses in an equally shabby manner. According to good authority, the blackcock is by no means particular in his choice of a wife, and is just as ready to marry out of his class as in it, for he has been known to mate with the grouse, the pheasant, and the willow grouse.

But whatever his moral shortcomings, he is a most truly excellent bird, whether for sport or for food, and very handsome withal. As is so generally the case with the feathered tribes, the male birds appear to get all the fun and wear all the fine clothing, whilst their unfortunate wives are condemned to do all the hard work and drudgery of the establishment, and to dress accordingly. Unfair as it may appear, I fear that such is by no means infrequently the case with human bipeds as well as feathered, though there are evident reasons why the custom should obtain amongst the latter, which are wanting with regard to the former.

Whereas the blackcock is an inhabitant of other countries than Britain, the red grouse is all our own, for nowhere is it to be found save in these islands. A truly royal bird, too, beautiful in plumage, affording the best of good sport under all circumstances, and incomparable of its kind for the table.

Although more especially confined to the Northern counties, it is to be found fairly well distributed throughout Wales. The Yorkshire grouse have always appeared to me to be superior to those of any other county. Why this

THE GROUSE

should be the case I am unable to say, unless they are able to secure a larger and better supply of food. I do not, however, think that they can lay claim to possessing any higher qualification from a gastronomic point of view than their brethren of other counties

The hen grouse is rather smaller than the male bird, which latter, unlike the blackcock, is an exemplary husband and parent. Grouse are peculiarly liable to disease. This has been attributed to various causes. Mr. Corballis, in his work ' Forty-five Years of Sport,' goes very near the truth, I suspect, in attributing it to the want of pure water for the birds on several of the moors, which are badly drained, especially in the vicinity of peat-stacks, and are, in a dry season, absolutely without a proper supply of pure water, which is so essential for the well-being of grouse.

He very wisely suggests as a remedy that means should be adopted to furnish such districts with water of good quality. Old and tough heather is also said to be a prolific source of disease. This evil is easily remediable by care being taken to burn the heather at stated periods, thus securing a sufficiency of tender food for the birds, if the burning is systematically carried out.

In winter, the plumage of the grouse undergoes a slight change, the under parts being frequently splashed with white.

The measurements of the capercailzie, blackcock, and grouse, are as follows:

Capercailzie -	Male, 36 inches. Female, 26 inches.
Blackcock - -	Male, 22 inches. Female, 15 inches (called the gray-hen).
Grouse - - -	Male, 15 inches. Female, 14 inches.

The ptarmigan, or white grouse, is not found in any part of Great Britain except Scotland, though it frequents various other parts of the world—Europe, Asia, and North America. It is, however, frequently confused with the willow grouse, a large and more common variety of the same order. In length, the ptarmigan measures some fifteen inches. In winter its plumage is white, save for the black eye-stripes which distinguish the male from the female. The summer plumage of the male bird is black above, with brown and white markings on the lower portion of the back, the wings and under parts being white; the wattle above the eyes is scarlet. At the same period the plumage of the female is buff above, barred and marked with black lines, and with white tips to the feathers. The transition plumage during autumn is singularly handsome, being a curious and beautiful blending of grays, browns, black, and white. In the willow grouse there is no black on the lores, as in the male of the true ptarmigan.

It is impossible to say when the pheasant first made its appearance in England, but it is stated to have existed in this country before the Norman invasion. It may, for aught that is known to the contrary, have been indigenous. Since those days, the pheasant has undergone a considerable change, and the old-fashioned English red bird is now but rarely seen, having been crossed with the Chinese or Japanese varieties. Beautiful as the result of this admixture of foreign blood most undoubtedly is, I am by no means so sure that either the sporting or edible qualities of the bird have been equally advanced.

Pheasants have frequently been known to mate with other birds, and it has been asserted that the hybrid offspring of such unions have proved fertile. Letters on this subject have, from time to time, appeared in the *Field*.

The number of pheasants annually reared at the present day in England alone is very great. The craze for good pheasant-shooting is rapidly increasing, and to such an extent as to make the preservation of pheasants a profitable investment to the landowners, who, for the right of killing the game reared by them, are able to secure rentals which appear well-nigh phenomenal, especially when the owner reserves the game shot for his own use. However, against all this it has to be remembered that the preservation of all game—pheasants more particularly—is very costly; and to state that every pheasant which is reared on an estate costs at least ten shillings is very much the reverse of an exaggeration, the average cost being over rather than under that sum. Therefore, when it is considered that the market-price of a brace of pheasants, *i.e.*, the price at which the game-dealer purchases them, does not exceed six shillings (indeed, the sum is very frequently even less), it will be seen that the landlord who shoots his own coverts makes the public a present of some twelve or fourteen shillings for every brace of pheasants which he sells to the game-dealer. This is a side of the question very generally overlooked by the public, and a fact for which the latter have every reason to be grateful. Were the 'land and game for the people' party to have their way, it would not, I take it, be very long before every variety of our British game-birds would become extinct.

The rearing and preservation of game at the present time may almost be regarded as an industry, by reason of the number of employés who are engaged for the purpose on the various estates throughout the country; but, as I have shown, in those instances where the shooting of an estate is not sublet, it is an industry which, although providing employment for a large number of persons, is by no means one of profit to the landlords. The demand for pheasants' eggs is nowadays very great, and, I fear, conduces largely to dishonesty.

Of all our British game-birds we could least afford to lose the partridge. An English farm without partridges would lose much of its attractiveness and homeliness, for the partridge is a homely bird in its habits and plumage alike, and, when unmolested during the breeding season, fearlessly ventures to approach close to our dwellings in the most confiding manner, as if there were no such festival in the sportsman's calendar as the feast of St. Partridge. There are few farms on which there is not at least one covey which elects to frequent the fields adjoining the homestead—at times even the garden itself—and so is often allowed to go free and untouched throughout the season.

The male partridge is a most worthy spouse and father, setting an example to the more flippant blackcock which the latter would do well to follow, and remaining in the bosom of his family throughout the season, unless previously disposed of by the sportsman. The number of partridges' nests annually destroyed during hay-harvest is very great, and even when the nests chance to be discovered before being cut out with the scythe, it is very difficult to preserve the eggs from injury, unless they are placed under a hen. It is useless to cut round the patch of grass in which the nest may be situated, for any such measures but too clearly indicate its position, and should it escape the poachers, the crows would speedily make a raid upon it. The partridge has more enemies than friends, and, all things considered, it is surprising that so many broods arrive at maturity. A friend of mine has noticed for several years past that partridges, during the time they are preparing to pair, appear never to feed. There is, in front of his house, a hillside, to which at that period partridges resort in considerable numbers, and he has observed them in this situation for several consecutive days, evidently very much occupied in the selection of their mates, but never feeding, as at other times.

Partridges have been frequently known to make their nests in the most unlikely places, and I myself remember to have been shown a spot under one of the sleepers of the Great Western Railway, near Shrivenham Station, in which a partridge laid her eggs and successfully hatched them, despite the fact that many trains, the Flying Dutchman being one of them, ran daily over the place.

It is much to be desired that the red-legged or French partridge would take its departure from this country, for, beautiful as is its plumage, it is a bird which is most detrimental to sport, and, being both powerful and pugnacious, is able to inflict serious damage on our own much-

THE QUAIL

respected little russet-coloured partridge, driving the latter altogether out of the field. For ordinary shooting or for edible purposes, it is of little value, but is said to afford good sport when 'driven,' being less liable to turn from the guns than the common partridge. The introduction of these French partridges into this country has proved anything but advantageous, since no one desires its presence, and, like many other nuisances, it thrives uncommonly well. In size it is larger by an inch and a half than the English bird. Its habits are also somewhat diverse from the latter, and it prefers to run rather than fly. It is also said to perch in a tree, or on the top of a tall hedge, when forced to rise. French partridges, though they are more common in the Eastern counties, are to be found in greater or less numbers throughout this country. The call-note is unlike that of the common partridge, being somewhat similar to that of the quail.

The quail is the only migrant of all our British game-birds; it visits this country in the spring and remains until October. In some seasons these birds are very plentiful, and then, perhaps for several years in succession, but few of them make their appearance. In 1870 there was a considerable influx of quail, and several were shot in Hampshire during that season. A few years ago we were favoured with another, though less remarkable, visitation. Where quails are abundant they afford excellent sport, for, though they are much given to run, when they are flushed their flight is swift and straight, and with the assistance of a well-trained dog they are easily induced to rise. Large bags of these birds are frequently made in India, more especially during the rainy season, when they are most plentiful. Enormous numbers of quail are annually taken in nets in the island of Capri during migration. The female is larger than the male.

Although not a game-bird, the present is, I consider, not unfitting for some reference to the land-rail, or, as it is otherwise and more aptly called, the corn crake. This bird is also a migrant, arriving in this country about the end of April or the beginning of May, and remaining until the end of September.

It is a remarkable bird in many respects, not the least so by reason of its weak, laboured flight, so apparently weak and slow as to excite wonder as to how it can possibly traverse the distance between this country and Africa. Macgillivray, the well-known naturalist, states that on one occasion, when shooting in the island of Harris, he shot at a corn crake, which he missed, and the bird flew off in a direct course to the sea, about four hundred yards distant, where it alighted and floated motionless, sitting lightly on the water like a coot, curiously enough falling a prey immediately afterwards to a black-backed gull. I have always thought that, if the corn crake thus possesses the power of being able to float and rest on the water, it may possibly be enabled to rest itself *en route* during its migration.

When the summer grass is growing long, the corn crake may be heard more or less throughout the land, especially towards evening, though it is by no means silent during the hours of daylight. The ease with which it is able to thread its way through the thickest herbage is extraordinary, moving as rapidly through the densest clover as if it were stubble. Many hundreds of these birds are annually killed during the partridge season in September. Their flesh is considered a great delicacy. The note of the corn crake is a hoarse kind of croak, very similar to the croaking of a frog, and by no means unlike the noise made by a fishing-reel when the line is being wound up. I have often enticed one of these birds to within a few paces of me by drawing the line from off my reel when fishing in the summer evenings. On May 4 I heard the corn crake, for the first time this year (1895), in a meadow in front of my house, and I could hear the same bird calling at 10.30 p.m.

In addition to the land-rail, or corn crake, the spotted and little crakes, the water-rail, the moor-hen, and the coot belong to the same family. The spotted crake cannot be described as common nowadays, though it is said to have been abundant before the country was as well drained as it is at the present time. Both the spotted and the little crake are migratory birds, arriving in the spring and leaving in the autumn. During several years' residence in Hampshire, a county exceptionally well watered, and suitable for nearly every description of water-birds, I only once saw a specimen of the spotted crake, and that had been procured by a friend of mine. The little crake is still rarer. In plumage the two birds much resemble each other, the colour being of a greenish-brown, with dark stripes on the back, and spotted with white, the spotted crake measuring between eight and nine inches in length, the little crake about half an inch less.

The water-rail, if not as common as the moor-hen, is, nevertheless, to be found wherever the latter birds are abundant, and may often be seen feeding on the banks of the rivers and in the meadows in company with them. Although not a migratory bird, it is more plentiful in some seasons than others, this being due to the fact that these birds are apt to shift their quarters in the autumn, moving southward, this partial migration, if such it may be termed, varying according as the weather is severe or the reverse, though I have frequently seen it running through the rushes and boles of the willows by the riverside, when snipe-shooting, in very hard weather. It is a shy bird, and when out feeding with moor-hens is ever the first to take alarm. I have frequently watched them creeping cautiously along the sides of the river-banks, threading their way through the rushes and sedges, and never venturing to emerge from their covert until they have by many examinations quite assured themselves that there is no enemy in sight. The water-rail is a smart, handsome bird, with his red bill and olive-brown back streaked with black, and contrasting well with the slate colour of the neck and breast, the white bars on the flanks, and the pale yellow of the vent. In length it is between ten and eleven inches.

Dixon, in his 'Rarer Birds,' describes the water-rail as being unsociable, and rarely if ever seen in the company of other birds. With all deference to the opinion of so well-known an authority on such matters, I cannot endorse the statement, as for several years past I have taken considerable interest in the preservation both of moor-hens and water-rails, and have noticed a very great increase in the number of both. I constantly watched them when out feeding in showery weather in the late spring and early summer, and, as I have stated, frequently saw them out in company with the moor-hens—indeed, I rarely ever observed any number of moor-hens feeding without some few water-rails being of the party.

Since the commencement of the present work, I have left the home to which I have so often referred, and which I loved so well, and I dread to think what may be the fate of the birds which for so long were the objects of my care, and were free to build and breed unharmed and undisturbed,* though in my new home I am fortunate in being surrounded by an even greater variety of feathered friends.

The river runs within a few yards of my house, and the moor-hens, which come out to feed in the moonlight, splash about almost at my door. At the present time of year (May) they are especially clamorous. Some two or three nights ago I stood in front of the house listening to them, and such a medley of sounds I have rarely heard inland. In addition to the moor-hens, which were literally shrieking in a way I have never before experienced, a corn crake was croaking in the water-meadows beyond the river, some plover were screaming over their nests, a sedge warbler was chattering away, and at intervals the song of a nightingale was audible from a distant copse. The moon was shining bright and clear, and where the surface of the water was broken by the long, trailing river-weeds as they rose and fell with the stream, it gleamed like silver; while from time to time a heavy splash and widening silvery rings showed where the trout were feasting on the sedge-flies. It was a scene to be remembered.

I had occasion in a former chapter to refer to the wanton destruction of kingfishers, and I have

* I grieve to add that, since writing the above, I have received information that the water-rails and kingfishers have all disappeared, and but few moor-hens are left.

DESTRUCTION OF KINGFISHERS, ETC. 253

within the past twenty-four hours received a letter from a friend, urging me to do all in my power to help him in his endeavours to check the ruthless slaughter of these birds, moor-hens and herons. He has already ventilated the subject in one of the sporting papers, and has met with some argument in opposition to his views. Now, my friend is not only a devoted lover of birds, but a more than ordinarily good fisherman, having been born on the banks of one of the very best little trout-streams in England, which belongs to his family. What he maintains is perfectly correct. Kingfishers do very little harm to a trout-stream, their food consisting very largely of sticklebacks, and for every small trout they devour, they kill a score of small coarse fish, such as bleak, dace, etc., fish which are far better out of a trout-stream than in it.

As regards the charges brought against the moor-hen, of being detrimental to the interest of a fishery, I believe them to be unfounded; they most certainly do not eat fish, nor do I believe that they eat the spawn of fish. Were they in the habit of so doing, they would congregate in the vicinity of the spawning-beds; and this is precisely what they do not do, ever preferring to frequent those deeper portions of the stream in which the spawning-beds are not situated.

As regards herons, I fear they are terrible thieves at certain times of the year, more especially during the autumn at low-water, when they are capable of causing the destruction of a large number of fish; nevertheless, they may well be tolerated, unless they are very numerous, but it is necessary to keep their number within a reasonable limit. Where a fishery is deteriorating, any and every cause but the correct one is usually assigned. As often as not it is due to pollution, the spawning-beds being choked up with filth and mud; and quite as frequently it is the result of indiscriminate poaching. Then, again, pike will work havoc in a stream; and, I venture to assert, tame ducks and swans will do as much harm as all the rest put together. I have been an ardent fisherman all my life, and so consider myself qualified to give an opinion on matters piscatorial; and I have never yet had reason to believe that moorhens are in any way harmful to a fishery, and it will require more than mere assertion to convince me to the contrary; were I capable of believing them to be inimical to the interests of a river, I could not love them as I do.

There are few birds which afford me greater pleasure and interest than moor-hens, and they are ornamental withal, for when in full plumage a moor-hen is particularly handsome, his orange bill and white tail contrasting well with the dark olive-brown and blue-black colour of the rest of his body as he dots his way across the stream.

MOOR-HEN SHOOTING

In some parts of the country where moor-hens are plentiful, it is customary to shoot them, the time of year most suitable for this kind of sport being the latter part of August. The following is the system adopted: Two gunners, one at either end of the boat, proceed up-stream in a large flat-bottomed punt, similar to the kind of boats frequently used on the Thames and rivers of a like character, a team of spaniels being used to beat the rushes on either side of the river. The services of a skilful punter are essential, especially if the current is at all rapid. The birds are mostly shot on the wing, though they frequently dive, remaining under water for a considerable time, now and again protruding the tips of their bills to take air. It requires a quick eye to detect the bubble on these occasions, as it is very insignificant.

Many birds are caught by the dogs, and the bag at the end of the day is often a heavy one. It is not sport of a very exalted order, as a moor-hen on the wing, even at its best pace, offers but a very easy mark. When killed at this time of year, moor-hens are excellent for the table; but they should be skinned soon after being killed, placed in cold salt-water for some twelve hours, and roasted.

I hope I may be exonerated from any apparent inconsistency in thus referring to the destruction of a bird whose preservation I have been previously advocating. I declaim against moor-hens being accused of being enemies to a fishery. It is an altogether different matter when they are destroyed for purposes of sport and for food, though whether regarded as a pest or a fit object for sport doubtless matters but little as far as the bird itself is concerned.

The coot, the bald-headed coot, as it is often termed, by reason of the patch of white on its forehead, is by no means as common as I remember it some thirty years ago. In some parts of England it was then nearly as plentiful as the moor-hen, and was frequent in most of our larger rivers and ponds. It is supposed that this diminution in its numbers is due to the increased amount of land which has been reclaimed and drained. This may possibly be a partial cause, but, nevertheless, it is but rarely to be seen nowadays in those streams in which it was formerly abundant. I am inclined to the supposition that the gun has had more to do with its present scarcity than drainage and reclamation of marshlands, since it was in the rivers, ponds, and lakes that it was invariably to be found, in preference to swampy lands intersected and fed by the smaller streams. During very severe weather it migrates to the sea-coast, but is a resident in this country. In some few counties it is said to be still fairly common, this being doubtless due to its preservation. It is longer than the moor-hen by five inches, and is an altogether more powerful bird, and infinitely more wary. It is also accused of eating the spawn of fish, but I very much doubt if the accusation is one whit more warrantable than in the case of the moor-hen. The plumage of the coot is of a blacker shade than that of the moor-hen, and the tail is of the same hue, but the wings are crossed with a white bar. The bill is flesh-coloured. Like the moor-hen, the coot is excellent eating; numbers are, or were, annually shot in the neighbourhood of Poole, in Dorsetshire.

Colonel Hawker states that the Poole gunners always endeavoured to shoot these birds as early in the morning as possible, the birds thus killed being superior in flavour to those shot later in the day, when the dew was off the grass. I am not aware if coots are as plentiful in that district as in the days to which Colonel Hawker referred, but I should be inclined to suppose not, since nowadays, wherever there is any bird, fish, or animal to be shot, captured, or hunted, there are twenty people intent on its destruction as compared with one formerly. The nest of the coot is very similar to that of the moor-hen, being constructed of reeds and rushes, but is remarkable for its strength and size. The eggs are considerably larger, though not unlike those of the moor-hen in general colour; but the reddish-brown spots are very much smaller, and more plentifully distributed than those of the latter bird.

The feet of the coot are peculiar, the three

front toes being furnished with flat round lobes, the feet of the moor-hen having no such appendages. The coot is therefore able to swim more powerfully and rapidly than the moor-hen, and is better adapted for encountering the strong streams and waves of the larger waters it frequents.

DWELLERS IN NESTS.

PART VII.

The Heron—Fight between a Peregrine Falcon and a Heron—Fatal Encounter between a Falcon and a Heron—Herons as Food—Swans as Food—Uses of Herons' Feathers—Varieties of Herons noticed in Britain—The Bittern—The Jack Snipe—The Common Snipe—The Solitary Snipe—Varieties of British Snipe—Snipe-shooting—Indian Snipe-shooting—Snipe when shot difficult to find—Snipe-crouching—Snipe returning to same Spot after being flushed—My first Woodcock—Migration of Woodcocks—A Strange 'Right and Left'—Dixon on Migration of Birds—Mortality amongst Birds on Passage—Woodcocks returning to the same Spot when flushed—Drawing a Woodcock—Use of Woodcock Feathers—Woodcock carrying their Young—British Plovers—The Golden Plover—The Ringed Plover—The Oyster-catcher—The Dotterel—The Kentish Plover—The Gray Plover—The Turnstone.

I ALWAYS feel somewhat ashamed of myself in abusing the heron (and I do so solely from a fisherman's point of view), for he is a truly interesting bird, and if somewhat ungainly at times, his plumage, though not brilliant, is very beautiful; but, as I have elsewhere remarked, he is a terrible fish-poacher, and where these birds are numerous they must be kept down, though it goes to my heart to shoot them. On the contrary, where they are few in number, they should be protected as much as possible.

In describing the heron as an ungainly bird, I fear that I may be thought to do him an injustice; and I may qualify the observation by saying that, in my opinion, he is graceful as well as ungainly. No bird is, perhaps, more grotesquely awkward in its movements than a heron when capering about on a river-bank after having captured a large fish which he is endeavouring to kill, and under such circumstances he appears by no means lovely in the eyes of the owner of a fishery; but standing in the water, watching for his prey or intent on its capture, he is a peculiarly striking bird, and when sailing high in air with legs outstretched and neck doubled back, he is truly noble and game-looking. His best points are exhibited when standing still or in flight, but when rising from the ground to get on the wing he is at his worst; it is at this time that the enormous length of his wings is most noticeable. He possesses so little body, and so much wing, neck, and leg, that it is not to be wondered at that he should require time for the due and decent disposal of all this paraphernalia. When in full plumage, an adult male heron is very handsome, and, to my mind, nothing can exceed the beauty of the delicate shades of ash and pearl-gray, which are in such perfect contrast with the bold dark markings of the cream-coloured plume, yellowish-green beak and yellow iris.

The heron is a wary bird, but there are times when he is so intent on his fishing operations as to render himself an easy mark for the gunner, especially amongst the deeply-cut furrows which so often intersect the water-meadows. Last autumn, one of my servants, observing a heron fishing in such a spot, picked up a stone and killed it as it rose. I preserved and mounted it, and a very good specimen it is of its kind, though, perhaps, hardly as fully matured as it might have been.

It has been stated by some naturalists of repute that herons are in the habit of holding a kind of parliament, and I have seen an illustration of one of these supposed 'assemblages,' in which a number of these birds were disposed in a semi-circle, with one patriarch standing in the centre of the group, as if judging the community. All such stereotyped gatherings are, of course, purely ideal. I have no reason to doubt the truth of the assertion that certain kinds of birds do hold a kind of parliament. That rooks do so I have from the lips of an eye-witness upon whose veracity I place every reliance, though I myself have never witnessed such a proceeding. Birds are often most brutally cruel to each other, as may constantly be witnessed amongst fowls or tame pigeons, which, for no apparent reason, will select some wretched individual and hunt it to death, at times pecking its very brains out. Amongst my own pigeons, I have from time to time noticed some one or two birds which systematically bully the rest. I tried various plans to prevent them, with no results, and at last hit upon one which I have found successful. This is to catch the bully and fasten a paper collar round its neck. Birds always select those of their number which have any peculiarity about them as objects of aversion, and the knowledge of this led me to try the experiment.

Like those of many birds intended to fly high in the air, the bones of the heron are hollow and without marrow, and their enormous wings and small, light bodies are admirably adapted for flight; but they are very slow in getting up steam. I had often heard it stated that when it is attacked by a falcon the heron endeavours to impale its assailant by so directing its beak as to transfix the latter in its stoop, but I am forced to admit that I was always somewhat sceptical regarding the statement until a friend of mine related the following, of which he was an eye-witness: One day, when riding along the highroad near his house to meet a friend who was driving over to see him, he observed a peregrine falcon attacking a heron, and so waited to watch the conflict. Each time the falcon struck at the heron, the heron dropped on the ground and pointed his bill upwards at the falcon, which, being thus foiled, immediately mounted again with extraordinary speed, the heron endeavouring meanwhile to make good its escape. This took place several times, with the result that the falcon was unable to strike at the heron. What the result of the encounter might have been it is impossible to say, as just then the birds were scared by the appearance of the carriage which my friend had gone to meet. The falcon discontinued the attack and sailed across the road in front of my friend, then struck at a hare, which it missed, and disappeared, the heron flapping off as fast as it could, doubtless thankful for the unexpected interruption to the duel.

When relating the above to another friend of mine, he informed me of an instance which had occurred to him some years previously when hawking, in which both falcon and heron were lost in a thick wood and not recovered until a long time afterwards, when their bodies were found, the falcon being transfixed on the beak of the heron.

I regret that I did not make a note of this occurrence at the time I was informed of it. It is my custom to do so, and I was under the impression that I had entered it in my note-book or elsewhere; but I am unable to find any record, or I should have been able to state the name of the place and approximate date.

In some districts in England herons are by the country people called cranes. I am at a loss to account for the confusion of the names, since cranes have not been common in any part of England since the sixteenth or seventeenth century, and have long since ceased to visit these islands.

I very much doubt if herons are fit for the table, though we read of their being cooked in the olden days. Birds which feed so exclusively on fish, etc., must necessarily have a strong and unpleasant flavour. I have never had the misfortune to be asked to partake of a cooked heron, though I have been fortunate enough to taste a swan, which is justly entitled to be considered a delicacy, whether roasted or made into swan soup; but even these birds require long and careful preparation and feeding before they are fit for the table. In no place do they understand the business of the fattening and cooking of swans better than in that most hospitable of all towns, Norwich. Some fifteen or sixteen years ago there was an old army pensioner who earned his living by fattening and preparing swans for the table. If I remember rightly, the birds were kept in a field close to the Cathedral, and the pens were visible from the windows of the officers' quarters in the old Cavalry Barracks.

The plume feathers of the heron, when dyed, are used in the manufacture of some salmon-flies, and the fibres of the back feathers, dyed and undyed, are useful for forming the bodies of some trout-flies.

VARIETIES OF HERONS IN BRITAIN

Naturalists mention some varieties of the heron, viz., the purple and the great white, the buff-backed, squacco, green, and night herons, as belonging to the list of our British birds. They are, however, so exceedingly rarely met with in these islands as to hardly deserve the title of British. I have never seen either of these birds alive in this country, though I was fortunate enough some few years ago to procure the entire breast and back of a very good specimen of the purple heron when purchasing some feathers for the manufacture of salmon-flies at the shop of a provincial bird-stuffer. Colonel Irby states that but one occurrence is recorded of the buff-backed heron being seen in Britain, and that was in Devonshire in 1805, and the squacco heron he describes as a straggler on migration.

This last-named bird is noticed from time to time, but is exceedingly rare; and the green heron has also but once been noticed, that being, according to the same author, probably an escaped bird. The night heron he states to be not uncommon on migration. He thus describes its plumage. Crown, nape, and back brownish-black, with green gloss; wings and tail ash-gray; crest usually of three, but rarely of as many as six long, narrow white feathers, pendent from nape; legs yellow; bill black; iris red.

Although nearly extinct in this country, it would

hardly be fitting to omit some mention of the bittern, which is scientifically classified amongst the heron tribe (the Herodiones). Time was when this bird was far from uncommon in Britain. It is, alas! now so rare as to excite the attention of the public in the newspapers. Persecution and drainage have been the causes of its being at present so infrequently seen in this country. One was shot in Berkshire, near Farringdon, during last winter, 1894-95, and its destruction was, I am glad to say, purely accidental; and, as I am given to understand, no one regretted it more than the farmer who, when waiting for duck in the twilight, killed it, not discerning what kind of bird it was.*

I believe that some few other specimens were also obtained during the past winter in various localities. No bird is, of its kind, more beautiful in colour or shape than the bittern, the rich brown, almost black, markings contrasting so perfectly with the lighter tan colour. The neck-feathers, which are long, soft and exquisitely mottled, partake rather of the character of a ruff than of a plume, and are continued further round the neck than in the heron, those on the crown and nape being black, forming a kind of crest, somewhat square and decided in shape. The note of this bird is hoarse and deep,

* A friend of mine also shot a bittern during the past winter within two hundred yards of my house.

THE BITTERN

and has earned for it the various names of bog-bumper, mire-drum, night raven. I have never seen a living specimen of the bittern in Britain, but have shot them in India, their shape, plumage, etc., being in every respect similar to the ordinary British variety. Colonel Irby gives the length of the bittern as being seven or eight inches less than that of the common heron. Like the heron, the bittern, when wounded, is a dangerous bird to handle, and can use its powerful beak with unerring certainty in self-defence.

Two other varieties of the bittern find a place in the list of British birds, viz., the little bittern and the American bittern, the former being but twelve inches in length, and the latter twenty-seven—nearly the same size as the common bittern. The little bittern, though common in some parts of France, is but a very occasional straggler to this country. The Rev. C. A. Johns states that they are so numerous in the marshes of Esonne, near Paris, that in the months of August and September, if a gun be fired, the valley re-echoes to a long distance with their harsh cries.

The American bittern cannot truly be said to be a British bird, though Colonel Irby states that more than twenty occurrences of its having been seen in Britain and Ireland are recorded. In plumage and size this bird much resembles the common bittern, but its bill is more slender, and the upper parts are more finely marked (vermiculated), the primary feathers being of a blackish-brown, *not barred*.

It was formerly very commonly believed that the handsome little jack snipe was the male of the common or full snipe. In these more enlightened days it is perhaps hardly necessary to state that no relationship or affinity, save that of name, exists between the two birds.

Its name, doubtless, gave rise to this erroneous impression. The other appellations by which it is known, viz., judcock and half-snipe, are far more appropriate. The jack snipe has never been known to breed in the British Islands, whereas the common or full snipe frequently does so, and in some parts of England, Scotland, and Ireland in considerable numbers.

The jack snipe is more common in the earlier and later months of winter than during the actual winter months, resting as it were during its passage on migration. It is supposed that this bird is more difficult to shoot than any other; in reality it is one of the very easiest of all birds to kill, and far more so than the common snipe. Its flight, though twisting, is feeble and slow; whereas that of the common snipe is equally peculiar, but very rapid. The truth is that both birds have earned the reputation of being difficult to kill, and so escape more frequently than they otherwise would do were the gunner a little more deliberate and cool. It takes very little to kill snipe, their skins and skulls being very delicate. There are two periods in the flight of a snipe when it offers itself an easy mark even to an indifferent shot, viz., when it first rises, and whilst it is turning against the wind, as is its invariable custom; and just after it has turned. It is at these times, just for a second, almost stationary. The plumage of all the three British varieties of snipe—the great or double, the common or full, and the jack or half snipe—is very beautiful, especially that of the two last-named, though I think the palm for general beauty and gracefulness may be awarded to the common snipe. When just killed, the upper plumage of the jack snipe is very brilliant, being an exquisite combination of rich brown, tan colour and deep shot-greens; but its lustre fades very rapidly and visibly.

Every year some few occurrences of the great or solitary snipe are recorded. It has never been my fortune to shoot one of these birds, though I believe that on two occasions I have flushed them when salmon-fishing in the river Test, in Hampshire. If they were not the solitary snipe, I am at a loss to know what else they could have been, for the time of year when I saw them was that when they are most likely to be met with, viz., September, during which month, and in the spring, they are on passage. Two years running, and in almost the same spot, I flushed one of these birds.

These three varieties of snipe severally measure as follows, viz. :

The great or solitary, $11\frac{1}{2}$ inches.
The common or full, $10\frac{1}{2}$ inches.
The jack, $7\frac{1}{2}$ inches.

Apart from size, the differences between these three birds are very distinguishable. The plumage of the solitary snipe is more sombre than that of the common snipe, and the belly is barred to the vent, the breast and belly of the common snipe being pure white. The back of the jack snipe is the most brilliant in colour; the bill is much shorter, and it is altogether a less slender and graceful bird than either of the other two varieties.

A snipe is essentially an aristocrat among birds. He is cleanly in his diet, graceful in shape, and, I think I may add, the very best of all birds to eat. He is a thorough gentleman, and affords more real sport to the gunner than any other bird I know. Some of the very happiest days of my life have been spent in tramping over the Irish bogs alone with a good setter, snipe-shooting. There is always so much satisfaction in knocking a snipe over; he is so worthy a quarry, and not the worst that can be said of him is that he is not heavy to carry. A fair-sized hare-pocket will hold a great many couple of snipe, and it is possible to travel over miles of country, enjoy excellent sport, and dispense with the services of an attendant. Snipe-shooting is one of the most delightfully independent of all kinds of shooting; it has ever been my favourite sport with the gun, and I must beg the reader to excuse me if I am somewhat over-enthusiastic regarding it.

I shall never forget my first day's snipe-shooting in India. I had never seen so many snipe in my life before. In about four hours a brother officer and I succeeded in bagging thirty-six couple and a half, besides some teal and a bittern. We lost many more from want of a retriever, being unable to find them in the long matted water-grass when they fell. This was by no means a large bag for India, but it was the best day I have ever experienced, either before or since.

Snipe have an awkward habit of falling into holes in rough ground when shot, and without a good retriever they are often excessively difficult to find. Their plumage also seems to harmonize strangely well with the colour of the ground, unless they chance to fall on their backs, when their snow-white under-plumage renders them conspicuous.

At times it is a difficult matter to get snipe to rise, though, as a rule, the reverse is more frequently the case. I have seen a snipe lower its body until it was perfectly flat, its neck and bill being stretched out as close to the ground as possible. Woodcocks are also given to disposing of their bodies in a similar fashion, from which it has been argued that both birds utilize their bills in rising, an idea as incorrect as it is absurd. It might just as reasonably be argued that a fox utilizes his brush to jump with, because he trails it on the ground when hard pressed.

It is a peculiarity of snipe that when they rise out of shot they very frequently return to the same spot; it is, therefore, well to watch the flight of a bird under such circumstances. It will be observed to soar high in the air, and at times well-nigh disappear, describing a circuitous course, and probably repeating the same line of flight two or three times, eventually dropping on, or near to, the very spot from which it rose.

Although I am unable to remember my first partridge, the memory of my first woodcock is indelibly impressed on my mind. I was at the time a mere boy, and on a visit to a friend in Cumberland, who owned some of the best shooting I have ever known—fine, wild, rough country, and well, though not too heavily, stocked with nearly every description of game, my host being one of the most generous and kindly-hearted of men, a rare good sportsman to boot, and never grudging to give up the best place, even to a youngster like myself, who was but little likely to do much execution. I had been placed at a forward angle of a warm-lying covert, and before I had waited many minutes the cry of 'Mark cock!' reached me: a shadow over the sunlit pasture behind me, and almost before I descried a woodcock flash past me and disappear amongst the fir-trees, I had recklessly emptied my gun-barrel at it, never for an instant being conceited enough to suppose that I had hit it. Great was my delight when the beaters came up and discovered the bird lying dead, and I received shillings all round for the first cock of the day. And such a woodcock as it was, too! Its weight was a record.

But, there, I will close the account of my performances, for though numberless opportunities presented themselves to me, I did not succeed in shooting another, so I have every reason to remember this, my first cock. Those Christmas holidays were happy days, days which never can return, for my kind host and my old schoolfriend, his son, are, I grieve to say, no more, the latter cut off when life seemed to offer all that was best and brightest.

It has, I believe, come to be recognized that there are two varieties of woodcock which visit this country, the one considerably larger and lighter in colour than the other. Some few birds remain with us to breed, and it is stated that these British-bred birds are larger and lighter in colour than those which come to us from abroad.

The exact period of migration of woodcocks varies, depending to a great extent upon the phases of the moon, but as a rule they begin to arrive in Britain about the third week in October. If they have encountered heavy gales during their passage, they drop into the nearest resting-places, and remain there for a few days to recover themselves; but having regained their strength, they proceed onwards to those districts which they find most suitable to their requirements. Hence it happens at times that a considerable number of woodcocks may make their appearance in a certain place, and a day or two afterwards not one will be visible. Of course, under such circumstances these newly-arrived birds are, generally speaking, in but poor condition after their long and toilsome flight.

I have previously referred to my having flushed a woodcock in the University Parks in Oxford. Contrary to the general habit of woodcocks, this individual bird did not shift its quarters, but remained in the vicinity for some months, and was afterwards seen on several occasions by the park-keeper. I have from time to time, when visiting Oxford since then, asked the keeper if any further instances of woodcocks settling in the same locality have been noticed by him, but none have been observed.

A Wiltshire friend of mine, who died some two years ago at a very advanced age, told me that when he was a young man, and before old Cranbourne Chase had been quite cleared away, he fired his right barrel at a woodcock which he had flushed, and at the report a stag jumped up out of the fern close to him, and this he killed with his left barrel—a very unusual 'right and left.'

Dixon, in 'Our Rarer Birds,' thus describes the

migration of birds as seen from a lighthouse at the periods during which they are on passage : ' No pen can do justice to the wonderful sights which may often be witnessed at some of these lighthouses, especially in autumn. The moon is shining brightly in a cloudless sky ; not a bird is in sight, not a sound is heard. Suddenly a bank of clouds spreads over the heavens, and soon afterwards just as suddenly a vast army of migratory birds make their appearance. Birds of many different species are flying in company. Skylarks have fraternized with owls, and redwings and fieldfares are mixed up with goldcrests and big, lumbering herons. The lantern is vignetted in a sea of fluttering birds. Some of them crowd upon the railings and balcony of the lighthouse, others beat and flutter against the glass ; but as soon as the sky is clear again, and the moon sheds light upon the sea and land, the little voyagers pass on, rising to the highest air, where doubtless many old familiar landmarks point out the Southern course this feathered army is bent on taking.' This description is charming, as is the entire work in question, and I cannot but recommend its perusal to the reader, if he be a lover of birds, for every page of it is full of interest.

Many hundreds, and indeed thousands, of our migratory birds annually lose their lives when on passage. The wonder is that any survive when the weather is stormy and the winds contrary. It is not surprising, then, that woodcocks, when they first reach our shores, are emaciated and exhausted. The 'shiny nights' in October always bring back to my memory Whyte-Melville's lines :

> 'The woodcock on a moonlit night
> Comes flitting o'er the sea.'

When flushed a second or third time, woodcocks are very apt to return to the place where they first rose; but this very much depends, I think, upon the position of the springs, for they generally make off to some holly-bush near a spring or moist ground, and when these are not forthcoming they will circle round again to where they were first flushed. It is curious how great repugnance some dogs evince to retrieve a woodcock, and it is with the greatest difficulty that they can be induced to do so. On first rising from the ground, the flight of a woodcock is slow and heavy, and by no means unlike that of an owl; but when well on the wing there is, perhaps, no bird whose flight is more rapid, or one which is better able to test the skill of the gunner.

May I be permitted to remark, for the benefit of the uninitiated, that the term of 'drawing,' as applied to a woodcock, has an altogether different signification to when it is applied to a hare, and that a woodcock is invariably cooked without being denuded of its interior economy? To 'draw' a woodcock means to remove the sinew

which runs through the leg into the thigh, and
this should be done as soon after the bird is shot
as possible. The process is a very simple one.
The leg is broken, and the sinew which is attached
to it is pulled out of the thigh, thereby rendering
that well-known epicure's portion more tender.

The wing-feathers of the woodcock are most
useful to the trout-fisherman, and satisfactorily
represent the mottled and freckled wings of many
of those water-flies on which trout love to make
their evening meal, viz., the large, fat sedge-flies,
caperers, etc., which make their appearance when
the sun is declining under the distant hills at the
close of a summer's day.

It has been stated that woodcocks are in the
habit of carrying their young on their backs. I
have never been fortunate enough to witness such
a performance, and was somewhat sceptical as to
the truth of such an assertion. Some few years
ago, however, a well-known coach-builder in
Southampton, who rented the shooting of a large
wood some miles distant from that city, and
in which few woodcocks are known to breed
annually, informed me that he had himself seen a
woodcock flying up and down a small brook
which runs through the wood referred to, carrying
one of its young brood on its back, and that it
repeated the performance until it had evidently
thus exercised the entire family. My informant
minutely described the place where he lay hidden
amongst the fern and made his observations,

and I have every reason to rely on his veracity. Swans carry their young ones between their wings, so perhaps woodcocks do the same. Some naturalists assert that these birds carry their young with their feet, stating that they have often been witnessed in the act. I am unable either to contradict or confirm the statement, but when the shape of the foot of a woodcock is taken into consideration, it would seem a difficult matter for it to grasp a young bird securely enough for the purpose of carrying it. The structure of the foot is not adapted either for grasping or perching. A woodcock never perches, for the simple reason that it is unable to do so, and when dead its claws do not contract as do the feet of perching birds, but remain extended. It is, however, most generally believed that woodcocks carry their young between their thighs, close up under their breasts.

Woodcocks frequently evince a curious and unaccountable partiality for certain localities. Year after year they will select one or two special coverts entirely to the exclusion of those adjoining, although the conditions of all may be apparently precisely similar. Some few years ago I flushed and shot a woodcock in a large covert in the county of Durham. For twenty years no woodcock had been seen in that particular wood, although the surrounding coverts may generally be reckoned upon to hold a fair number of these birds every season. Two years subsequently I was again shooting on the edge of the same wood, and flushed a woodcock out of the fern, which I also secured, thus fully breaking the tradition. I have never been able to understand why the said covert was avoided by woodcock so persistently, for it has all the requisites which might be supposed to attract these birds. Two years running a friend of mine killed a brace of woodcock 'right and left' in the same spot in a covert in Hampshire. I am well acquainted with the place, and have often shot the covert in company with my friend. Of course there is a reason for the marked predilection of woodcock for certain coverts and certain spots in them, that reason being probably due to the supply of food and water being more to their liking. Again, although the supply of food in one place may be equally plentiful as in another, and the water apparently the same, the springs may be brackish or hard.

The members of the plover family which are included in the list of British birds are no fewer than fifteen in number, viz. :

    1. The stone curlew.
    2. The cream-coloured courser.
    3. The golden plover.
    4. The Asiatic plover.
    5. The gray plover.
    6. The dotterel.
    7. The ringed plover.
    8. The little ringed plover.
    9. The Caspian plover.

10. The Kentish plover.
11. The killdeer plover.
12. The peewit or lapwing.
13. The sociable lapwing.
14. The oyster-catcher.
15. The turnstone.

Of these fifteen, Nos. 1, 2, 4, 5, 6, 8, 9, 10, 11, 13, 15, are migratory, the remainder—viz., 3, 7, 12, 14—are resident.

The cream-coloured courser, Asiatic plover, little ringed plover, Caspian plover, killdeer plover, and sociable lapwing are rare.

I have previously referred to the stone curlew and peewit. Of the remaining seven, the dotterel and the Kentish plover arrive in the spring and remain with us until the autumn, and so may be termed summer visitors, the gray plover and the turnstone arriving in the autumn and leaving in the spring. I may as well here remark that, with the exception of the peewit, gray plover, and turnstone, the members of this family are without the hind-toe common to most birds. The remembrance of this fact will assist identification. We have thus four varieties of this tribe which are resident in this country, and five which are migratory, viz. :

Resident
{
The golden plover.
The ringed plover.
The oyster-catcher.
The peewit.
}

Migratory { The stone curlew / The dotterel / The Kentish plover } Spring to autumn.
{ The gray plover / The turnstone } Autumn to spring.

Next to the peewit, the golden plover is, perhaps, that variety most generally distributed throughout Britain. Although a resident, many of these birds shift their quarters in the autumn, moving southwards, and retiring northwards again in the spring, some remaining to breed in the Southern counties. Their habits much resemble those of the peewit, moving about in flocks; but their cry is different, partaking more of the character of a whistle. The plumage of this bird is subject to a very remarkable change. During summer the chin, throat, breast, and belly are black, the upper parts also very dark and spotted with yellow. This colouring is in the winter replaced by brown above spotted with yellow, the under parts being nearly white. The gray plover is also very similar in plumage to the golden plover, and undergoes a similar transformation, with this exception, viz., that the upper parts are spotted with white instead of yellow in *winter;* in spring they are white, barred with black.

I was fortunate in obtaining two excellent specimens of the golden plover in winter dress, male and female, with a 'right and left,' a few years ago when partridge-shooting in Hampshire. I only regret that they were not better mounted, for the plumage is very perfect. The birds were feeding in a ploughed field, and I happened to be on the flank of the line. I was much struck with the indifference of the flock to my presence, rising and settling again almost immediately, thereby affording me every opportunity for approaching them. On other occasions I have at times known them very much the reverse, being wary and difficult to come at. Although the food of the golden plover is much of the same character as that of the peewit, there is no comparison between the value of the two birds from a gastronomic point of view, the flesh of the latter bird being far inferior and, in my opinion, never altogether free from a somewhat strong and unpleasant flavour; that of the golden plover being equal, if not superior, to that of any bird which finds a place on the table. Colonel Irby states that he has seen golden plover with black markings peculiar to the summer plumage showing early in January, and remaining till late in September.

Taking the resident birds of this species in the order in which I have named them, we come to the ringed plover, or, as it is otherwise called, the ringed dotterel, whereas the golden plover and the peewit are more especially inland birds. The ringed plover is most generally, though not invariably, to be found by the flat stretches of sea-coast and salt-marshes. This is one of the smallest of the plovers, being between seven and eight inches in length, the common plover or peewit being thirteen inches. In plumage and size the ringed plover is not very unlike the Kentish plover, but the collar or ring of black which encircles the neck of the former bird, and from which it derives its appellation, is not complete in the Kentish plover, the entire breast of the latter being white. The two birds might, to an inexperienced eye, be very readily mistaken for each other. The ringed plover is very generally distributed throughout Britain in those portions of the coast which furnish it with suitable feeding-grounds.

The oyster-catcher, equally well known by the more appropriate name of sea-pie, is with the stone curlew the largest of the plover tribe, the length of both birds being equal, $i.e.$, sixteen inches. Why the appellation of oyster-catcher should have been given to this bird I am at a loss to understand, since, though it feeds on mussels and such-like shellfish, it is altogether incapable of opening an oyster, whereas, from its pied plumage, the name of sea-pie is more truly descriptive. As Dixon remarks, 'This singular bird may best be described as the magpie of the shore, its black and white plumage, brilliant orange bill, and pink legs, making it a very conspicuous object along the precipitous coast.' Whereas the ringed plover is chiefly to be met with on the flat sea-shores, the oyster-catcher prefers the more rocky portions of the coast, for the reason that it is on the rocks that it finds the chief portions of its food. It is a strong, active bird, but very wary and difficult to approach, its powerful bill being singularly well adapted for the purpose of procuring its food. Dixon gives the following pathetic account of the affection of which these birds are capable for each other: 'In summer it is generally observed in pairs, and few birds are more attached to each other. If one of the birds is shot, its companion flies round and round above its fallen comrade, uttering its shrill mournful pipe, and every now and then swooping down and almost touching its body, utterly regardless of its own safety. I have seen the oyster-catcher fly about for hours above the body of its mate, which was lying in the sea, slowly drifting with the tide; and sometimes several birds will come upon the sad scene and chant the death-knell of their poor companion. Who shall say, after this, that the "lower animals"—as man is pleased to call them—are not capable of displaying sentiment as true and as tender as his own?' I have inserted the foregoing extract in the hope that the heart of some eager shore-gunner may be softened towards these birds, which, after all, are neither fit for food, sufficiently beautiful in plumage, nor rare enough, to tempt any but the cockney sportsman to seek their destruction.

The dotterel, a bird at one time fairly common in certain districts, may nowadays be classed, if

THE DOTTEREL

not amongst our rarer birds, at all events amongst those which may be termed uncommon. I can myself remember the time when the dotterel was generally to be seen on the hillsides of Cumberland and the Northern counties. Saunders states that this decrease is mainly due to the esteem in which its feathers are held by the makers of artificial trout-flies, rather than to the greed of the ornithologist or egg-collector. This may have been the case in former years, but I do not think that the demand for the feathers of this bird has, for many years past, been very considerable, inasmuch as the dressing of artificial trout-flies is very different to what it was fifteen or twenty years ago, the feathers of the starling and other birds being used instead. And who can say that starlings are less common than they were? On the contrary, they are infinitely more numerous than ever. So I am inclined to suppose that the diminution in the numbers of the dotterel must be due to some other cause. Even in those days when dotterel feathers were considered indispensable, their use was restricted to the manufacture of but very few trout-flies, certainly not enough to account for so marked a decrease as has been apparent during recent years, and since the demand for them has been so much lessened. Nor can it, as far as I can see, be argued that the feathers of other birds have been substituted *because* of the decrease of the dotterel, inasmuch as the dressings of the present patterns of trout-flies are infinitely truer to nature than formerly. There must, of course, be a reason for the present scarcity of the dotterel, but what that reason may be I am not prepared to suggest. The fact remains, and it is one to be deplored. I should suppose that it is far more likely to be due to the increasing number of 'pot-hunters,' and the well-known tameness of the bird, which admits of its being easily approached, and so offering itself an easy mark. The majority of these birds which still elect to take up their abode with us during the warmer months of the year are to be found in Scotland, chiefly in the Highlands, some few being occasionally seen on the sea-coasts of England during the periods of their migration. It is said to be esteemed a delicacy as an article of food, but as I have never had any experience of its edible qualities, and hope I never may—at all events during its present scarcity—I am unable to corroborate the assertion.

The Kentish plover is another member of the plover tribe which is becoming annually more and more scarce. As I have before remarked, the plumage of this bird is very similar to that of the ringed plover, except that the collarette of black, so noticeable in the ringed plover, is interrupted by the white breast. It takes its name from its having been formerly common in Kent, although it was by no means rare in other localities, viz., Sussex, Yorkshire, Devonshire, Cornwall, and in some of the Channel Islands.

THE GRAY PLOVER 287

The gray plover, which with the turnstone is one of our autumnal visitors, is, as I have stated, similar in plumage to the golden plover. In size it is larger by two or three inches, measuring eleven and a half inches. Like the golden plover, the under parts change to black in summer, the upper parts being mottled and barred with black and white, and the tail-coverts white, this colouring, in like manner as is the case with the golden plover, being replaced in winter by white on the under parts, the yellow spots on the upper plumage being represented by white. The two birds are thus liable to be mistaken for each other. The gray plover is, however, of stouter build than the golden plover, and there is also in addition one unfailing characteristic which serves to identify it, viz., the possession of a short hind-toe. It is more common in the Eastern counties than elsewhere. I believe that I have also observed it in the Isle of Anglesey.

One more member of this family remains to be noticed, also an autumnal visitor, the handsome, active, busy little turnstone, otherwise known as the tangle-picker. This bird also possesses a hind-toe, though the peculiarity of its plumage is sufficient to enable it to be readily distinguished. The bill is short, pointed, powerful, and well adapted for the purpose of enabling it to procure its food, which consists for the most part of small shellfish, the bird turning and tossing over the stones and seaweeds in its search for them. In spring the head, neck, upper part of the breast, and shoulders, are black and white, the back and wings chestnut colour and black, the rump white, banded with black, the legs and feet orange-red. In winter the chestnut colour is less conspicuous, and the colour of the legs less vivid. It is fairly common on most of our coasts, more so, perhaps, in Lincolnshire, Norfolk, Suffolk, etc., though it is to be found more or less in all those localities which furnish it with suitable feeding-grounds. The Rev. C. A. Johns refers to an account which appeared in vol. ix. of the *Zoologist*, of the *successful* efforts of two of these little birds to turn over the dead body of a codfish, nearly three and a half feet in length, which had been imbedded in the sand to the depth of some two inches. Another author states that it is easily tamed. It is doubtless very intelligent, as may be gathered from the foregoing account, for, though excessively powerful for its size, it must be able to utilize its strength to the best advantage.

DWELLERS IN NESTS.

PART VIII.

The Avocet—The Black-winged Stilt—The Phalaropes—The Water Ouzel—The British Scolopacidæ—The Dunlin—The Redshank—The Curlew—The Little Stint—The Dusky Redshank—The Whimbrel—The Curlew Sandpiper—The Black-tailed Godwit—The Ruff—The Common Sandpiper —The Knot—The Sanderling—The Green Sandpiper— The Purple Sandpiper — The Bar-tailed Godwit — The Greenshank.

THE avocet, although now excessively rare in this country, was formerly plentiful in the Eastern counties, and to be met with in other parts of the kingdom.* The cause of this diminution is stated by one author to be partly due to the reclamation of fenland, but chiefly to the especial demand by dressers of artificial fishing-flies. The Rev. C. Johns says: 'This bird has become so rare, that having recently applied to two several collectors

* Since writing the above, a friend tells me of an avocet which he saw and shot at in Devon, within the last few years. The distance was too great for him to secure the bird, which he had stalked for some time.

in Norfolk, once the headquarters of the avocet, to know if they could procure me a specimen, I was told by one that they were not seen oftener than once in seven years; by the other, that it was very rare, and, if attainable at all, could not be purchased for less than five pounds.' Pennant says: 'These birds are frequent in the winter on the shores of this kingdom; in Gloucestershire, at the Severn's mouth; and sometimes on the lakes of Shropshire. We have seen them in considerable numbers in the breeding-season, near Fosdyke Wash, in Lincolnshire.'

Saunders, in his 'Manual of British Birds,' thus refers to the present scarcity of the avocet: 'Reclamation of fenland gradually circumscribed its haunts; a large colony at Salthouse was destroyed, as Mr. J. H. Gurney was informed, in consequence of the demand (especially from Newcastle) for avocets' feathers for dressing artificial flies; and egg-collectors also contributed to the decrease of the species, which by 1824 had probably ceased to nest in England.'

It is impossible to gainsay such well-known authorities, but, as a fisherman, I am at a loss to understand for what purpose the makers of artificial flies, whether salmon or trout flies, could have required the feathers of the avocet. The plumage of the bird is black and white, neither of which colours is used, except very sparingly, in the manufacture of either salmon or trout flies.

Indeed, I know of only two trout-flies in which a white feather is used, and those could be dressed just as well with any ordinary white feather, such as is obtainable from a white pigeon; also, amongst the legion of salmon-flies, there are but one or two patterns requiring white feathers, and these are generally procured from the swan. Fishermen and their requisites have doubtless something to say regarding the diminution of some birds to a certain extent, as is the case with the Canadian wood-duck, but I cannot bring myself to believe that the present rarity of either the avocet or the dotterel is attributable to the cause assigned to the extent supposed. I have been a keen fisherman all my life, manufacturing my own flies, whether for salmon, trout, or grayling, and having fished, more or less, over Great Britain and Ireland, am well acquainted with the various patterns of fishing-flies and the materials used in their construction. The dotterel is, or was, at one time used for the manufacture of some few North-Country trout-flies, and there was doubtless a demand for its feathers. There were, in fact, some nine or ten different varieties of flies for which these feathers were used. However, be this as it may, the avocet may be said to be very nearly unknown in Britain at the present time, more's the pity, for it is an exceedingly graceful and interesting bird. The reader is, I fear, but little likely to meet with it in Britain. It is said to breed in some parts of the

Continent, as well as in Asia, Africa, and America. In length it is about eighteen inches. Its plumage, as I have stated, is black and white, and it is web-footed. The shape of its bill is very peculiar, being extremely slender, long, and curved upwards. Its motions when feeding are singularly graceful and curious: it sways its body from side to side as it walks up the shallow streams in search of food, which it collects by utilizing the sides of its bill, thus swinging its body and bill alternately. It is truly a matter for regret that it has ceased to make its home in this country, but as a fisherman I cannot bear to think that the needs of the 'gentle craft' are so largely to blame as is supposed for the extinction of this graceful and beautiful bird.

The black-winged stilt is another rare bird, which is only, as an irregular wanderer on migration, very occasionally met with in Britain. It appears to have been at no time common in this country. It is, perhaps, one of the most peculiarly-shaped of all our British birds, the length of its legs being nearly as great as its entire body, giving the idea of extreme weakness. It is plentiful in the South of Spain, Sicily, and some other parts of the Old World.

There are two varieties of the phalarope which are occasionally to be met with in Britain. One, the gray phalarope, which is more frequent in its visits, sometimes appears in considerable numbers *from the autumn to the spring;* the other, the red-necked phalarope, and somewhat rare (though stated by Saunders to have become more common in Norfolk during the last five-and-twenty years), which visits this country *from the spring to the autumn.*

Some three years ago a specimen of the gray phalarope was shot by a friend of mine as it rose from the banks of a pond on the Wiltshire downs close to the village in which I was then residing ; but, I regret to say, it was completely spoiled by the local bird-stuffer. I saw the bird soon after it was killed, and it was in excellent condition, and but little injured, rendering the circumstance all the more to be regretted. The gray phalarope is, however, by no means uncommon in Britain, though in the South-western counties it is of rare occurrence. Saunders records instances of large numbers of these birds having been killed at various times, upwards of 500 in 1866. They appear to visit this country at very irregular intervals, but at these times a considerable influx takes place. The following years have been remarkable for these immigrations: 1866, 1869, and 1886. Nor do these visits seem to be always confined to similar localities, though they appear to have been chiefly in the South and South-eastern counties. In winter, the forehead and crown are white, the nape gray, and there is a white bar across the wing. The female is larger than the male, the under parts being of a reddish-chestnut, the beak orange - yellow, the crown blackish. The length of this bird is about eight inches. The feet of both varieties of the phalarope are peculiar, being lobed like those of the coot. The red-necked phalarope is also called, from this formation of its feet, the lobe-foot. The Rev. C. A. Johns states that 'the most marked habit of these birds seems to be that of alighting at sea on beds of floating seaweed . . . swimming about in search of food, or running with light and nimble pace after the manner of a wagtail,' and that 'they are often met with thus employed at the distance of a hundred miles from land.' The length of this bird is somewhat shorter than that of the gray phalarope, being about seven inches and three-quarters, and the male is rather smaller than the female. Colonel Irby thus describes its plumage in spring : Chin and throat white ; a bright rufous patch on each side of the neck, extending almost across the throat. In winter the forehead and the greater part of the crown are white, cheeks and under parts nearly pure white ; the nape, and a streak through the eye, sooty - brown. I have never had an opportunity of observing this bird when alive, and am indebted to Mr. Saunders' work for the description of its winter plumage. It is, indeed, rarely that any specimens in museums and collections are, unless freshly preserved, thoroughly reliable as to the colour of the plumage, as the latter is so very liable to fade. There are other varieties of the phalarope, but they are American. Dixon states that the male red-necked phalarope is in the habit of incubating the eggs instead of the female.

Wherever there are rocky streams the water ouzel is to be seen, one of the cheeriest, happiest little birds we have, and the only one of our water birds which can boast of any musical talent; like the robin, he sings most when other birds are silent —during the autumn and winter months. He is a lively, active bird, his every movement being quick and sprightly; even when standing on some rock or pebbly shore, his head and tail are in constant motion. To the fisherman or rambler by the riverside he is a well-known and familiar little friend, when suddenly alarmed on one bend of the river, winging his course straight up or down stream to the next, and screeching as he goes, much after the manner of the blackbird, save that the note of alarm is less mellow, though his song, if not remarkable for any very great variety, is soft and sweet and low. In length the water-ouzel measures but seven inches, or rather less, but his robust little body and pert bearing convey the impression of greater size. In shape and general demeanour, he very much resembles the wren. He flies rapidly, and, like the kingfisher, in a direct line, seeking his food amongst the water crustacea, water spiders, beetles, etc. Two varieties of this bird are met with in Britain, differing but slightly in plumage, and similar in size, both being dark-brown in the upper parts, and with the chest and throat white, the breast of the more common variety being of a chestnut colour, whereas that most frequently met with in the Northern counties is without this colour on the breast. The water ouzel is one of the few of our British water birds which is not frequent in the Eastern counties, the streams in those districts being unsuitable for its requirements. It is also known by the name of dipper, water crow, water blackbird, water pyet. Although not web-footed, the water ouzel is an accomplished swimmer and diver, using its legs and wings for the purpose. It is asserted that it is in the habit of walking under water in the bed of the stream, a performance which I have never had the opportunity of witnessing, though I think it is highly probable that such is the case, since, not being web-footed, and feeding in the manner above described, a bird which is able to remain for so long a time under water would be by this means enabled to procure a larger and more varied supply of food. It is stated that the water ouzel is addicted to the crime of eating the spawn of fish. Such may be the case. I am unable to contradict the statement, but considering that these birds, though not uncommon, are nowhere very plentiful, I am of opinion that it may well be left free of the streams it loves to frequent, and which it so much graces. It doubtless does good in some way or other, and I for one should indeed grieve were it to be exposed to persecution, even if its guilt were ever so strongly established. The bad name which attaches to many birds is but too readily accepted merely as an excuse for their slaughter.

The list of British Scolopacidæ, to which belong the avocet, black-winged stilt, the phalaropes, woodcock, solitary, common, and jack snipe, and to which reference has already been made, embraces also the following : Eleven sandpipers, three stints, the greenshank, yellowshank, redshank, and dusky redshank, two godwits, the sanderling, knot, dunlin, ruff, curlew, and two whimbrels.

The list is too numerous for me to refer to each individual variety, it may, however, be useful to the reader to give it in detail :

Avocet.
Black-winged stilt.
Gray phalarope.
Red-necked phala-
Woodcock. [rope.
Solitary snipe.
Common snipe.
Jack snipe.
Red-breasted snipe.
Common sand-
    piper.
Green sandpiper.
Broad-billed sand-
    piper.

Curlew sandpiper.
Purple sandpiper.
Pectoral sandpiper.
Bonaparte's sand-
    piper. [piper.
Buff-breasted sand-
Bartram's sand-
    piper.
Solitary sandpiper.
Wood sandpiper.
Bar-tailed godwit.
Black-tailed godwit.
Greenshank.
Redshank.

Dusky redshank.
Yellowshank.
Little stint.
Temminck's stint.
American stint.
The knot.

The dunlin.
The ruff.
The curlew.
Whimbrel.
Eskimo whimbrel.
Sanderling.

A long list, but many of its members are too rare to call for any special mention at the present time—such, for instance, as the following:

    The broad-billed sandpiper.
    The pectoral sandpiper.
    Bonaparte's sandpiper.
    Bartram's sandpiper.
    The wood sandpiper.
    The solitary sandpiper.
    The buff-breasted sandpiper.
    The yellowshank.
    The Eskimo whimbrel.
    The American stint.
    Temminck's stint.

Of the remaining sixteen birds, these only are residents:

    The dunlin.
    The redshank.
    The curlew.

The ruff was formerly a resident, but is now so rare that it has ceased to be regarded as such, and is only to be met with from the spring to the autumn, when on passage.

BRITISH SCOLOPACIDÆ

The following, therefore, are either visitors from the spring to the autumn, or visitors when migrating during that period :

1. The little stint (on passage, spring and autumn).
2. The dusky redshank (on passage, spring and autumn).
3. The whimbrel (on passage, spring and autumn).
4. The curlew sandpiper (on passage, spring and autumn).
5. The black-tailed godwit (on passage, spring and autumn).
6. The ruff (on passage from spring to autumn).
7. The common sandpiper (spring to autumn).

In like manner, those birds named below are either visitors from autumn to spring, or visitors on passage at those periods :

1. The knot (autumn to spring).
2. The sanderling (autumn to spring).
3. The green sandpiper (autumn to spring).
4. The purple sandpiper (autumn to spring).
5. The bar-tailed godwit (autumn to spring).
6. The greenshank (on passage, autumn and spring).

I have thus classified the foregoing birds in order to assist the reader in more readily ascertaining when, or during which periods of the year, the several varieties may be looked for. I propose to refer as briefly as possible to each individual bird, giving merely its measurement, localities in which it is most frequent, and any peculiarities which I consider worthy of mention as being likely to aid identification.

The dunlin is one of the most common of our smaller shore-birds, and is to be met with nearly everywhere—along the coast, on tidal rivers, etc.—and frequently in great numbers. Its length is eight inches. Its change of plumage is so remarkable, that formerly two different varieties were supposed to exist—*i.e.*, the dunlin and the purre. In summer the plumage is reddish-brown above, marked with black, the under parts being black. In winter the upper parts are of an ash-gray hue, and the under parts white. During the summer —viz., May, June, and July—the dunlin leaves the coast, and betakes itself to the high moorlands to breed, more especially in the more Northern counties. It is an exceedingly sprightly and pretty little bird, and when in winter plumage, and in flocks, the white under parts, glistening in the sunlight, present a peculiarly pleasing effect, more especially when seen flying across the blue water of some small shore-bay. It is also known as the ox-bird, a name also given to the sanderling. In summer plumage the lower part of the breast is black.

The redshank, a larger bird than the dunlin, and measuring between ten and eleven inches in length, is very similar to the dunlin as regards the

THE REDSHANK

localities it frequents during the winter, and those to which it retires during the breeding season, though less confined to the Northern counties during the latter period. Although a resident, a considerable number of these birds arrive in this country in the autumn from the Continent. The plumage in winter is also diverse from that in summer, the latter being light brown above, streaked and barred with brown, secondary feathers whitish, rump white; tail-feathers also white, barred with black; legs and feet red (in the mature bird). In the winter plumage the upper parts are ash-colour, the rump and under parts white, streaked and spotted with ashy-gray. A somewhat slender and very graceful bird. Writing of these birds, Dixon remarks: 'They are conspicuous objects when perched on the top of a tuft of cotton-grass or rushes, and look very pretty as they trip round the margin of the pools, or even run along the rough walls and fences in their anxiety and excitement. The male bird at this season may often be seen soaring into the air, and descending with wings and tail expanded, uttering a shrill note very rapidly; and he often begins these flights from a stump, wall, or a tree, and returns to the same place, much after the manner of the meadow pipits that live upon the moors with him.'

Saunders says: 'Its flight is quick, though somewhat wavering, the white band on the extended wing being very conspicuous.'

The curlew is considerably the largest member

of the family to which it belongs, and, I think I may add, by far the most wary and difficult to approach. Curlews may be met with more or less frequently on all of our higher downlands and moors throughout the spring, summer, and autumn months, occasionally remaining inland as late as November and December in very mild seasons and so long as food is plentiful, when they betake themselves to the sea-coasts and marshes until the spring, when they return to their breeding-grounds. After corn harvest they frequent the stubble-fields in considerable numbers, and are at that period of the year excellent eating; but when shot in the winter near the sea they have an unpleasantly strong and fishy flavour. Wild and wary birds, with a wild and plaintive cry, they are fitting inhabitants of the desolate marshlands and mud-flats which they frequent. Often when sitting in my smoking-room late at night in the autumn and early winter I have heard them whistling overhead, the sound being audible down the chimney. At one time a curlew was in the habit of passing over the house regularly every night at the same hour; and many a time when returning home over the downs from shooting, in the dusk of an autumn evening, when the lights in the village below were beginning to shine out from the cottage windows, I have heard the cry of a curlew, and could perhaps descry the bird winging its way far overhead in the clear though darkening sky. I know no bird more difficult to stalk than the curlew; the most carefully-laid plans so frequently end in failure, unless there happens to be a strong wind blowing from the birds, and suitable covert to enable one to approach within reasonable gunshot distance; and these are precisely the conditions which the curlew takes special care to avoid affording, generally selecting the most exposed portion of some large field in which to feed, and ever ready and watchful to take alarm. The plumage is a very pale brown streaked and blotched with dark brown. The bill is very long, and curved downwards. The name of the bird is derived from its cry, 'Cŭrlēe, cŭrlēe.' The country people generally pronounce it as spelt, 'C'lōo.' It may frequently be found nesting in company with the peewit and stone curlew or thick-knee plover, on the ploughed fields of the cultivated downlands, and, like the plover, its eggs are never more than four in number, of an olive-green blotched with brown.

Although I have included the little stint in the list of those members of the Scolopacidæ which are less rare than others, it is, nevertheless, by no means common throughout the country, being most frequently to be found in that home of wild-fowl, Norfolk, and the adjoining counties. In plumage it is very similar to the dunlin, but it measures only some six inches in length. Its visits are confined to the periods during which it is on migration, viz., the autumn and spring. Apart from its smaller size, it may be distinguished from the dunlin by its breast being of a light gray colour, streaked with brown ; its bill is also straight, whereas that of the dunlin is slightly curved downwards.

The dusky, otherwise called the spotted redshank, is another visitor during its migration in spring and autumn, measuring twelve inches in length, with exceedingly long, dark-red legs. The base of the lower part of the bill is also of the same colour. The plumage, which in summer is nearly black, except the rump and tail feathers, which are white, the latter barred with gray, changes in winter to an ash-gray in the upper parts, mottled with white ; the under parts are of a pale gray, nearly white. Its visitations are almost entirely confined to the Eastern counties.

The whimbrel may be briefly described as being very similar to the curlew, though considerably smaller, measuring about seventeen inches in length. Its plumage differs from that of the curlew, more especially in the colour of the crown of the head, the latter being dark brown with a pale brown streak from the base of the bill over the eyes ; and the feathers of the vent are also, perhaps, whiter. In all other respects, in shape, general bearing, and colour of the plumage, the two birds are very much alike. The whimbrel is also a visitor during its migration in spring and autumn, and in some counties it is so regular in making its appearance in May as to have earned the name of Maybird. It is most frequent in the Southern and Eastern counties, and also in some parts of Scotland. It is frequently to be seen in company with the curlews on the salt-marshes and long stretches of mud-flats so frequent on the South and East coasts.

The curlew-sandpiper can hardly be called a common bird, neither is it rare. Its visitations occur during its migrations in spring and autumn, more especially the latter. Like the whimbrel, it is more frequently noticed in the Southern and Eastern counties. It is a small unpretentious bird, measuring seven inches in length, and its plumage, like so many of the family to which it belongs, is subject to considerable alteration, that worn in the spring, a reddish brown with black markings, giving place in the autumn to a gray colour on the upper parts and white on the under, the rump being white. The shape of the bill is, like that of the curlew, long and curved downwards, from which peculiarity it derives its name. It frequents the salt-marshes and sand-banks, but is less inclined to be gregarious than the other members of this genus.

The black-tailed godwit, another of our visitors during its spring and autumnal migrations, was, like the ruff, at one time a resident in Britain in the Eastern counties. It is one of the largest of the Scolopacidæ, measuring from sixteen to twenty inches in length. The winter plumage is of an ash-brown above and grayish-white in the under parts; the vent white, the belly barred with blackish-brown. In summer this colouring changes to a reddish-fawn on the head, neck, and breast, the belly white and barred with blackish-brown. The bills of both varieties are remarkably long, and are perfectly straight; the females are larger than the males. The tail of this bird is black, and serves to distinguish it very readily from the bar-tailed godwit. Both birds frequent much the same localities as the preceding varieties of this genus. The black-tailed godwit is, however, by far the less common of the two.

Time was when the ruff and his wife, the reeve, were plentiful in this country, and numbers of them were annually exposed for sale in our poultry markets. Unfortunately, they were so esteemed for table purposes, and their numbers have been so terribly reduced, that nowadays this bird is regarded as a rarity; indeed, it may be said that none remain to breed in Britain, and the few which are annually noticed are no more than visitors on migration from the spring to the autumn. It is sad to reflect upon the long list of birds, formerly so plentiful, which are now rapidly becoming extinct in this country, owing to the greed of the gourmand or the collector; and of all these, surely none is more interesting than the ruff. The pugnacity of the ruff is proverbial. It has been stated that so continuous and fierce were the

THE RUFF

contests which daily took place during the pairing season that the turf was worn bare on their fighting-grounds. The peculiar collar worn by the male bird is quite sufficient for its identification without any further reference to its plumage. This ruff, which extends round the neck of the cock, is of every shade of purple, black, chestnut, gray, and white, and the same beauty of colouring extends also along the back. The female, though very handsome, is without the ruff, and of more sombre attire. The male is larger than the female, being twelve and a half inches in length, as compared with ten and a half. After moulting the male bird sheds the ruff, and both birds are very similar in plumage—viz., buff-coloured, marked with dark brown above, and grayish-white in the under parts. They frequent marshy and swampy localities. The reclamation of land by drainage is said to have had much to do with the decrease in the numbers of this bird. Such may be the case; I fear, however, that the demands of the poulterers have been the cause of its present rarity.

The summer-snipe, or common sandpiper, is a well-known frequenter of most of our streams, and although not a resident, there are but few weeks from early spring-time till late autumn in which it may not be seen winging its way from one bend of the river to another, its white breast gleaming in the sunlight as it turns in its flight. Now and again it will stop to rest on some miniature headland, when it might, from the motion of its tail, be mistaken for one of the wagtails, and this peculiarity serves to distinguish it from the other sandpipers. These birds have been, during the past spring (1895), remarkably numerous on the stream which runs close to my house, and I have seen as many as three and four pairs of them in the course of an afternoon, doubtless nesting under the leaves of the plant called the butter-burr, which grows in profusion in some of the meadows, and which they are said to avail themselves of for the purpose. In flight this bird conveys the impression of being much larger than it is, it measuring no more than seven and a half inches in length. It is plentiful in the Southern and Eastern counties, and especially so in the North, Scotland, and Wales. The plumage is thus described: Upper parts of a greenish-brown, flecked and barred with brown, the outer tail-feathers tipped with white, and with black bars; chin and under parts white, neck and breast ash-colour, with darkish streaks.

The knot, which is a winter visitor to this country, arriving in the autumn and departing in the spring, is more or less plentiful during that period on the mud-flats and sand-banks of England, especially those on the East coast. It is also said to visit the Solway in great numbers, though less generally distributed in Scotland than in the other parts of Great Britain and Ireland. Its name is said to have been derived from King Canute, or

Knut. It is a trustful, fearless little bird, of about ten inches in length. It has never been known to breed in this country. Its winter plumage is ash-gray above, and the under parts white, with brownish streaks or flecks. In summer the crown and neck are of a reddish-brown, streaked with dark brown; the back streaked and spotted with black, red, and gray, the feathers edged with white; the cheeks, throat, and breast of a chestnut colour.

The sanderling, another of our visitors from autumn to spring, is smaller than the knot, measuring but eight inches in length. The plumage also undergoes a change during moult. In spring the upper parts are rufous and black; the head, throat, and upper breast rufous, marked with black. In winter gray above, white below; rump ashy-gray. The visitations of the sanderling are somewhat fitful, and though a visitor from the autumn to the spring, it does not often remain with us throughout the winter. A peculiarity which will readily assist the identification of this bird is that it has no hinder toe. It frequents the low-lying, sandy parts of the coast.

As I write, I have a specimen of the green sandpiper, which I shot a couple of seasons ago, before me. It may be met with, though it can hardly be described as a common bird, in any of our rivers, except during the months of June and July. It is most plentiful during August. It has, however, never been known to breed in these islands, though it does so on the Continent, making its nest in old trees. In length it measures some nine and a half inches. It is a slender, graceful bird. Its plumage apparently undergoes no change. The upper parts are of a greenish-brown, with very small white spots; the head and shoulders of a dark ash-gray; round the eyes a light whitish-gray; the chin white; the breast white, thickly streaked with dark gray; the under parts white; the legs dark green; the rump white; outer tail-feathers white, the lower portion of the tail with broad black bars; the bill is long, and slightly curved downwards at the tip.

The small white spots on the dark green back, and the *broad* black bars across the tail, are distinctive marks by which this bird may be identified. This and the common sandpiper are perhaps more frequently to be met with inland than the other varieties of sandpiper.

The purple sandpiper is frequent throughout the rocky coasts of Great Britain and Ireland throughout the winter. It is a smaller variety than the green sandpiper, measuring but eight inches in length. The winter plumage is of a black-brown above, and dark mottled brown in the under parts, the upper parts changing in summer to a dark brown-gray, nearly to black, spotted with reddish colour, and the feathers tipped with a yellowish-white; throat, neck, and breast gray, with pale brown streaks; legs and feet yellow. *The hind-toe of this bird turns inwards.* It selects for its feeding-grounds those localities in which seaweed is plentiful, feeding on the small crustacea, etc., which cling to it.

The black-tailed and the bar-tailed godwits are similar in shape, both possessing the same long, slender, and up-curved bill, the same peculiarly-shaped head, not unlike that of the woodcock in the setting-on of the bill at its base, though the neck is longer and more slender than that of the woodcock. The bar-tailed godwit is the more common of the two. It is said to be most plentiful on the Northumbrian coast throughout the winter, and in Norfolk during its migration in spring. As I have before observed when referring to the black-tailed godwit, the females of both varieties are larger than the males. The bar-tailed variety is, however, the smaller, measuring from fifteen to sixteen inches, as compared with from sixteen to twenty inches. In summer the plumage of the bar-tailed godwit is of a red colour below, the upper parts streaked with brown and black; the rump white, with brown streaks; the tail a yellowish-white, with dark brown bars. In winter the under parts are white, the upper grayish-brown, the tail barred. The length and peculiar shape of the bill is alone sufficiently characteristic to denote the godwit, the colour of the tail-feathers plainly indicating which of the two varieties, whether the black or bar-tailed.

The greenshank, though it may be almost called a resident in Ireland, is rarely to be seen in England save during its migrations *in autumn and spring*. It frequents the shores and lakes, feeding on small fish, crustacea, worms, beetles, etc., and may at times be found in the water-meadows and pastures. It is one of the largest varieties of the genus to which it belongs, measuring fourteen inches. As its name indicates, the colour of its legs is greenish-brown. It is said to breed in the North of Scotland, but rarely remains with us throughout the winter, except in the West of Ireland. In summer the plumage of the head and neck is pale gray streaked with dark brown; the feathers of the back very dark brown with pale gray margins; the rump white; the tail-feathers white, with dark brown bars, and mottled with the same colour; the under parts white, streaked and spotted with grayish-brown on the throat and breast; the bill is slightly curved upwards.

In winter the upper parts are grayer, the under parts white. It is a handsome, graceful, and game-looking bird, and able to swim and dive Like the curlew, to which bird it bears some resemblance, it is wary, ever selecting some spot from which it can readily survey the approach of an enemy.

DWELLERS IN NESTS.

PART IX.

British Wild-geese—The Gray-lag Goose—The White-fronted Goose—The Bean Goose—The Pink-footed Goose—The Snow Goose—The Red-breasted Goose—The Brent Goose—The Bernacle Goose—Other British Varieties of Anatidæ—The Sheldrake—The Wild-duck—The Shoveller—The Teal—The Red-breasted Merganser—The Gadwall—The Pintail—The Widgeon—The Pochard—The Tufted Duck—The Scaup Duck—The Golden-eye Duck—The Long-tailed Duck—The Scoter—The Velvet Scoter—The Surf Scoter—The Goosander—The Smew—The Garganey—Plumage of Immature Males of the Duck Tribe.

EIGHT varieties of the wild-goose visit, or are known to have visited, this country, either from autumn to spring or at some time during the winter, and so have the right to be styled British birds. They are as follows:

1. The gray-lag goose (not common).
2. The white-fronted goose (frequent at times; local).
3. The bean goose (common).
4. The pink-footed goose (common, but local).
5. The snow goose (rare).

6. The brent goose (very common).

7. The bernacle goose (not infrequent, but local).

8. The red-breasted goose (very rare).

As the gray-lag goose is said to have been the progenitor of our tame variety, it must at one time have been not only very common, and in the habit of breeding in Britain, but also well distributed. Now, however, it is by no means a common bird anywhere in these islands, and is only known to breed in the Hebrides and the extreme North of Scotland. It is the largest of the eight varieties, measuring thirty-five inches in length. Its distinguishing characteristics are as follows: Plumage—white round the base of the bill; breast, whitish, with a few black marks; head, neck, and upper parts, grayish-brown; under parts, dirty white; rump and wing-covert, bluish-gray; bill, legs, and feet, flesh-coloured; the tip of the bill (the 'nail,' as it is termed), white. It is to be met with in England only from the autumn to the spring, when it wanders Southwards.

The white-fronted goose, otherwise called the 'laughing goose,' measures in length but twenty-seven inches. It is a particularly handsome bird, perhaps more so than any of the other seven varieties. It derives its *first* name from the white on its forehead and the white *nail* at the tip of its bill, which latter is of an orange colour (the legs and feet being also of the same hue), its *second* name from its peculiar note. It arrives

THE BEAN GOOSE

in this country late in the autumn, remaining until the spring, and is more especially frequent on the Southern and South-western coasts, and on the West coast of Ireland. It is more plentiful during very severe winters.

The bean goose approaches the gray-lag goose very nearly in size, being but one inch shorter in length, viz., thirty-four inches. It may be readily distinguished from the gray-lag and white-fronted varieties by the colour of its bill, which is *orange-coloured* with a *black nail*. It is stated to have derived its name from its habit of feeding inland during the daytime, and from its partiality to all kinds of grain crops, though I am inclined to suppose that the appellation of bean goose must have a different origin. In open weather these birds seek their food inland, betaking themselves to the coast should frost intervene, their movements varying with the wind and weather. It is common enough in Ireland, and frequent on our East and extreme Southern coasts. It is, for a goose, a by no means ungraceful bird. Its plumage generally is darker than that of the gray-lag or white-fronted goose.

The pink-footed goose is chiefly to be found on the East coast of England, and on both the East and Western coasts of Scotland, but it does not visit Ireland. This bird is that generally known as the gray goose, the feathers of which were in olden days in such request for the winging of arrows. The colour of its plumage resembles that of the bean goose. The bill is pink, the nail black; the legs and feet are also pink. In length it measures twenty-eight inches.

The snow goose is a rare visitor. It is the only variety which is white. The bill, legs, and feet are red. It is twenty-three inches in length. An instance is recorded of its having been domesticated and crossed with the common tame goose.

The red-breasted goose may be described as a *very rare* visitor to this country. It is a small goose, measuring but twenty-two inches in length. The very few specimens of this bird which have been obtained have been from no one particular part of the country. Its plumage is peculiar, and Colonel Irby briefly describes it as follows: 'Fore part of chest and sides of neck, brick-red; white patch between the eye and the bill.' This description is sufficient for its identification, and so will serve the present purpose, and one more full and detailed would be too lengthy. I may, however, add that the fore part of the neck, the upper breast, and the ears, are red; the crown, the back part of the neck, and from below the eyes to the gullet and the back of the neck, are black, the division between the several portions being outlined with white; there is also a peculiar patch of white between the eye and the base of the bill; the upper parts are blackish, the belly white, the lower breast black; the bill, legs, and feet dark brown.

The brent goose is the commonest variety we

THE BRENT GOOSE

have, visiting us during the winter in great numbers, and more or less frequent throughout Great Britain. It is rarely seen inland, but seeks its food on the muddy and sandy shores, and is most numerous on the East coast. It measures about twenty-three inches. The head, neck, and throat are black, with a curious triangular patch of white on either side of the neck; the upper parts are of a brownish-black, the under parts of a slate-gray; the vent white.

The bernacle goose—the bar goose, as it is at times called—is a winter visitor, chiefly to the Western coast of Great Britain and the East coast of Ireland. It is by no means a common bird. Some authors state that its name is derived from the peculiar black mark round its eye, which, being on a white ground, presents the appearance of a pair of spectacles, or 'bernacles,' as they were formerly termed; others, that it was supposed to be hatched from the bernacles found in salt-water. The sides of the head are white; the forehead, neck, shoulders, and upper breast black; the under parts gray; the vent white; the back blue-gray; the bill, legs, and feet black. In length it is twenty-five inches.

Including three varieties of the eider duck, three of the scoters, the goosander, three varieties of the merganser, and the smew, there are, in addition to the eight varieties of the wild-goose already mentioned, and three of the swan, to which I do not intend to refer, no fewer than thirty-one different varieties of the Anatidæ, all of which are either regular visitors to Great Britain or have a place in the list of our British birds. It is impossible to do more than briefly refer to each of the less rare varieties in the present instance, merely noticing such characteristics as may enable the reader to readily identify any specimens he may see or procure. I think it as well to give the list *in extenso* :

1. The sheldrake.
2. The ruddy sheldrake.
3. The wild-duck.
4. The gadwall.
5. The shoveller.
6. The pintail.
7. The teal.
8. The American green-winged teal.
9. The American blue-winged teal.
10. The garganey, or summer teal.
11. The widgeon.
12. The American widgeon.
13. The red-crested pochard.
14. The pochard.
15. The White-eyed pochard.
16. The tufted duck.
17. The scaup.
18. The golden-eye.
19. The buffel-headed golden-eye.
20. The long-tailed duck.
21. The harlequin duck.
22. Steller's eider duck.
23. The king eider duck. [duck.
24. The common eider
25. The scoter, or black duck.
26. The velvet scoter.
27. The surf scoter.
28. The goosander.
29. The red-breasted merganser.
30. The hooded merganser.
31. The smew.

ANATIDÆ, RESIDENT AND MIGRATORY

Of the foregoing, some are resident, and some are migratory; some few are too rare to necessitate any further reference. In this latter category may be included:

1. The ruddy sheldrake.
2. The American green-winged teal.
3. The American blue-winged teal.
4. The American widgeon.
5. The red-crested pochard.
6. The white-eyed pochard.
7. The buffel-headed golden-eye.
8. The harlequin duck.
9. Steller's eider duck.
10. The king eider.
11. The common eider.
12. The hooded merganser.

Of the remaining nineteen varieties, the following are *residents:*

1. The sheldrake.
2. The wild-duck.
3. The shoveller.
4. The teal.
5. The red-breasted merganser.

Those which visit us *from the autumn to the spring* are:

The gadwall (breeds in Norfolk).
The pintail (sometimes breeds in Ireland).
The widgeon (many breed in Scotland).
The pochard (breeds in a few places).

The tufted duck.
The scaup.
The golden-eye.
The long-tailed duck.
The scoter.
The velvet scoter (a few breed in North of Scotland).
The surf scoter.
The goosander (some breed in Scotland).
The red-breasted merganser (resident in Scotland and Ireland).

The garganey, or summer teal, visits us *from the spring to the autumn.*

The smew makes its appearance *during the winter only.*

Commencing with those residents, which may be termed true wild-duck, the sheldrake heads the list, as being the largest. The pintail exceeds it in length, but the tail-feathers of the latter have to be taken into account, the sheldrake measuring from twenty-five to twenty-six inches, the pintail from twenty-four to twenty-eight.

Another name for the sheldrake is that of burrow duck, from its habit of utilizing the burrows of the rabbits which are so frequently to be found on the sandy portions of the coasts and near the sea-shore.

The name of sheldrake is stated by Willoughby to be derived from its variegated plumage, the word *shelled*, in the Eastern counties parlance, being still used to convey that meaning. Saunders also states that 'the prefix "sheld" is given by Ray as an East-Anglian equivalent for "particoloured."'

The sheldrake is, as are most of the varieties to which I shall have occasion to refer, plentiful on the coasts of Norfolk, Lincolnshire, etc., though by no means infrequently to be met with on the other coasts of Britain which are of a similar character and adapted to its requirements. It is an excessively handsome bird. Its plumage is as follows: Head and neck green; lower part of neck and upper breast white, forming a collar; lower breast and shoulders chestnut; wings white, green, and black; under parts white, a dark brown line traversing the breast and belly; legs and feet flesh-coloured; the bill flesh-coloured, as is also a fleshy knob at its base.

The wild-duck is so familiar to everyone as to need no description either as to its size, plumage, or habits. Suffice it to say that it is thickly and generally distributed throughout Great Britain and Ireland. A very great difference exists in the plumage of the male and female of most of the varieties of the Anatidæ, the males being, as a rule, far more gaily clad than the females, this being probably a provision of the Creator to guard the females from molestation during the breeding season. It may possibly interest the reader to know, if he is unaware of the fact, that, smart as is the mallard during the rest of the year (probably one of the handsomest birds we have), yet during the breeding season he lays aside his gay clothing, assuming a plumage very similar to the female. This change has been observed to take place in the case of mallards which have been domesticated, and at the usual time of year when the plumage of the wild mallard undergoes its annual transformation. In May the change commences, and about the middle of October the normal dress is resumed.

Wild-duck often lead their broods into extraordinary places, and a year or two ago a wild-duck with her young ones strayed into the greenhouse of a friend of mine. This season, a brood of young wild-ducks was discovered in the very centre of the village cricket-ground. A friend of mine, supposing the old duck to have wandered to a neighbouring withy-bed, took the tiny creatures, which had evidently been very recently hatched, to the brink of the river which, at the point opposite the withy-bed, is both strong and wide, where they immediately took the water, and, utilizing the eddies in the stream to assist their passage, completed their voyage in safety, the duck joining them shortly afterwards.

It is not often possible to bring up young wild-ducks under a hen. They thrive fairly well up to a certain stage, after which they generally sicken and die, though I have succeeded in preserving them in health until about half-grown. The food and confinement are alike unsuitable for them.

THE SHOVELLER AND TEAL

Wild-duck they are, and wild they must be in order to thrive as they should.

The shoveller, although it has the right to be styled one of our resident birds by reason of a certain number of the variety remaining in this country to breed, may also be classed as a visitant during the colder months of winter. It breeds principally in Lincolnshire and Norfolk, and is also to be met with in the Scottish Lowlands as well as in some parts of Ireland.

The plumage is thus described by Colonel Irby: 'Head and neck green; shoulders pale blue; iris yellow.' Length, twenty inches. The male bird, like the mallard, assumes the plumage of the female during the summer, viz., a dark brown. The shape of the bill is peculiar, its width at the tip being double that at the base.

The teal is almost as well known in Britain as the wild-duck, and, although not as numerous, is very plentiful throughout the winter, many birds also remaining to breed in the Northern counties of England, as well as in Scotland and Wales. It is unnecessary for me to describe the plumage of a bird with which everyone is so well acquainted. The plumage of the male bird undergoes a similar transformation to that of the female, as in the case of the wild-duck.

Although belonging to the Anatidæ, the merganser can hardly be regarded as a true duck. Its bill, instead of being flat like those of the true ducks, is longer, more pointed, slightly turned down at the tip, furnished with sharp sawlike edges, and is therefore well adapted for seizing the small fish upon which it feeds. In length it measures from twenty-two to twenty-four inches. The plumage is as follows: Bill red; legs and feet orange; head and neck black, with a long black crest or plume; back black; white collar round the neck; wings with a great deal of white on them; at the shoulder of the wing several white feathers, edged with black; lower part of the neck saffron colour, ermined with black; under parts white. The female is smaller than the male; the head and neck of a red-brown colour; wings white, with a black bar across them. The merganser is more or less frequent on all of our coasts, large lakes, and also in Ireland. It breeds in some parts of Scotland. In hard winters it is by no means uncommon, at such times congregating in large flocks. The male bird changes its plumage during the breeding season. Dixon thus refers to this bird: 'Whatever food is secured under the water is always brought up to the surface to be swallowed, and usually, as soon as it has disposed of its capture, the bird drinks, and rises half out of the water, and flaps its wings. The red-breasted merganser lives entirely on animal substances.' And again; 'A favourite haunt of the red-breasted merganser, abounding with its food, is where the trout-stream from the distant hills falls into the loch.' The merganser is a handsome and interesting bird,

THE GADWALL AND PINTAIL

but, as may be supposed from the fishy nature of its diet, is absolutely unfit for food.

The gadwall, the first on the list which I have given of those ducks which visit us from the autumn to the spring, is by no means common at any period, although a considerable number of these birds are preserved and breed on one estate in Norfolk. It measures twenty inches in length. The general colour of its plumage is gray, the shoulder of the wing chestnut; the back feathers dark gray edged with light gray; head and neck light gray with dark markings; lower part of neck dark gray; breast and belly white; legs and feet dark orange-colour. This plumage is exchanged during the breeding season for that of the female, viz., brown and gray.

The pintail is one of the handsomest of our British ducks. It is, though not rare, by no means common or widely distributed. It is chiefly to be found on the South coasts of England, as also, at times, on the lakes and rivers of the Southern counties. It is, perhaps, more frequent in the South of Ireland, where it is also said to breed. Its name is derived from the two very long centre feathers of the tail. Its length is from twenty-four to twenty-eight inches. The head and back of the neck are of a brown chestnut colour, a white stripe on either side of the neck. The lower part of the neck, breast, and under parts, white; back and sides light gray mottled with dark gray; the vent white; black under the base of the tail; the wings buff-coloured, the upper wing-feathers edged with black and white, and a dark coppery-green wing-spot; the bill, legs, and feet slate-gray.

The plumage of the female, which is also assumed by the male in the breeding season, is of a brown colour above (mottled), and white below. Saunders states that it does well in confinement, breeds freely, and that it has been known to mate with the widgeon and common duck, the produce of a cross between the pintail and the mallard being singularly handsome.

Next to the common wild-duck, the widgeon is, perhaps, more generally and plentifully distributed throughout Britain and Ireland during the winter months than any other variety of the genus. Large numbers of these birds find their way to the poulterers' shops, being caught in the shore-nets on the East coast during the autumn. The note of this bird is familiar to all wild-fowl gunners, and is peculiar, being a kind of whistle, from which fact it possibly derives its name. Its length is twenty inches. It may readily be distinguished by the yellow colour of the crown of its head, from which it is sometimes termed the golden-headed widgeon. With the exception of the forehead and crown, the head and neck are of a dark chestnut colour with small dark green spots on the cheeks and back of the neck; the upper part of the breast is white, the lower gray; the back and flanks light gray

THE POCHARD AND TUFTED DUCK

pencilled with darker gray ; the wings light gray, with a green spot ; the wing-coverts are white.

The female is brown and gray above ; the head and neck light brown, mottled with dark brown ; wings grayish-white with a gray spot. The male changes its plumage to a great extent to that of the female. The legs and feet of both sexes are dark brown, the bill lead-coloured.

The pochard (the *ch* pronounced as *k*) is a fairly common visitor during the winter, though some birds remain with us to breed. It measures from seventeen to nineteen inches. The head and neck are red chestnut ; the breast black ; the upper parts mottled with black and white, the under parts grayish white ; tail-coverts black ; bill black, with a band of blue across the middle ; legs and feet blue-gray. In the female the chin is white, the head, neck, and breast of a dull brown. It is most frequent on the East coast, though by no means uncommon elsewhere. It is plentiful in Ireland.

The tufted duck, although chiefly visiting us from autumn to spring, breeds in some parts of Britain, more particularly in Nottinghamshire, where it receives protection during the breeding season. It is also said to have been known to breed in Northumberland, Lancashire, Yorkshire, Norfolk, Sussex, and Dorsetshire, as well as in some parts of Scotland and Ireland. It is a smaller bird than the pochard, measuring but seventeen inches. It is readily distinguishable by the long purple-black crest of feathers from which it derives its name. The head, neck, and upper breast are of a similar colour; the upper parts of a duller black, the under parts white, except the under tail-coverts, which are black; the bill is pale blue; the legs and feet dark blue; the wing has a small white bar on its lower edge. In the female the prevailing colour of the upper parts is brown; the under parts are brownish-gray; to this plumage the male changes during the breeding season. Writing of this bird, Saunders, in his 'Manual of British Birds,' draws attention to the curious fact that the males of this and many other varieties of the duck tribe do not change fully, if at all, to the female plumage during the breeding season unless they have mated.

The scaup duck, another of our autumnal visitants, is said to breed on Loch Leven. I conclude that it most probably selects St. Serf's Island for the purpose, in common with the numerous other varieties of water-birds which there retire for the purpose of breeding. It is fairly common throughout the winter on our coasts. I shot a specimen of this duck on the moat of the old fort at Tilbury, opposite Gravesend. It is of somewhat sombre plumage, the head, neck, and breast being black; the upper parts freckled with gray and white, the under parts white; rump and tail brown; bill pale blue; legs and feet grayish-blue. The female has the breast and neck dark brown; the upper parts freckled with lighter brown and gray; the belly dirty white; the bill lead-coloured. The length of this bird is eighteen inches. The head of the young male does not attain to a full glossy-black until over three years of age.

The golden-eye, one of the handsomest and smartest of the family to which it belongs, is to be found on most of our coasts during the winter. According to Yarrell, the adult male birds are less numerous than the females and young birds of the year; they at times frequent the estuaries and rivers near the sea, and are occasionally procured both in decoys and by gunners on inland waters. The same authority states that this bird is a regular visitor to Ireland during the winter months. As its name implies, the eye is of a golden yellow. Colonel Irby thus sufficiently describes its plumage:

'*Male.*—Head and neck glossy green; feathers on crown slightly lengthened; *small white spot* at base of bill; scapulars white; wing-spot white. The breast and belly are white.

'*Female and Young Male.*—Head and neck ash-brown; no white spot on head; wing-spot white, divided by a black line. The length of the adult male is from sixteen to nineteen inches.'

I have often seen these birds exposed for sale in the poulterers' shops, and numbers of them are taken in the wild-fowlers' nets on the East coast. Bewick, in his 'Water-Birds,' gives a description of a variety of duck which he calls the morillon. More modern ornithologists have, however, ascertained that the morillon is none other than the female and immature male of the golden-eye. The error doubtless arose from the fact of the mature males being so much less frequently met with, and so different in plumage to the duck and young drake.

The long-tailed duck, or calloo, as it is termed in the Orkneys and Shetlands, is not uncommon on the East coast of England, and fairly common in North Britain from November to April. The long tail-feathers, from which it derives its name, are fourteen in number, and are about ten inches in length, the entire length of the male bird, including these, being from twenty-two to twenty-six inches. According to Colonel Irby, the winter plumage of the male and female birds is as follows:

'*Male in Winter.*—Scapulars white; rump black. Two *centre tail-feathers* black, and about five inches longer than the rest, which are white.

'*Female in Winter.*—Crown and chin dark brown; sides of head dull white; patch on each side of neck dark brown; tail not elongated.'

It is a handsome, graceful, and somewhat peculiar-looking bird, and '*in summer* the forehead, forecrown, and sides of the head *of the male* are sooty-gray, the space round the eye whitish; throat, neck, and breast black; the back black margined with rufous. *The female* is grayer in summer than in the winter.'

Some few pairs of the scoter, or black duck,

remain in this country to breed. It is, however, chiefly during the autumn and winter months that this variety of duck is most plentiful on our coasts, for it ever prefers the sea, and, except during rough weather, avoids the shelter of the bays and inland waters. Saunders states that 'at times its flocks blacken the sea between this country and Holland, and are also very plentiful throughout the English Channel.' It is most common on the East coast of England, the coast of Lancashire, the Solway, and the North-eastern coast of Ireland. Its plumage is very sombre, the upper parts being of a glossy, the under parts of a duller black. The bill is of the same hue, with a longitudinal stripe of orange colour from base to point. The plumage of the female is of a brownish-black shade. The length of this bird is twenty inches.

The velvet scoter is of the same size as the common scoter. Indeed, all three varieties of the scoter are of the same dimensions, and very similar in colour. The velvet scoter is less common than the common scoter. Both birds frequent much the same localities. The plumage of the velvet scoter is of a velvet-black. The bill is orange-coloured; the legs and toes of the same, the webs black. Below the eye there is a white crescent-shaped spot, and also a white bar across the wing. The female is of a brownish-black colour, a whitish patch in front of the eye and another behind it; the bar on the wing less white than that of the male; the bill lead-coloured; the legs and toes of a dull red. All three varieties of the scoter are expert divers.

The surf scoter is somewhat rare in Britain, and those individuals which visit us from time to time hail from North America. Saunders states that it is most frequently found on the Western coasts, 'where the influence of the Gulf Stream predominates.' The general colour of its plumage is black, a patch of white being conspicuous on the forehead, and another on the nape of the neck; the bill, the legs and toes are orange-red. The plumage of the female is of a brownish shade of black, and sometimes with two white spots on the cheeks; the colour of the legs and toes is orange-yellow.

The goosander, the red-breasted merganser, and the smew, are all three what are termed mergansers, or sawbills, their bills being straight and slender, with the edges serrated, like the teeth of a saw, but turned backwards for the purpose of enabling them to seize and retain the fish upon which they feed. Both the goosander and the red-breasted merganser have the same peculiar habit of rising half out of the water and flapping their wings after having captured a fish, though I do not think that this is also a characteristic of the smew. All three varieties frequent the large lakes and inland waters. The goosander is the largest of the three, measuring twenty-six inches in length, as compared with twenty-four, the length of the red-breasted merganser, and seventeen, that of the smew. Although by no means a common bird in any part of Britain, it cannot be considered a rarity. A few are said to breed in Scotland, but this, from all accounts, seems to be doubtful; its visits are chiefly from the autumn to the spring. Colonel Irby thus describes its plumage:

'*Male.*—Head and upper neck glossy metallic black, slightly crested; lower neck and under parts white; rump and tail *ashy-gray;* bill blood-red; iris red.

'*Female.*—Head and upper neck light chestnut, crested; above slate-gray, below white; wing-spot white.'

In hard winters the smew is by no means infrequently to be met with in all parts of Britain on our rivers and lakes. Those birds, however, which venture inland are chiefly females and immature males. It is a singularly smart-looking and handsome bird.

In winter its plumage is as follows:

'*Male.*—Black, gray, and white; head and neck white, slightly crested; black stripe through eye to nape; rump ash-gray.

'*Female.*—Head and nape chestnut, crested; above slate-gray; black patch from bill to eye; rump grayish-black.

'*Young Male.*—Like female, but has no black patch between eye and bill.'

The adult male is seventeen inches in length.

A remarkably good specimen of an adult male was shot by a friend of mine on the river Test in

Hampshire during excessively severe weather some four or five years ago. I received it from him together with some wild-duck he kindly sent me. I had it preserved and mounted by Mr. Cullingford, of the Durham University Museum, and returned it to the sender. The contrast between the black and white in the plumage of the adult male bird is very striking and handsome, a creamy tinge pervading the white, and adding considerably to the beauty of the bird. The smew is more duck-like in shape than the goosander and red-breasted merganser, altogether a trimmer, neater-looking bird.

The garganey, otherwise called the summer teal, visits this country between the spring and autumn only. It is seldom found in Ireland, and both in England and Scotland it occurs chiefly on the East coasts, Lincolnshire, Norfolk, and Suffolk being the counties to which its visitations are almost entirely restricted; nor does it appear to extend its migration very far North in Scotland. Referring to this bird, Dixon says: 'The drainage of fens and marshes has robbed the garganey of nearly all its nesting-places in England. Like the teal, it is remarkably trustful and tame. . . . Water is by no means essential to the nesting-place of this pretty bird.' And again: 'The eggs are . . . undistinguishable from those of the teal. The down in the nest, however, will readily identify them. It is brown, with long white tips.' Saunders states that the eggs of the garganey are more creamy-white than those of the common

THE GARGANEY

teal, with no tinge of green and that it nests regularly in the Norfolk Broads, and also in other parts of the same county, where, owing to protection, it is on the increase. Handsome bird as is the common teal, the garganey is equally if not more so, and more graceful in shape. In size it is rather larger than the teal, measuring from fifteen to sixteen inches in length, as compared with thirteen to fifteen.

The plumage of the *male* bird in spring is as follows: Forehead, crown, and nape dark brown. From above the eye, and running nearly parallel with this dark colour, is a white stripe extending nearly the entire length of the neck; the cheeks and neck are of a reddish-brown, variegated with fine horizontal white lines; the breast pale brown, with dark brown horizontal lines; the belly white; under tail-coverts black and white, freckled and barred; tail dark brown; the back dark brown; the scapulars long, black striped with white; the wing green, with two white bars; the primary feathers brown. The plumage of the female much resembles that of the female of the common teal, but without the green on the wing, the shoulders being tinged with gray. The male changes its plumage to that of the female during the breeding season.

Before closing this chapter, it may be as well to draw the attention of the reader to the fact that nearly all the immature males of the duck tribe resemble the females in their plumage until after the first moult.

DWELLERS IN NESTS.
PART X.

British Laridæ—The Black Tern—The White-winged Black Tern—The Sandwich Tern—The Roseate Tern—The Arctic Tern—The Common Tern—The Little Tern—The Larinæ—Sabine's Gull—The Little Gull—The Brown-headed Gull—The Common Gull—The Herring Gull—The Lesser Black-backed Gull—The Glaucous Gull—The Iceland Gull—The Kittiwake Gull—The Ivory Gull—The Stercorariinæ—The Great Skua—The Pomatorhine Skua—Richardson's Skua—The Long-tailed or Buffon's Skua—The Alcidæ, or Auks—The Great Auk—The Razorbill—The Common Guillemot—The Black Guillemot—The Puffin—The Little Auk—The Divers—The Great Northern Diver—The Red-throated Diver—The Black-throated Diver—The White-billed Northern Diver—British Grebes—The Great-crested Grebe—The Red necked Grebe—The Lesser-crested or Slavonian Grebe—The Eared or Black-necked Grebe—The Little Grebe, or Dabchick—The Petrels—The Fulmar Petrel—The Great Shearwater—The Sooty Shearwater—The Manx Shearwater—The Storm Petrel—The Fork-tailed Petrel—The Cormorants—The Common Cormorant—The Shag—The Gannet.

THE family of Laridæ are divided into three classes, viz. :
1. The Sterninæ.
2. The Larinæ.
3. The Stercorariinæ.

The first (the Sterninæ) includes the several varieties of tern, the characteristics of which are the *small size of the legs and feet*, and *the length of bill*, which *equals or exceeds that of the head*.

The second (the Larinæ) are characterized by *the strength and size of their legs and feet, their bills* being *shorter than their heads*. This subdivision includes the different varieties of the gull.

The third (the Stercorariinæ) are recognizable by their having the upper mandible hooked at the point, its base being covered with a skin. This subdivision includes the four varieties of the skua, the 'robber gulls,' as they are termed.

In the Larinæ we have no fewer than thirteen varieties, varying in length from eight and a half to twenty-one inches:

1. The black tern.
2. The white-winged black tern.
3. The whiskered tern.
4. The gull-billed tern.
5. The Caspian tern.
6. The Sandwich tern.
7. The roseate tern.
8. The Arctic tern.
9. The common tern.
10. The little tern.
11. The sooty tern.
12. The lesser sooty tern.
13. The noddy tern.

Of these thirteen, six are either rare or too uncommon to refer to, viz.:

The whiskered tern (very rare).
The gull-billed tern.
The Caspian tern.
The sooty tern.
The lesser sooty tern.
The noddy tern.

The black tern, which at one time bred on the coasts of our Eastern counties, now only visits us during its migration, and those which do so confine themselves chiefly to our Eastern and Southern shores. The period of its visitation extends from April to October or November. Its plumage in the autumn varies considerably from that of the spring.

In the *latter season* the head, neck, breast, and belly are black; the rest of the plumage slate-coloured; the bill black; the legs reddish-brown.

In the *autumn* the forehead, throat and nape of the neck are white; the under parts white barred with gray. Its length is ten inches.

The white-winged black tern, a peculiarly beautiful bird, has the head, neck, breast, and belly black; the vent, tail and tail-coverts white; the legs are scarlet, the bill dark red, the back gray; the shoulders of the wing white, the rest of the wing of a pearly-gray colour. It measures nine inches and a half in length. This bird is described as an irregular visitor during migration, specimens having been recorded during May, June, October, and November. It has been observed in Norfolk, Sussex, Hampshire, Dorsetshire, Cornwall, Yorkshire, Durham, and also in Warwickshire; two instances have been recorded of its having visited Ireland. In winter the head, neck, wing-coverts, and under parts are white.

The Sandwich tern, according to Yarrell so called from Sandwich in Kent, the place where it was first observed, is one of the largest of the British terns, measuring fifteen inches in length. Colonel Irby thus describes its plumage : 'Head black; tail white; bill black, with yellow tip; legs black.'

This description is sufficient for identification, but it hardly conveys a full impression of the extreme beauty of the bird, the back, or 'mantle,' as it is termed, being a pearl-gray; the throat and under parts white (according to Saunders, 'often suffused with a lovely salmon-pink); the rump and tail are also white. It is a summer visitor, although it is known to breed in the Farne Islands, in one locality in Cumberland, one or two parts of Scotland, and near Ballina in Ireland.

The roseate tern, though not a rare variety, is by no means common. It is one of the most graceful of this graceful family, and one of the largest, measuring from fifteen to seventeen inches in length. It derives its name from the delicate rose-colour of its under parts. The back, or 'mantle,' is of a pale gray. Yarrell thus describes the plumage of the adult bird in summer : 'The bill from the point to the nostrils black, thence to base red; top of head black; neck all round white ; back, wing-coverts, and quill-feathers ash-gray; outer webs of primaries dark gray, inner webs lighter ; tail-feathers very long, extending beyond the ends of the wings, the colour pale ash-gray ; breast and under surface of the body white, strongly tinted with a delicate rose-colour; legs, toes, and their membranes red.' The plumage of the young bird varies in some particulars, 'the bill being orange-yellow at the base, the back and wing coverts being of a bluish-gray barred with dark gray, the feathers tipped with yellowish-white.' It is to be regretted that this bird is gradually becoming more scarce; Saunders attributes this as due in a great measure to 'the increase of the larger stronger-billed common tern . . . three colonies of the roseate tern having' (according to his informant, Dr. Bureau) 'successively given way on the coast of Brittany in the course of a few years.' According to the same authority, this tern arrives late in May, and leaves earlier than the other terns.

Writing of the Arctic tern, Yarrell states that it was at one time confounded with the common tern, the main differences (to which he draws attention) existing in the length of the bill being a quarter of an inch shorter than that of the common tern, the legs being orange-red, and the under surface of the body a dark gray. Colonel Irby thus further describes the plumage of this tern: 'Crown black; below as gray as the back . . . bill and legs coral-red. Breeds much further North than the common tern, and as far South as the Humber in Great Britain, and Kerry in Ireland.' It is said to be the only tern which is known to nest in the Shetland Isles. It is, during migration, to be found throughout the greater part of the British coast. Its length is fifteen inches.

As its name implies, the common tern is the variety most frequently met with in Britain; but it is by no means the least beautiful of the terns. It measures in length fourteen inches. The bill and legs are orange-red, the bill nearly black at the tip; the head and nape black; the back, or 'mantle,' pearl-gray; rump white; tail white and gray; under parts whitish.

The little tern is the smallest of the terns, measuring but eight and a half inches in length. It neither breeds largely nor very far North in Britain (as far as Aberdeenshire). It is chiefly a summer visitant, arriving in May and leaving in September or early in October, frequenting the low-lying shores from Kent to the mouth of the Humber on the Eastern Coast, and from Cornwall to Lancashire on the Western coast, of England. Its plumage in summer is thus described by Saunders: ' Bill orange-yellow, tipped with black; forehead white . . . crown and nape black; mantle pearl-gray; wing-feathers gray . . . tail and under parts white; legs and feet orange.'

Of the Larinæ (the gulls), no fewer than fifteen varieties are included in the list of British birds, viz. :

    1. Sabine's gull.
    2. The wedge-tailed gull.
    3. The little gull.
    4. Bonaparte's gull.

5. The brown-headed gull.
6. The Mediterranean black-headed gull.
7. The great black-headed gull.
8. The common gull.
9. The herring gull.
10. The lesser black-backed gull.
11. The great black-backed gull.
12. The glaucous gull.
13. The Iceland gull.
14. The kittiwake gull.
15. The ivory gull.

Of these, the following only are residents in this country (the kittiwake but partially so):

1. The brown-headed gull.
2. The common gull.
3. The herring gull.
4. The lesser black-backed gull.
5. The great black-backed gull.
6. The kittiwake gull.

The following are too rare to invite our attention:

The wedge-tailed gull.
Bonaparte's gull.
The Mediterranean black-headed gull.
The great black-headed gull.

It has been but seldom that an adult specimen of Sabine's gull has been noticed in Britain, though several instances of young birds have been recorded from time to time in different parts of Britain and Ireland. The tail of this gull is forked; the head and neck of a dark gray, with a black collar; the mantle slate-coloured. In winter the crown and forehead change to white. In length it measures fourteen inches.

The little gull, the smallest of the British gulls, measuring but twelve inches, is somewhat irregular in its visits to Britain, being most frequently met with on the Eastern coasts of England and Scotland after heavy easterly gales, being doubtless driven thither from Russia, although it has been from time to time observed in the Channel and Ireland. Since its visitations are almost entirely confined to the winter, it will perhaps be of more service to the reader to describe its plumage at that season: The head is white, the nape streaked with gray; the mantle pale gray; under parts white, with a pink tinge; legs and feet vermilion. In summer the head is black.

The brown-headed gull, less aptly also termed the black-headed gull, is one of our resident gulls; it is common on all the low-lying portions of the British and Irish coasts. Like many of the same family, the colour of the head changes in winter to white, with the exception of a gray patch behind the eye. In summer the head is of a sooty-brown colour (according to Colonel Irby, this colour is retained from the beginning of March to the beginning of August); the mantle blue-gray; tail white; under parts white, with a pink tinge; the primary feathers white in the *centre*, and dark edges to their *inner* webs.

Saunders thus writes of this bird : 'To the farmer this gull is a benefactor, devouring large numbers of grubs and worms, while it has been seen to capture cockchafers and moths on the wing ; in fact, it is almost omnivorous.' From its hoarse cackle, it is often called the laughing gull ; also the peewit, or peewit gull. It is sixteen inches in length.

Like the brown-headed gull, the common gull may frequently be seen feeding on the arable lands of our farms, and is common enough on all our coasts from the autumn to the spring, at the latter season migrating north of the Border for the purpose of breeding. In its summer plumage the head, tail, and under parts are white ; mantle dark gray ; the longest primary feathers are tipped with black, the black portion being starred with three white spots ; the bill and legs greenish-yellow, the former yellow at the tip. In winter the head and neck are streaked and spotted with brown ; the legs pale brown. In length it averages from eighteen to eighteen and a half inches.

The herring gull, another resident, is one of the largest of the British gulls, measuring from twenty-two to twenty-four inches in length. It is plentiful on all our coasts. It, like the brown-headed and the common gulls, may also be frequently seen feeding inland in the corn and turnip - fields. These birds are said to be terrible poachers of the eggs of the gannets and guillemots, swooping down on the nests of the latter birds the instant they are alarmed off them. The head and neck are white; the mantle pale gray; legs and feet pink; tail and under parts white.

In winter the head and neck are streaked with gray.

The lesser black-backed gull may also be described as a common resident. In length it measures from twenty-one to twenty-three inches. The head and neck are white; mantle very dark slate-colour, almost black; legs and feet yellow; the tail and under parts white.

In winter the head and neck are streaked with dusky brown. This gull is stated to be addicted to destroying the eggs of game, an accusation which is, I fear, but too well founded.

The glaucous gull is a winter visitor to the British Isles. It is a large, powerful bird, measuring some thirty-two inches in length. It is most frequent in severe winters, and in the Northern half of England and Scotland. It is said to be rare in Ireland. Its plumage *in summer* is entirely white, except the mantle, which is pale gray; the bill is yellow, the legs and feet pink.

In winter the head and neck are streaked with ash-gray.

The visitations of the Iceland gull are confined to the winter months, and principally to the Scottish coasts, though in very heavy weather it has been observed in the extreme South of England; such instances are, however, somewhat exceptional.

In winter plumage the head and neck are streaked and spotted with gray; the mantle is pale gray; the bill yellow; secondary feathers with white tips; legs and feet yellowish-pink. Its length is twenty-two inches. It is somewhat similar to the glaucous gull in plumage, but is a smaller and more graceful bird.

The kittiwake gull is distinguishable from the other gulls by having no hind-toe. It is partly resident, nesting amongst the rocky cliffs wherever such exist throughout the coasts of Great Britain and Ireland, and ever selecting the most precipitous and inaccessible places for the purpose. Dixon, in 'Our Rarer Birds,' thus makes mention of this gull : ' High above the roar of the waters, as they dash against the solid walls of cliff, the kittiwake's unmistakable cry is heard, sounding like *get-away-ah-get-away*, and the birds may be seen clustering on the rocks far down the awful depths, only a few feet above the restless waves.' The kittiwake never leaves the sea, save for the purpose of breeding. It rears its young on the stupendous boundary walls of the vast ocean, and when domestic duties are over, it leaves the rocks and wanders far and wide over the wild and lonely watery wastes. The kittiwake must be known to all those who have any acquaintance with the more rocky portions of our coasts, though probably to many observers a mere gull, ' and nothing more.' Yet it is a bird whose ways and mode of life are full of interest. It will follow the ships at sea day and night on untiring wing, ever on the look-out to seize any refuse which may be thrown overboard, and apparently never moving its outstretched wings, sailing along in the wake of some Channel steamer which plies between England and Ireland, to again return with the next ship.

It measures some fifteen inches, rather more than less, and the summer plumage varies somewhat from that worn during the winter. At the *former season* the head, neck, tail, and under parts are white; the bill greenish-yellow; the feet nearly black; the mantle dark gray.

In winter the nape and hinder part of the neck are slate-gray. At both seasons the primary feathers are tipped with black.

The ivory gull may be described as a rare winter visitor. Saunders states that but some thirty specimens have been procured in the British Islands, half of which appear to have been adults. Hailing from the Arctic regions, the visitations of this bird have been more frequent in the Northern portion of Britain than elsewhere. Its plumage is entirely white, the legs black. A peculiarity noticeable in this gull is the web which connects the hind-toe and the leg. It measures eighteen inches in length.

Of the Stercorariinæ, or predatory gulls, we have four British varieties, viz. :

1. The great skua.
2. The twist-tailed or pomatorhine skua.
3. Richardson's skua.
4. The long-tailed or Buffon's skua.

Of these, the first, the great skua, breeds in the Shetland Isles. This bird is the largest of the four above-mentioned varieties, measuring from twenty-four to twenty-five inches in length. It is but rarely seen inland except in very severe weather, remaining out at sea. It is unknown in Ireland. The plumage of the upper parts is of a dark brown, that of the under parts somewhat lighter in colour; the legs and feet are black, the latter furnished with sharp, hooked claws; the quills of the primary feathers are white at their bases, and these are very noticeable when the wings are outstretched.

The twist-tailed or pomatorhine skua is a visitor chiefly to our Eastern coasts, from the autumn to the spring, and occasionally, after heavy weather, may be met with at some distance inland. It derives its first name from the peculiar upward twist of its tail-feathers. Colonel Irby states that two forms or races of this bird are found, both dark brown above, the dark form as dark below as above, the light form white below, barred on the flanks and the tail-coverts with dark brown; white on the throat, tinged with golden yellow, and sometimes extending round the nape. In length it measures twenty-one inches; the two centre tail-feathers *slightly* longer than the others.

Richardson's or the Arctic skua is said to breed in Scotland, and on some of the Northern Scottish islands. Similarly to the pomatorhine skua, two forms or races of this bird have been observed—one dark, the other light. Colonel Irby states that the name of Arctic as applied to this bird is a misnomer, since it breeds and migrates further South than any of the other Northern skuas. Including the centre tail-feathers, its length is twenty inches. The *dark* variety is of a sooty-brown colour in plumage. The *light*, in which the centre tail-feathers are but three inches longer than the others, has the crown black; the upper parts brownish-gray; the sides of the neck white; the under parts white; the legs slate-gray.

The plumage of the long-tailed or Buffon's skua is the same as that of the light variety of Richardson's skua. Colonel Irby remarks that there is this difference between the two birds, apart from that in their measurements, viz., that 'it is said that the nostrils of Buffon's skua are nearer the frontal feathers than the tip of the bill; whereas in Richardson's skua the contrary is the case. In length, inclusive of the tail-feathers, the long-tailed skua measures twenty-three inches. It is said to be comparatively common on the East coast of England. Its visitation occurs from the autumn to the spring.'

The following constitute the list of the British auks (the Alcidæ):

    1. The great auk (extinct).
    2. The razorbill.
    3. The common guillemot.

4. Brunnich's guillemot.
5. The black guillemot.
6. The little auk.
7. The puffin.

The great auk is extinct. The last specimen obtained in Britain was over sixty years ago, the last foreign one over fifty years. But two specimens of this bird exist in Britain, viz., one in the British Museum, and one in the museum of Trinity College in Dublin.

It is very doubtful if Brunnich's guillemot can be included in the list of British birds.

Of the seven birds included in the foregoing list, the following are residents in Britain:

1. The razorbill.
2. The common guillemot.
3. The black guillemot.
4. The puffin.

The little auk is a winter visitor.

The peculiar shape of its bill, from which its name is derived, is, apart from any other characteristics, sufficient for the identification of the razorbill. The bill is large and powerful, the upper portion curved downwards, though not overlapping the lower, rising in a very distinct curve, with three grooves across it, and a curved white line across the centre on either side, and running upwards to the centre of the front portion of the eyelid. It is a bird which is common on almost every portion of the British coast wherever there are rocky cliffs. Flamborough Head is a well-known resort of these birds, which breed there in vast numbers in company with the guillemots. The tail of the razorbill is long, and turns upwards. In its summer plumage the head, neck, and upper parts generally are greenish-black, with a distinctly-marked white bar across the wings; the under parts white.

In winter the black loses the glossy green shade which pervades the upper parts of the summer plumage, and the throat, neck, and cheeks turn white. The length is seventeen inches.

Expert swimmers and divers as are all the members of this family, their movements on land are slow and awkward, by reason of the peculiar position and shape of their legs and feet.

Wherever the razorbill is found, the common guillemot is sure to be present in even greater numbers. The bill of this bird is straight, strong, and sharply pointed. The summer plumage is dark brown above; a slightly-marked short white bar across the wings; the breast and under parts are white. In winter the white extends to the throat and sides of the head. In length it measures about eighteen inches.

The black guillemot is rarely met with except on the West coast of Scotland. It is plentiful in the Orkneys and Shetland Isles. Its length is fourteen inches. In spring the plumage is sooty-black, with a large white patch on the wings; the legs and inside of the mouth are orange-red.

In winter the head and nape are white, speckled with brown; the back barred with black and white; the under parts grayish-white.

The puffin is common on all the more rocky portions of the British and Irish coasts. During heavy weather many of these birds are driven inland, unable to withstand the force of the gales. I have seen specimens which have been thus driven miles inland in Hampshire, and also on the Wiltshire downs; and numerous instances are annually recorded of their being picked up either dead or in an exhausted condition at distances far more remote from the sea-coast. The bill of the puffin is peculiar, being short, thick, and with both the upper and lower portions equally arched and grooved with orange colour. In summer plumage the crown, nape, and neck are black; the chin and sides of the head white; the under parts white, with a black collar round the neck; the upper part of the back and wings dark grayish-brown; the lower part of the back and tail black; the legs are orange-coloured. In winter the bill is smaller and without the orange colour visible in the summer plumage, the base of the bill being shed in the autumn. The length of this bird averages twelve inches.

The little auk, a winter visitor to Britain, is more frequently met with on the Northern coasts, though from time to time some storm-beaten specimen is found in more Southern localities. The bill is short, thick, and broad at the base. In summer the upper plumage is black, as are also the head, neck, and throat; the under parts white; a white spot over the eyes; the ends of the secondary and sides of the scapular feathers are edged with white, giving the appearance of a white bar across the wings. In winter the chin, throat, and front portion of the neck are white. The little auk is a somewhat diminutive bird, measuring but eight and a half inches in length.

Of the British diver there are four varieties, viz. :

1. The great Northern diver.
2. The red-throated diver.
3. The black-throated diver.
4. The white-billed Northern diver.

The last-named, the white-billed Northern diver, the largest of the four, is rare.

The great Northern diver, a visitor chiefly from the autumn to the spring, is more frequent on the North-western and Western British coasts. Now and again a stray bird may be met with far inland during very hard winters. A relation of mine shot one about three miles from Oxford some years ago, but, as a rule, the older birds keep well away from the shore. I know no bird which has the appearance of being able to encounter the force of rough wild water and weather more than this. The very texture of its plumage seems to be specially adapted to withstand the heaviest storms, and its shape, strength, and general bearing are all indicative of its habits.

It is, in my opinion, one of the grandest of all our British birds. In length it averages from thirty to thirty-three inches. Its plumage in winter is brownish-black above, spotted with white; the under parts white; the eye red. In spring the head and neck are purple-black, two broad black bands encircling the neck, the intermediate portion of the neck being black with longitudinal white streaks.

The red-throated diver is almost entirely confined to Scotland and the North-west of Ireland, frequenting the lochs, rivers, and their tideways. It is the smallest of the British divers, measuring but from twenty-one to twenty-three inches. Dixon remarks of this bird : ' When alarmed it gradually sinks itself lower and lower into the water, until almost every part but the head is concealed below the surface. . . . Its wild, unearthly cry, like a human being in pain, startles the naturalist, especially at dusk, as it sounds loudly over the water in these wild mountain solitudes. Particularly vociferous does this bird become at the approach of rain.' In some districts the red-throated diver is called the 'rain goose,' on account of its clamouring in the manner above stated. Like all birds of this class, it is ungainly when on land, but especially graceful when swimming about. In spring the throat is gray, the lower portion of it being of a chestnut colour ; the under parts white ; the back of the neck streaked with black and white ; the

THE BLACK-THROATED DIVER

back is dark brown speckled with white; the bill is short, pointed, yet strong, and slightly curved upwards.

The black-throated diver is rarely seen south of Scotland, where it breeds in one or two localities, except during the winter, when from time to time a few birds may stray southwards. It can hardly be called rare, though it is decidedly uncommon. It is a singularly handsome bird. In summer the crown and hinder part of the neck are ash-coloured; the chin and throat of a purple-black; the sides of the neck striped with black and white; the back is black barred with white; the wings blackish-gray spotted with white; the under parts white; the bill black; the legs and feet brown; the irides red. In length it measures from twenty-five to twenty-six inches.

The white-billed Northern diver is too scarce a bird to claim our attention.

Of the five British grebes, but two are resident. The grebes are distinguished by possessing no tails, and by their feet being lobed. The following is the list of those which are entitled to rank as British birds:

1. The great crested grebe.
2. The red-necked grebe.
3. The lesser crested grebe.
4. The eared grebe.
5. The dabchick, or little grebe.

The great crested grebe and the dabchick are the only two which are resident; the remainder are visitors from autumn to spring. The plumage of all five varieties is different in summer and winter.

The great crested grebe is considerably the largest of the family, measuring twenty-two inches in length. It frequents the large fresh-water lakes of England and Ireland, being only very occasionally met with in Scotland. It is a beautiful bird, though of somewhat peculiar appearance by reason of its crest and the tippet which surrounds its face. In its summer plumage the crown and the crest are dark brown ; the cheeks white ; the tippet chestnut-coloured, with a black margin ; the upper parts are dark brown ; the under parts white and lustrous, like satin. In winter the crest and tippet are scarcely visible.

The red-necked grebe cannot be said to be common in any part of Britain. Breeding in the North of Germany and Denmark, those birds which visit us migrate to us from thence during the months which intervene between the autumn and the spring. It is said to be most frequently noticed on the East coast of Great Britain, and also in Cornwall. Like the rest of the grebes, it is a handsome and graceful bird when swimming. The crown, nape, and back part of the neck are black ; the chin and throat gray; the front portion of the neck chestnut-red ; the upper parts brown, the under parts of the soft, shining white which is characteristic of all the grebes. A white streak divides the gray colour on the cheeks from the black on the head, crown, and nape. This white streak, which is so conspicuous in the summer plumage, is absent in that of the winter; the red portion of the neck also turns to gray at the latter season. In length it measures sixteen inches and a half.

The lesser crested, Slavonian, or horned grebe is another of the grebe family, which is a visitor from autumn to spring on the East coast of England, and on both Eastern and Western coasts of Scotland. It is said to breed on some of the lochs in Ross-shire. It is a most peculiar-looking bird, the head, from the bill to the nape, being adorned with a large tuft of chestnut-coloured feathers on either side, which, circling backwards, form a kind of tippet of black, which meets under the neck, extending to the base of the under part of the bill; the neck, breast, and flanks are also of a chestnut colour; the upper parts brown, the under parts white; the bill is black, with a whitish tip. The crest is absent during winter, and, like the red-necked grebe, the chestnut colour of the neck turns nearly gray. It measures thirteen inches in length.

The eared or black-necked grebe is more frequently found in the Southern and Eastern counties of Norfolk and Suffolk than in the Northern part of Britain, and from autumn to spring. It is a smallish bird, measuring but twelve inches in length. The under parts are white; the head and neck black, with a patch of golden-red feathers on either side of the head; the upper parts dark brown; the shape of the bill is peculiar, being curved slightly upwards, though in length proportionately much the same as those of the other grebes. The golden patches on the side of the head change to gray during the winter, as does also the black on the neck.

The dabchick, or little grebe, is a well-known resident, and frequents, in greater or less numbers, every river, lake, and pond of any size throughout Great Britain and Ireland. It is the smallest of the grebes, measuring only about nine inches in length. It is a shy, wary little bird, a wonderful diver, capable of remaining an immense time under water, and I fear a sad enemy to a fishery, its character as a spawn-eater being all too well deserved, since during the fish-spawning season it is so frequently to be observed in the vicinity of the spawning-beds. Were it not a matter of some difficulty to approach within gunshot distance of this bird, it would doubtless long since have been exterminated on those streams where the fish are strictly preserved. In summer plumage the head, neck, and upper parts are dark brown; the chin black; the cheeks, sides, and front part of the neck chestnut colour; the under parts nearly white. In winter the chin is white, that portion of the neck which is chestnut in summer changing to brown.

It may perhaps interest the reader to know (if he is not already aware of it) that the family of petrel (Procellariidæ) derive their name from the

Italian *petrello*, or Little Peter, by reason of these birds appearing to walk on the water and at times to sink into it when hunting after the fish on which they feed.

There are twelve varieties of the petrel which are included in the list of British birds, viz. :

1. The fulmar petrel.
2. The capped petrel.
3. The collared petrel.
4. The great shearwater.
5. The sooty shearwater.
6. The Manx shearwater.
7. The dusky shearwater.
8. The white-faced or frigate petrel.
9. Bulwer's petrel.
10. The storm petrel.
11. The fork-tailed petrel
12. The long-legged or Wilson's petrel.

Of these, the four following varieties are resident in Britain :

1. The fulmar petrel.
2. The Manx shearwater.
3. The storm petrel.
4. The fork-tailed petrel.

The capped petrel, the collared petrel, the dusky shearwater, the white-faced or frigate petrel, Bulwer's petrel, and the long-legged or Wilson's petrel, are too rare to claim our attention.

The fulmar petrel, the largest of the family, measures some nineteen inches in length, equalling in size some of the larger gulls. A peculiarity of this bird is its faculty of squirting an oily substance from its bill when seized or attacked, this oil being used by the parent bird for the purpose of feeding its young. It is well known to the crews of whaling-ships, as it is ever in close attendance wherever whaling or sealing is going on, feeding ravenously on the dead carcases of the whales and seals at every opportunity. It is rarely found save off the Northern and Eastern coasts of Britain, generally keeping out to sea and clustering around the fishing-smacks. The head, neck, breast, and belly are white; the back, wings, tail, and vent of a gray colour; the bill is of a yellowish colour; the legs and feet ash-gray. It breeds in some of the northern islands of Scotland.

The great shearwater visits these islands at times during the autumn, but its visitations are so irregular that it cannot be described as being other than an uncommon, if not rare, bird. It has been more frequently noticed off the coasts of Cornwall, Devon, Dorset, and Ireland, being well known to the Irish sea-fishermen by reason of the avidity it displays in devouring the pieces of fish with which their hooks are baited; and, from all accounts, it is a gross, greedy feeder, and a powerful bird whether in flight, swimming, or diving. The bill is dark brown; the head and nape ash-coloured brown; the cheeks, chin, throat, sides of the neck, and the breast are white; the back of the neck nearly white; the back, wing-coverts, and rump are dark brown, the feathers tipped with light gray; tail dark brown; legs and feet pale pink. In length it measures eighteen inches.

The sooty shearwater is uncommon. In length it measures between seventeen and eighteen inches. In colour it is entirely brown, the upper parts being somewhat darker than the lower; the colour of the legs is somewhat peculiar, being brown on the outside and yellow on the inner. It has been observed principally off the North-east coasts of England and Scotland, more especially that of Yorkshire, and also off some parts of the Irish coast. It is, however, a bird of which, apparently, not very much is known, having until quite recently been confounded with the young of the great shearwater.

Despite its appellation, the Manx shearwater is by no means confined to the Isle of Man, but is very general throughout the coasts of Great Britain, as well as some parts of the coast of Ireland, though its breeding quarters are chiefly on the Western British coasts. In length it measures from thirteen to fifteen inches. The head, back of the neck, back, wings, and tail are black-brown; the breast white; the sides of the neck mottled with grayish-brown; the under parts white; the bill brown; the legs and feet are of a yellowish flesh-colour.

The storm, stormy petrel, or Mother Carey's chicken, is the smallest of our web-footed birds.

Although an ocean-loving bird, it is by no means infrequently found as far inland as our Midland counties during the prevalence of heavy gales, which, from its diminutive size, it is unable to weather. Specimens have from time to time been shot in the neighbourhood of Oxford. Yarrell also states that between two and three hundred were shot near Yarmouth after severe gales in 1824; that some three or four were caught in the streets of Coventry, and three procured near to the town of Birmingham. The same author says that the stormy petrel breeds in the Scilly Isles, on some of the islets on the Western coast of Ireland, St. Kilda, and the Isle of Skye. I myself have seen this petrel on two or three occasions far out at sea, though never within several miles of any coast. The name of Mother Carey's chicken is said to be a corruption of 'Mater Cara.' Saunders, in his 'Manual of British Birds,' mentions the occurrence of large numbers of storm petrels between the latter part of October and the earlier days of November, 1883, on the East side of England, and the same in the first week in October, 1886. In length this delicately-formed little bird measures but six inches. The plumage of the upper and under parts is black; the bases of the tail-coverts slightly edged with white; the sides of the vent are also white; the bill, legs, and feet are black.

The fork-tailed petrel is slightly larger than the storm petrel, measuring seven inches and a half in length. The tail of this bird, as its name implies, is long and forked. The upper parts are slaty-black; the under parts dead black; the upper tail-coverts white; the wing-coverts and the margins of the secondaries tinged with ash-colour. It has been noticed on most parts of the British coast, more especially on the East coast and off the coast of Cornwall. It is also frequent in Ireland.

There are three varieties of the cormorant, all of which are resident, viz. :

1. The common cormorant.
2. The shag or green cormorant.
3. The gannet.

The common cormorant, which is the largest of the three, measures thirty-six inches in length. It may be said to be more or less abundant on most of the coasts of Britain and Ireland. Although a bird of the sea, it nests inland. Near Towyn, in North Wales, there is a rock of peculiar shape called the Bird Rock, a notable nesting-place of the cormorants; also in Ireland, between Cork and Youghal, there is another well-known place which they frequent at Castle Martyr; and there are doubtless many other similar localities which they frequent in greater or less numbers during the breeding season. A few years ago, when on a visit near Durham, I constantly noticed one of these birds on the river Wear. It spent its days fishing in the river, but towards evening returned regularly to roost at a cottage on the opposite side of the stream. I often watched it preening its feathers on a stump or bough of some tree overhanging the water preparatory to its homeward flight. It was well known in the neighbourhood, and allowed to wander unmolested. Captain F. H. Salvin, of Whitmoor House, near Guildford, employs several cormorants for catching fish, they being trained for the purpose. I have before me a sketch of these birds, kindly sent me by their owner, and taken from a picture by Mr. Hook, as also another sketch representing a day's fishing with them. This variety of cormorant is, when in full plumage, a peculiar-looking bird; the bill is long, powerful, and hooked at the point; the upper part of the head and the neck black; the back of the head and upper neck crested, or rather maned, with long, untidy-looking white feathers in spring; the throat and cheeks white; the mantle brownish-black; the under parts blackish-purple; a white patch is very apparent on the thighs during the spring only; the pouch in the throat is yellow.

The shag is readily distinguishable, not only by its smaller size, measuring but twenty-seven inches as compared with thirty-six, but also by the shining black-green colour of its plumage, and in spring by the peculiar crest which curves forwards. Unlike the cormorant, it rarely wanders inland. It is common on the Western British coast, and also on a great portion of the coast of Ireland. This bird is a most expert diver, and may frequently be noticed fishing near the shore, under the lea of some headland or cliff where the water is deep and fish are plentiful.

The gannet, otherwise known as the solan goose, is perhaps the most interesting of the three varieties of cormorant. It breeds on Lundy Island, in Wales, several parts of the coast of Scotland, and also in Ireland. I have seen them in countless numbers off the West coast of Scotland. The Bass Rock on the Eastern coast is a well-known resort of these birds. It is most interesting to watch a number of gannets when fishing. Hovering in the air at an immense height from the water, they appear to fall rather than to swoop, so direct and sudden is the action, down on to their prey, the splash of the water being visible from a long distance, the birds rising and falling like a shower of snowballs. The difference of plumage between the adult and young birds is very marked. In the former the head and neck are of a yellowish-white, the rest of the plumage being white, with the exception of the longer wing-feathers (the primaries), which are black. In the latter the upper parts are dark brown spotted with white, the under parts being white thickly covered with dark brown spots. In length it measures from thirty to thirty-four inches. The bill is of a different shape to that of either the common cormorant or the shag, being more pointed, and, although slightly curved downwards, without the hook at the tip, so marked a characteristic of those birds.

BRITISH FIELD SPORTS.

Salmon-fishing—Trout-fishing—Grayling-fishing—Rook-shooting — Otter-hunting — Partridge-shooting — Nerves and Straight Powder — The Cruelty of Bad Shooting — The Cruelty of Long Shooting at Hares—Allowance—Cruelty to Wounded Game—Crippled Game—Retrievers—Pheasant-shooting—An Old-fashioned Day—A Day with the Rabbits in Downland — Rabbit-shooting — Snipe-shooting — Fox-hunting.

To the all-round sportsman each season as it arrives brings some new pleasure. While the ash-buds are still black, the salmon are running up the rivers, lusty and strong after their annual trip to the sea. The spring water is icy cold, and the bleak wind which, driving up the more exposed reaches, sends the spray into one's face as it whistles round the rocks, rattling the very rod-rings, makes casting difficult and toilsome. And there, just in the most unapproachable spot, lies the 'taking place' of the pool. At last a temporary lull affords the long-wished-for chance for getting out the requisite length of line; the fly goes out on its mission straight and true, and just as it works round into the very point of the tail formed by the junction of two off-sets from the big rock, there is a roll, a tug, followed by a shriek of the reel as the line goes whizzing out, and we are hard and fast in a fresh-run fish. No 'kelt' this time, and as he swings back from his rush, and feels the steel in his jaws, he gives a mighty bound up-stream, his lustrous sides glistening in the bright, spring sunlight, sending the spray right and left as he again strikes the water.

Anxious moments these! The least kink or fouling of the line would ruin everything, and so rapid have been his rush and return that it has been a difficult matter to reel up fast enough. He means to get rid of that hook or die hard, and so, as a last resource, he works his way doggedly up-stream to the foot of the rock, and there remains, sulking and immovable as the rock itself, against which he is endeavouring to cut the gut casting-line. Moved he must be, or he will succeed in his efforts; but move he will not. At last one of a few well-directed stones thrown by the gillie goes unpleasantly near his nose as it sinks to the bottom, and, with another, but steadier rush than the first, he turns downstream. And now it is a hard matter to keep pace with him, as he swings down the rapids and heads for a smaller pool lower down; there his strength begins to fail; each effort grows weaker, till he is at length brought round into the still backwater, and in another minute or two the gaff is in him and he is flopping and struggling on the bank, taking the gillie all his time to hold him while he deals him his death-blow on the head. There he lies, a beautiful clean-run fish of twenty-five pounds' weight, and with the sea-lice still adhering to his sides.

And we ourselves—are we cold? No! steaming and quivering with excitement, and the long continued strain. This is sport worth living for, sport which can never pall, and which more than compensates for hours, perhaps days, of unsuccessful toil.

A few weeks later. The elm-trees are already half clothed with tender green; the oak and the ash are competing for the honour of first leaves, and we stand beside some Southern trout-stream, this time armed with but a slender rod and line compared to those with which we fought and captured the big fish: for now we have to deal with a quarry of lesser size, though one which demands even more art and skill to capture. The alder-flies are hatching out, and here and there the smaller fry have already opened the ball. One by one the larger fish work up the shallows, now and again snapping at a fly as they make their way to their accustomed feeding-places. Under the sedges, on the far side of the stream, a slight circle, a mere bubble, perhaps, marks the spot where some more wary veteran is quietly taking toll of the flies, as they come sailing and fluttering down on the surface of the water. Let us leave him in peace for a few minutes, and watch him till we have matured our plan of campaign and prospected our surroundings. It is by no means a place in which it is easy to put a fly well over him, so as not to drag and scare him. Still, he is, apparently, too good a fish to leave untried, and he is now well on the feed, so it will be well to 'take him while he is in the humour.' Making a few false casts, just to measure the exact length of line required, the final throw is made, the fly falling a trifle short of the required spot. Letting it float well away down-stream, we make another attempt, with the addition of a little more line. The fly floats temptingly enough until within an inch or two of his nose, and then is carried away from its course by a small side-current. Still he goes on feeding, evidently unaware of the fraudulent concoction of feathers and silk which is again already on its way to deceive him. And this time all goes well; he sees it, and, wary old dog though he is, he has formed the conclusion that it is a real live alder, and, in the quietest and most methodical way, has sucked it down, but before he has time to discover his mistake, the steel barb is driven into his leathery jaws. With a rush and a shake of the head he makes off to the roots of a willow-tree which have before befriended him on a similar occasion; but greenheart and good gut are this time too much for him, and his career is arrested; so, after one or two unavailing efforts, he tries a change of tactics, and runs suddenly into the weeds in the middle of the steam; unfortunately for him, they are too thin to afford him any assistance; a steady but persistent pressure gradually forces him down-stream, and in less than no time he comes floundering into the landing-net, a full two-pounder.

And now the surface of the water is constantly broken by the circles made by the fish, which are well on the feed; and as the rise cannot last for long, we must needs make the most of the opportunity. At the mouth of one of the surface-drains, down which the water is pouring from the meadows, another good fish has been making merry with the alder-flies, and he, too, falls a victim to his appetite, much to the satisfaction of one of his poorer relations, who has been longing to step into his shoes, and who promptly takes the vacant place as soon as we have moved on, and matters are again quiet. And so the sport proceeds, with more or less success. Now and again things are apt, as indeed they must be, to go a bit wrong, and more than one good fish contrives to give us the slip—at one time walking off with the greater part of a new, but faulty, casting-line. Such minor *contretemps* but add to the excitement of the sport, and if fish were always to be caught without trouble of some kind, fishing would be but tame work; after all, the bag is quite heavy enough by the time the 'rise' is over —and three brace of well-conditioned trout should, surely, be enough to satisfy any but a glutton.

Greed and gluttony are at all times detestable, and a greedy or selfish sportsman is a person to be avoided as a most intolerable nuisance. With the man who never knows when to stay his hand no one can sympathize; he is universally disliked by all true sportsmen. Such individuals are frequently excellent shots and good fishermen, but they should none the less be kept at arm's length. Who has not, at some time or other, been unfortunate enough to find himself placed alongside some jealous shot, who, not content with shooting the birds which rise to his own gun, persistently shoots those on the right and left of him throughout the day? I have more than once unloaded my gun, and carried it under my arm, on such occasions, but the Graball family are not easily abashed. So it is by the river-side : they will not scruple to fish or, worse still, wade through the very water another person may be, by right of previous occupation, entitled to. It may be charitable to attribute such conduct to over-keenness for sport, but it is all the same in reality none other than over-caddishness, and due to an utter absence of those attributes which are usually described as gentlemanly feeling, and which are so characteristic of a true sportsman.

When 'the leaves are paling yellow or kindling into red,' and the hoar-frost is glistening on the grass in the rays of the autumn sun, the grayling, so aptly styled the 'lady of the stream,' is able to afford the best of good sport to the fisherman, and, where the fish run large, as is the case in some of our Southern chalk streams, sport well worth the having, and, to my mind, in nowise inferior to that of trout-fishing may be enjoyed. Woman-like, the grayling is by no means averse to a little finery, and loves a daintily-dressed and tinselled fly.

Grayling-fishing not only demands the use of fine tackle, but delicate handling as well, for the mouths of these fish are small, tender, and easily torn with rough usage. And they can fight bravely and long. I have known them spring out of the water well-nigh as boldly as any trout, though, as a rule, they utilize their large back fins to resist the pressure of the rod when hooked, not infrequently spinning their bodies against the stream, and thereby twisting the slender gut in a most perilous fashion. And who can do justice to the exquisite colouring of a freshly-caught grayling, especially when in full condition, as in November, the month of all months in the year when these fish are at their very best?

Ere the brown stems of the elm-trees are hidden amid the fresh green leaves of early summer, there is work for the gun or pea-rifle, for the young rooks must be shot if the interests of the sable community are to be preserved. Rook-shooting may not be sport of a very exalted kind—indeed, it may not be considered worthy of a place in the category of our British sports; but it has its charms, chiefly due to the time of year, and also, perhaps, because it affords the opportunity for using one's gun in a legitimate and necessary cause once more before it is finally relegated to its case for the summer months.

To bring down a rookling from the topmost bough of a tall elm-tree in a neat and workmanlike manner with a single bullet from a pea-rifle demands a true aim and steady hand; and one bullet should be enough, since more would but shatter the bird, and ruin its fitness for a pie. A rook-pie when properly made is truly a 'pretty dish'; but when its preparation is entrusted to incompetent hands, it is but a sad affair, especially if the crowning ingredient, the cream, is omitted, or the birds have been badly shot or riddled with bullets. I think that the present is a fitting opportunity for giving the instruction necessary to make a rook-pie in the orthodox fashion.

The birds must be plucked and skinned as soon as possible after they have been killed; the thighs and breast (the only portions which are utilized) removed, and placed in milk-and-water for at least twelve hours; then put them into the pie with a few slices of tender steak, a few hard-boiled eggs, and pour a teacupful of cream over the whole. Lastly, the pie should not be cut until it is quite cold. Young rooks when required for cooking should be shot with a gun, inasmuch as they are thus less liable to be shattered than when killed with a rifle.

Rook-shooting may be by no means despicable sport when the rookery is situated in some outlying copse, and the birds are shot at the right time—*i.e.*, when they can fly fairly well, but not strongly enough to take themselves off *en masse* at the first report of a gun. And in order to ascertain the exact period, the growth of the young birds must be carefully watched; for though perhaps unable to fly one day, a few days later on they may be too strong on the wing. When, however, they are taken at the proper stage of their growth, they can afford very fair sport to a gun placed outside and well away from the copse, as they fly through the openings between the tree-tops, and especially if they have the additional advantage of a light breeze to aid their flight.

To most people early rising is distasteful, but the charms of a summer morning by the riverside are sufficient to atone for the discomfort of having to scorn one's pillow just when dull sloth appeals most strongly to our sympathies, and especially when the deep, melodious note of some veteran hound, proclaiming the trail of an otter, peals down the valley.

Nor does hound-music ever sound so full and rich as when otter-hunting. It may be that the water has power to affect it, but I often think that the note of a hound, when on the line of an otter, is pitched in a lower tone than if the same hound were hunting a fox, a stag, or a hare.

But since we are up for a purpose, we must be

moving, for the scent holds good through the dewy grass, and there is no time to be lost, so for the next mile or two we are scuttling through the meadows, and negotiating the intersecting fences as best we can; now plunging through the water at a shallow, up the steep bank and over the rails into the highroad, across the bridge, and on again up the meadows to the pool below the mill, where, amongst the roots of an old willow-tree, the otter has taken refuge, though not for long, for, escaping through a hole at the back of the hollow trunk, he again slips into the water, only just in time to avoid being tackled by a young hound. At length his course is nearly run; every point by which he could escape has been stopped, though he has twice made an attempt to force the line of human legs which guard the shallow. One could wish that his life might be spared, for the proceeding is now little better than a rat-hunt, with all the odds against the rat.

The sport of the thing is over, and five minutes later the otter is struggling in mid-air, having been dexterously polled by the master. Alas, poor beast! more sinned against than sinning, his worst crimes have been the slaughter of a goodly number of eels and a few fish.

But the sun is high, and getting unpleasantly warm; the dews have dried off the meadows, and the scent is fast failing. Most of us begin to experience the feeling known as a sinking, or, in other words, a craving for food, for it is several hours since we so hastily partook of the slender meal which had to do duty for our usually substantial breakfast; and although some few more ardent sportsmen elect to remain with the hounds as they proceed further up-stream, the majority of us arrive at the conclusion that home and the prospect of food offer irresistible attractions, and so homeward bend our steps.

Partridges are still partridges, and turnip-fields are much the same as they ever have been; but partridge-shooting at the present day is a very different kind of sport to what it was some thirty or forty years ago. Nor can it be said that the present style of sport possesses the same attractions as when stubbles were real honest stubbles, the straw nearly up to one's knees, with plenty of pickings left for the birds, instead of the closely-shaven and closely-raked fields of the present day. It was in those days not only possible to approach within shot of the birds in the stubbles, but the sport in them was often little inferior to that in the roots. Breech-loading guns have usurped the place of the dear, delightful old muzzle-loading weapons, with their charming appointments of powder and shot flasks, though it must be confessed, as far as the loading part of the performance was concerned, no one could desire to return to the use of a muzzle-loading gun; the process of loading was necessarily slow, not to say dangerous, especially in cold weather, when one's finger-tips were numbed and well-nigh useless. But even these disadvantages were not without some merit, inasmuch as the delay afforded opportunity for rest and breathing-time. Under the present system there is too much hurry and pressing forward. More birds are doubtless killed, but more powder is wasted, and more game crippled. And lastly, though not least, what has become of the well-broken pointers and setters which formerly added so greatly to the pleasure of shooting? Gone, never to return, and, except in the grouse districts, well-nigh unattainable. Certainly one-half of the pleasure of shooting in former days consisted in watching the dogs at work. Few things were more pleasing than to see a staunch, well-broken dog stop suddenly short in his quartering, and lash round to his point with every muscle fixed and rigid as if carved in stone. We can only bewail the introduction of reaping-machines, and the causes which have brought about so radical a change in one of our most popular field-sports, and sigh for the days of auld lang syne.

Under the present system, the stubbles, such as they are, must be walked over in order to put the birds into the roots, or whatever description of covert may be available for the purpose; and this walking for hours, often under a broiling sun, and with little or no shooting to speak of, is not only toilsome, but desperately monotonous, work, occupying a considerable portion of the day; after a morning so spent, one's energies are not a little slackened, and just at the very time when they require to be freshest. The luncheon-hour affords a welcome rest; and a shooting-luncheon, no matter howsoever simple the repast may be—the simpler the better—can be a most enjoyable meal. But the most abstemious person cannot always settle down to steady shooting immediately afterwards, and so there is none too much time for the more serious part of the day's performance, as the birds begin to grow restless, and anxious to move on to the stubbles, about five o'clock, even during the earlier days of September, and as the season advances there is not much to be done in the roots after three or four o'clock.

I may be over-conservative in my ideas of sport, perhaps antiquated; but I have never been able to reconcile myself to the use of the artificial kite. I am well aware that there are times when partridges are so numerous, and yet so wild, that it is necessary to have recourse to the adoption of some extraordinary measures in order to bring them to the guns. I cannot but think that, wherever it can be arranged, the system of driving is preferable to the use of the kite. Those open lands on which it is most difficult to approach the coveys when wild are admirably suited for driving. A kite is not easy to manage satisfactorily—the wind may drop, and down it comes; the string may become entangled; all sorts of mischances may occur, as, indeed, they generally contrive to do—but even when all goes smoothly and well, half of the birds never rise at all, and either remain, skulking and terrified, among the roots, or double back between the guns.

At the same time, the difficulty of arranging and successfully carrying out a partridge-drive is by no means inconsiderable, for partridges cannot be driven like grouse; they will not always go in the required direction; they have an awkward habit of turning away from the guns at the last moment, and under the most favourable conditions take a deal of hitting. Nevertheless, I think it may be conceded that the driving system is that more worthy of the British sportsman.

When birds are wild, it is doubtless not a little exasperating to see covey after covey rise at such a distance as to render clean shooting a matter of the greatest difficulty, for there is but scant time in which to bring the gun to the shoulder and take aim, and the powder must needs be of the straightest description. The first part of the performance is easy enough; but, alas! it is the straight powder which is so frequently wanting, and straight powder is, after all, but another name for what are commonly termed 'nerves.' We can —most of us, at all events—shoot well, even brilliantly, when armed with a walking-stick; but the instant the latter is exchanged for a shot-gun or rifle, the performance is apt to deteriorate. Happy he who is so constituted as to be absolutely unaffected by the rattle of a covey as it rises out of the roots; and well indeed would it be for the birds if we were all equally phlegmatic, for their cruellest foe is the man whose nervous temperament is so highly strung as to interfere with his ability to hold his gun straight. The amount of suffering which a heedless or slovenly shot is capable of inflicting during a day's shooting is simply terrible, and if such an individual could but be brought to realize this, his night's rest, unless he be exceptionally hard-hearted, would be somewhat disturbed. Little do such persons reflect, when enjoying the comforts of the smoking-room fire, how many wretched cripples are crawling about in agony by reason of their want of skill or carelessness, and I cannot but think that were they to foster such reflections as these, rather than put them aside, they would find them wholesome aids to the permanent improvement of their shooting.

It is sad to see birds going away with their legs shattered and dangling. Hares, perhaps, suffer proportionately more than birds at the hands of their would-be slayers; nor do I think it any exaggeration to assert that, out of every ten hares killed during an ordinary day's shooting, seven of them have their hind-legs broken, while of those which escape many do so but to die miserably. No one who is able to shoot, even tolerably, ought to miss a hare in the open, always provided that the distance is not unreasonable, in which case it is unjustifiable to fire at it at all. Yet how few there are who can refrain from letting drive at a hare at sixty, or even seventy, yards! The poor animal is much more likely to be peppered and blazed at by anyone who can put in a barrel at *any* distance, jubilant rather than regretful if he can conscientiously assert that he has hit it. This kind of thing, although it may not be premeditated cruelty, is none the less horribly cruel. I am quite willing to admit that it is almost invariably the result of pure thoughtlessness and excitement. We cannot, it is true, all be crack shots; but we can, at all events, refrain from shooting at game, whether it be ground or winged, at unwarrantably long range. There is no credit in making an unduly long shot; the performance is indicative less of skill than want of experience and true sportsmanlike feeling.

More game is missed, and more suffering is inflicted, by shooting low and behind the object than well forward and above it. Low shooting is generally attributable to the gun being unsuitable to the user—*i.e.*, not sufficiently straight in the stock—shooting behind from the want of proper allowance. It is rarely indeed that a miss is the result of aim being taken too far *in front* of the object. The speed at which birds can travel when well on the wing is very great. It may be asked, What allowance is it requisite to make on a crossing shot at, say, forty yards' distance? It is a question which has been asked time after time in our sporting papers, yet one which it is impossible to answer accurately. I think, however, that it may be assumed that, as a general rule, the allowance should never be *less* than a yard, an allowance which may be doubled at fifty yards, and trebled, or even quadrupled, at sixty, if the bird is going strongly and down-wind. This allowance may be perhaps considered excessive. I would advise the reader *to try it, and to note the result*. For the sake of a beginner, I may further remark that it is a wise plan, when taking a crossing shot, to first cover the object with the gun, and then, without pausing in the swing, to carry it to the full extent of the allowance. By the time that the finger has pressed the trigger, and the charge has travelled the distance, not one grain of it will be too far forward. I do not, however, presume to offer either advice or instruction in the art of shooting. I merely desire to prevent the infliction of unnecessary suffering to birds and animals. It may be argued that all sport is cruel, and, with careless and slovenly shots, the charge is, I fear, undeniable; but when the gun is in the hands of a workman, there can be no method of taking game less cruel than by shooting it, and, as I have before remarked, no true sportsman can ever experience the slightest pleasure in the mere taking of life. It is the skill which is required to take it which affords him gratification, and so the truer his aim, and the cleaner his shooting, the better he is pleased.

With reference to the monster bags of which we hear from time to time, I have nothing to say. The subject is one which I leave to others to censure or praise just as they think fit, and I therefore reserve my own opinion respecting it.

It is, of course, possible to frame an excuse for anything and everything. I do, however, earnestly desire to draw attention to the gross and inhuman cruelty which wounded game so frequently suffers at the hands of keepers and their assistants, and it is high time that all sportsmen should combine to suppress it with the most resolute and unsparing hand. Birds which have not been killed outright are not infrequently placed on the game-stick while yet alive and fluttering, or, if any attempt is made to put them out of their misery, it is probably effected by the keeper, or one of the beaters, biting their heads. Hares and rabbits are not always quite dead before they are 'harled.' This is no exaggeration ; I merely state facts which anyone who is in the habit of shooting can witness for himself, if he takes the trouble to watch the disposal of wounded game. Nor is my experience limited or confined to any particular places. I assert that these inhuman practices are not merely occasional, but frequent ; and, since we are human, it behoves us to be humane, and to suppress their longer continuance. The power to do so is in the hands of the owners of shootings, and they need but use their eyes to see the necessity which exists for their exerting that power. A guest can but remonstrate with the offending individual.

Crippled game is often left to die, and no really energetic attempt made to recover it ; and this is, I take it, due in a great measure to the scarcity of good retrievers. Barely one retriever out of twenty so-called is worthy of the name. The rubbishy, ill-broken animals which are brought into the field, in no way to the furtherance of sport, but rather to its detriment, cannot be called retrievers. They may be, and often are, dogs of high pedigree and great beauty, but they are sadly deficient in nose and intelligence; such natural abilities as they possess have not been made the most of by the breaker, and but few of them are to be trusted 'at heel' without a slip. It seems as if the art of dog-breaking were becoming extinct. A well-broken retriever is a very valuable animal, and not to be purchased for a low price; nor is a retriever trained without the exercise of some trouble, experience, and patience. Strange to say, the most highly-bred dogs are often the worst retrievers, and a clever mongrel, no matter how plain he may be, is worth any number of handsome, well-bred, but useless animals, which, though capable of taking high honours on the show-bench are useless in the field. 'Handsome is as handsome does,' and appearance and breeding are but of slight avail when it is desired to recover a wounded bird quickly and quietly. My own experience inclines me to the belief that the better bred a dog may be, the bigger fool he frequently is. Nose and brains a retriever must have, and if he does not possess these, he is not worth a charge of powder and shot for sporting purposes. The intellectual powers of a dog may be cultivated to a very extraordinary extent, but no trainer can supply lack of nose-power. The mongrel very frequently possesses these two essentials in a higher degree than his more patrician relative. Where a retriever possesses the necessary qualifications naturally, the trouble of training is, of course, very greatly lessened; but in any case, in order that a retriever may serve his master to the full extent of his powers, it is essential for him to be his close and constant companion, as he will thus be the better able to understand his desires and intentions.

Nor is it necessary for a retriever to be a large dog; a spaniel, if properly educated, is capable of performing all the duties of a retriever, save that these dogs cannot stand wet and cold for any lengthened period. There are those who advocate the use of large and powerful retrievers because of their ability to carry a hare. As I have previously remarked, a hare should, under all ordinary circumstances, be killed clean. If, however, the animal should get away when hard hit, and can possibly be retrieved, a servant should be sent with a dog for the purpose, for to allow a retriever to give chase to a wounded hare is a most grievous mistake, and the evil effects of such a practice are very generally recognized. I have bred spaniels for several years, and am of opinion that, provided they possess the requisite qualifications of intelligence and scenting power (the latter far more general amongst spaniels than retrievers), and are well and carefully trained, they will be found capable of performing all the duties of a retriever just as efficiently as a dog of that breed, be more handy, more generally useful, and equally companionable. At the same time, it must be remembered that, of all dogs, a spaniel is the most difficult to train properly, and a really well-broken retrieving spaniel may, as far as its pecuniary value is concerned, vie with any ordinarily good retriever.

Large bird as is a pheasant, it is, nevertheless, astonishing how very easily it can be missed, for when well on the wing, its flight is very rapid, and a high 'rocketer' takes a deal of hitting. No description of shooting demands more judgment of pace and distance than high 'rocketing' pheasants, and especially if there is a strong wind blowing at the time. The apparent height from which a crack shot can bring down his bird is astonishing. Here, again, it is a matter of *allowance*. The birds, as they come skimming along, appear to be flying much higher than they really are, but the pace at which they can travel is tremendous, far in excess of the highest speed of which a partridge is capable. It is but a few days ago that I read an account of the relative speed of the two birds. A partridge was seen to enter a field in full flight, and almost immediately afterwards a pheasant followed in the same direction; but before the field had been covered by the partridge, the pheasant had overtaken and outstripped it. Of course circumstances alter cases, and where the guns can be placed well away from the covert, and the birds are not flying very high, pheasant-shooting requires no more skill than that of any other game; when, however, there is but little space to shoot in, or the guns are of necessity placed close in under the covertside, a considerable amount of skill is required to shoot pheasants in a clean and masterly fashion, and the man who can do so can probably hold his own with a gun under all circumstances.

At every season of the year an English covertside has many attractions, but never, perhaps, does our English woodland scenery appear more beautiful than on a bright winter's morning, when the sun is shining through the glades and grass-grown rides, lighting up the stems and branches of the trees, tipping the russet-coloured ferns with gold, and making each moss-grown bank appear like a mound of jewels. And when, in addition to all these charms, there is the prospect of sport, whether it be with horse and hound or with a gun, it is happiness to be there.

And there can surely be too much of a good thing. A covert can be too well stocked with game. The pleasantest days I can recall have ever been those when there was just enough shooting to keep one's interest from flagging. A good steady retriever at heel and one gun offer far greater attractions to me than the use of a couple of guns and an attendant loader. Overmuch shooting savours of the shambles; there is too much of the business element for real pleasure; the incessant slaughter is sickening, and after a time the perpetual firing becomes monotonous, and tiring to body and nerves alike.

To stand at the head of some warm-lying covert on such a morning as I have attempted to describe, and while the sticks of the beaters as yet sound but faintly in the distance, is delightful. As we move up to the post assigned to us, a jay flies screaming and chattering out of an elm-tree; a heavy flapping of wings, and some wood-pigeons steal away; a blackbird goes screaming across the turnip-field and down the hedgerow; a squirrel, which had been busily feeding on the nuts which strew the ground under the big beech-tree at the corner of the ride, hurriedly scrambles up the trunk, and, scampering along an overhanging branch, disappears. The fern is trembling at the side of the ditch, and a second later a ruddy old dog-fox trots leisurely away into the turnips. The old scoundrel has been out on the spree, and overslept himself. At all events, we may be sure he has been up to some rascality. It's lucky for him that it is not a hunting-day, or his well-whiskered mask might ere nightfall have adorned the kennel-door. While we have been watching him, a hare has given us the slip—so much the better for the hare. A rabbit is coming straight towards us along the outside of the ditch, apparently unconscious of danger; as the gun comes up, it stops for a second, turns to the bank, and the next instant rolls head over heels; almost before there is time to load, another, which had evidently been lying at the head of the wood, probably driven forward by the fox, bolts away on the left, and he, too, bites the dust. And now the beaters are coming nearer, and one by one the guns drop out of the rides and take up their posts along the outside of the wood. As yet but a comparatively few pheasants have broken away on the farther side, but as the beaters, changing their front, begin to circle round, the birds are forced forward to the guns, and for the next half-hour there is plenty of shooting, for, in addition to the pheasants, the rabbits are scuttling about in all directions, the mixture of ground and winged game affording excellent gunnery practice. One moment a pheasant rises, rattling out of the ferns, and swings out through the oak-trees across the little valley, the next a rabbit has to be stopped ere he can reach the turnips. Nor have the back guns been idle, for many of the birds have fallen to their share, and at least one half of the rabbits have slipped back between the beaters.

Forty brace of pheasants, three woodcock, and a long line of rabbits, together with a sprinkling of hares, to five guns. Not a very extraordinary bag, perhaps, but, surely, ample to satisfy any ordinary individual, and the afternoon work still lies before us. It is, however, time to unload and adjourn for luncheon, little less welcome to ourselves than to the beaters, who have had some rough and tough work, and need rest and refreshment before encountering that which yet awaits them.

In the valley the mist lies cold and chill; the trees have long since paid their last tribute to the autumn gales, and strew the ground in discoloured heaps, or swirl slowly round and round in the backwaters of the river-pools. Everything appears damp, dejected, and to have resigned itself to the grasp of approaching Winter. Mud and slush reign supreme in the lanes, and wage war against all who brave them on foot. The stile-path through the meadows below the church is under water, and the stepping-stones across the brook are no longer visible. Up on the downs, which in the heat and glare of the summer sun looked so brown and parched, the grass is fresh and green, and the firm clean turf bids welcome to all comers.

I love the downs at all seasons, but never so well as when the autumn skies are blue and the air clear, crisp, and invigorating. Life up there seems life at its best. One feels free and superior to the lower world, with its petty vanities and vexations. All below seems close, stuffy, and narrow-minded.

Barren and lifeless as the downlands appear in

the distance, a closer acquaintance with them can reveal a profusion and variety of life but little suspected by those who are strangers to such districts. Although it is somewhat late in the season, many a wild-flower still holds its own. The gentian still blooms, and here and there dropwort and wild mignonette retain some few graceful blossoms. Twice I have gathered cowslips in mid-October, and later still many a goodly bouquet of wild-flowers. For the most part, the down flowers are small, lowly-growing, and unpretentious little plants. In May the milk-wort makes its appearance, and, surely, no one of our British wild-flowers is more beautiful and delicate—here a patch of white, there pink, but most frequently of deepest sapphire hue, dazzlingly bright in its purity and depth. On the lynches, as the country-folk term the hillsides, and where the wild orchises abound in the spring-time, the hares love to make their forms. A covey of partridges, rising with much fuss and whirring, sail away across the valley, and flutter down on the spur of a distant hill. At the head of a gorge a pair of kestrels are hovering and circling. As we near the rough, overgrown hedge which serves as a boundary, two magpies (luckily *two*) dart out, and with quivering tails make off to the fir-copse beyond the gorse-covert which lies below the crest of the opposite hill.

The contours of the ground are peculiarly interesting, and, when the valleys are filled with mist, it requires but little stretch of imagination to follow out the lines of headlands, bays, and gulfs, as when the sea was there in very truth; and in the flints which are so thickly spread over the short, sweet herbage, countless marine fossils may be found. Is not, indeed, each grain of the chalk which underlies the surface in itself a shell of rarest beauty?

Here and there the lines of some Roman camp are plainly visible, the position invariably one which no General of modern days could improve upon; and as we survey the scene, we seem to see the stalwart sentinel pacing to and fro on his post, the thin blue columns of smoke curling upwards from the camp-fires, to hear the clanging of hammer on anvil as the armourers are hard at work shaping sword and spearhead, and note the well-guarded bullock-carts as they slowly mount the hill, the wooden wheels creaking and groaning under the load. And then all has vanished, and the fairy-rings alone remain to mark the spots where stood the tents of the now deserted camping-ground.

That long, low mound betokens the grave of some ancient warrior-chieftain; the well-known lines in 'Westward Ho!' recur to mind, and it is 'the old Norse Viking, in his crown of gold,' who sleeps beside us.

On many of the hillsides the gorse grows thick and strong, acres and acres of it, providing a stronghold for many a stout fox, seldom indeed proving faithless when the hounds go there to draw. And despite the foxes, which are, perhaps, 'none too few, but all too many,' the rabbits swarm and hold their own. Leggings, the keeper, may aver to the contrary, but foxes and rabbits can exist together in the same covert, and in very tolerable amity. Leggings doubtless finds rabbits more profitable than foxes!

Rabbit-shooting in these large patches of gorse is often first-rate sport. The rabbits must be kept within bounds for the sake of the crops, and so periodical parties are organized for the purpose. The gorse is cut into large square patches by rides which intersect each other at regular intervals, and with the assistance of some four or five couple of dogs (every cur in the village being requisitioned for the purpose), to keep the rabbits moving, and a strong line of beaters to prevent their breaking back, there is plenty of work for half a dozen guns.

It is by no means easy to stop a rabbit going full swing across a ride, especially if the ride is a narrow one, and it is a feat which requires no little practice to accomplish. There is no time to bring up the gun to the shoulder from the hip; it must be kept close up under the arm, ready to drop into its place the instant a rabbit shows. A novice at the work, though, perhaps, a fairly good shot under other circumstances, will find that it is possible to expend a good deal of powder and shot, with very small results. The majority of the rabbits killed on these occasions will be found lying a yard or two inside the opposite patch.

Gorse rabbit-shooting is hard and hot work both for beaters and dogs, and especially so for the latter, the dead spines of the gorse penetrating their feet, and it takes an exceptionally bold and resolute dog to work continuously under such circumstances. The dogs also suffer greatly from thirst, for there is but little air amidst the stems and undergrowth, and it is not only humane, but wise, to afford them frequent opportunities for being watered during the day. Where the covert is thick and high, it is necessary to keep the ale-jar circulating freely amongst the beaters to induce them to face it, and it frequently happens that from the time they enter a patch of gorse until they emerge thereform, they are unseen, though by no means unheard, the combined effects of gorse and John Barleycorn being manifested by the most discordant yelling and shouting, a part of the performance which they consider to be essential to success, and the summit of their happiness is attained should one or other of their number go down in the thorny mass. Everybody enjoys the fun, except the rabbits, which get a rough time of it, for those which go to ground are speedily pulled out, the loose, light soil favouring the operation; the dogs catch a great many, and those which cross the rides are either killed, peppered, or frightened out of their wits.

For my own part, I prefer this kind of sport without the beaters, and with the assistance of some few couples of well-broken, resolute spaniels. The beaters spoil good dogs by pressing them forward too rapidly, and also by shouting. The other system is doubtless more amusing, but I like to hear my dogs give tongue, and to let them do the work themselves.

The old-world sport of hawking still survives in our down-country, nor could any description of ground be more suitable for it. More than one of our Downshire roads still bears the name of Hawking Road or Hawkers' Path.

The badger still makes his home in the neighbouring woods or on the rougher hillsides. Long may he be left in peace! for though he bears an evil reputation, and smells most foully, he is a clean and inoffensive beast, and 'more sinned against than sinning.'

Time was when the great bustard was no rarity on our Southern downs. A brace of such birds would be a goodly burthen for any ordinary man.

But the evening breeze is rising, and blows keenly, and we must turn our heads homewards. As the sun sinks beneath the skyline, the hillsides change from green to olive colour, and the gorse looks black in the fast-fading light. High overhead a curlew whistles plaintively as it wings its way to the stubbles; here and there a light shines out from some cottage window in the distant village; the sheep-bells tinkle in the folds in the valley, and the day is gone.

Rabbit-shooting is a sport by no means to be despised. On the contrary, the humble cony can afford as much real sport as any other description of game. As the late Sir John Astley remarks in his 'Memoirs,' 'A bunny in a hurry takes a deal of hitting.' Where should we be without our wild rabbits? Nine times out of ten, half the bag is made up of them. Such jolly, happy little beggars as they are, too, it almost seems a shame to kill them; and yet they are so terribly tempting as they skip across the tussocks of grass or bolt through the ferns. I think that the so-called (miscalled) sport of rabbit-coursing, as practised in some parts of the country, cannot be too strongly condemned. It is gross cruelty to confine a number of wretched animals in boxes or cages solely for the purpose of running them down with terriers. The rabbits are cramped, weakly from want of food and proper air, and are unable to run sufficiently well to have a chance of saving their lives. I could wish that this and every sport of a similar character were rendered illegal; nor can I find it in me to make excuse for any sport which necessitates the capture of any wild animal or bird solely for the purpose of hunting it to death or shooting it. Such a proceeding is cruel, and therefore un-English.

Of all sport with the gun, it may, I think, be conceded that snipe-shooting is able to offer as many attractions as any other. Unfortunately, it is just one of those sports which is annually becoming more difficult to procure, inasmuch as the gradual reclamation and drainage of land in those districts which formerly provided excellent feeding-grounds for snipe and other marsh-loving birds has driven them to seek their food in other places, and every acre of such ground is eagerly snapped up by some of the many votaries of the sport. Ireland, of course, remains much as it was, in so far as the ground is concerned; but I fear, from all accounts, that Irish shooting of any kind is not what it used to be, and the preservation of game is difficult. A few years ago a friend of mine, who owns a considerable estate in one of the Southern Irish counties, told me that, on proceeding to shoot over one of his snipe-bogs one morning, he met a man with a gun just leaving the bog, and was informed by him that it was useless his going there to shoot, as he had only succeeded in getting a few snipe, and that he was the third person who had been over the ground that morning. All of these three individuals had been poaching, neither of them having right or permission to set foot on the land. I have already referred to the many happy days I have spent in wandering over the Irish bogs, my sole companion a steady old setter. Delightful days, never to return, alas! Miles of bog and heather to wander over, scarce a care in the world, and the almost certainty of good sport when the weather was suitable and the birds were well in. As a rule the walking was good and sound. Where, however, the crust which covers the surface of the bog is so thin as to be treacherous—and such are ever the best feeding-grounds for snipe—half of the pleasure of the sport is spoiled, for who can shoot well and steadily when in constant fear of being entombed in mud?

Were I offered my choice between good snipe-shooting and the very best shooting of any other description, I should most unhesitatingly pronounce in favour of the former. A snipe is such a truly sporting bird; it requires some skill to shoot, is beautiful in its shape and plumage, and is one of the very best, if not *the* best, of birds for the table.

It is during October and November that the greater number of foreign snipe arrive in Britain. Though many birds remain here to breed, during their residence in this country they are constantly shifting their quarters according as the weather may affect their feeding-grounds. So long as these remain soft they are content, but with frost or easterly winds, they are off to other more suitable localities. People often express surprise at these sudden arrivals and departures, but the reason is a very simple one. Wherever the ground is most suitable for snipe to feed, there they are generally to be found;

their bills are tender, and not adapted for piercing any but the softest soils in their search for food, which consists of worms, insects, small snails, etc. In wet weather they may frequently be found in the turnip-fields and on the higher grounds, the supply of food being there plentiful and easily procured. The slightest frost, by hardening the soil, will suffice to send them down into the valleys to seek for food in the ditches and watercourses.

It is not, I imagine, generally known that snipe are addicted to perching. Such, however, appears to be the case. Saunders, in his 'Manual of British Birds,' thus refers to this habit: 'Occasionally it perches on trees, etc., though the fact has been dogmatically disputed by persons of limited experience.'

Snipe-shooting in the tropics, India especially, is proverbially good, and the account of the large bags made there must appear well-nigh incredible to those who have had no experience of the sport in such countries. I am bound to admit that I myself was somewhat sceptical until I had the opportunity of seeing and judging for myself.

The Indian full snipe is precisely similar to the British. It is, however, better fed, and, consequently, not quite so active a bird. So well fed and heavy are they that, when picked up, their breasts may often be found to have burst by reason of their weight. It would be difficult to imagine a more delicate bird for the table than an Indian snipe.

Snipe-shooting is said to be a knack. If so, it is one which is not difficult to acquire by anyone who is a fairly good shot. Half the snipe which escape the gun are missed by being too hurriedly fired at. Twice during its flight does a snipe offer itself a comparatively easy mark, viz., when it first rises, and just as it turns into the wind. It is for this reason that snipe-shooting with the assistance of a steady pointer or setter is rendered so much easier than when the birds are merely walked up, the opportunity for taking the bird as it rises being thereby afforded. It is thus necessary to be either quick or slow. I cannot myself lay claim to be considered other than a very average shot; nevertheless, I have always been able to hold my own when snipe-shooting. When one considers how very delicately a snipe is framed, how extremely thin is its skull, how slender and brittle are its bones, and therefore how easily it is killed, it becomes evident that there is no necessity to shoot hurriedly at it, provided the sportsman watches for the opportunity it offers as it turns up wind. Being but a small bird, a snipe often appears to be much farther off than it really is, and this is especially the case when the light is uncertain.

When so much has been written in praise of fox-hunting, it would seem somewhat superfluous for me to attempt to add anything by way of eulogy. Nevertheless, since any treatise bearing on British sports would be incomplete without some reference to it, I can hardly, without running the risk of appearing indifferent, abstain from making some few observations regarding a sport which is of such great value to the country generally. In these advanced days a class of persons has arisen whose object is apparently to decry all those sports in which they themselves are unable to participate, that of fox-hunting in particular. These would-be detractors allege, by way of excuse for the line which they have adopted, that fox-hunting is cruel. Now, without attempting to enter into any argument upon the subject, I may as well at once admit that there is more or less cruelty, as we understand it, in all sport. Even fishing may be described as cruelty; and without doubt fishing with a worm or any living bait is, when the torture which the living lure is compelled to suffer is considered, most horribly cruel. I am not at all sure that, when one sport is balanced with another, fox-hunting is not perhaps the least cruel of all. But be this as it may, we cannot afford to relinquish our national field-sports, and it would indeed be a sorry day for England if fox-hunting were to be abolished. At the present time such an event appears highly improbable from the action of any adverse party; the votaries of the sport are more numerous than ever, and if any danger to its interests exists, it is rather to be apprehended from the fact of this excessive popularity than from any other cause. Where one man hunted thirty years ago, a dozen do so at the present day, and the attendance at the meets of some of the more fashionable packs has become so enormous as to cause no little anxiety to the Masters and hunt-committees, as to how best to confine it within reasonable limits.

It may be considered as beyond all dispute that, socially or financially, the presence of a well-organized and well-managed pack of hounds in a neighbourhood is of the very greatest benefit to the inhabitants. If I remember rightly, I think that the sum which it was estimated was annually lost to a certain district in Ireland consequent upon the abolition of a well-known pack of hounds was some forty thousand pounds. I am acquainted with the district referred to, and, judging from my own experiences, I should say that this sum was by no means exaggerated. The result has been most disastrous to the poorer inhabitants, all of whom, in a greater or less degree, participated in the former prosperity.

Despite the annual increase in the number of men who hunt, it is nowadays a matter of no little difficulty to procure the services of efficient Masters for the various packs of fox-hounds in the kingdom. The continued agricultural depression has, of course, contributed very largely to such a condition of affairs. Incomes being thereby reduced, subscriptions are consequently lessened or altogether withdrawn. In the most prosperous times there were but few packs in which the money subscribed was sufficient to defray the working expenses, the result being that the Masters themselves were compelled to meet the deficiency as best they could ; in other words, to pay the money out of their own pockets. Thus, it is evident that, if the position of a Master of Hounds was not all *couleur de rose* in former days, it is still less so at the present time.

Apart from any such expenditure as a Master of Hounds may generously be disposed to incur for the benefit of his neighbours, the actual labour which devolves upon him in his endeavours to show sport is very considerable ; and this is more especially the case if he does not employ the services of a professional huntsman, since it is necessary for him, in order that he may know his hounds and that they may know him, to be constantly with them, out of season as well as in season. The responsibility is also heavy, for it behoves him not only to maintain the necessary establishment in as high a state of efficiency as the resources at his command will permit, but he must also contrive, by the exercise of tact and cordiality, to maintain friendly relations with all of those with whom he has to deal—landowners, farmers, labourers, keepers, etc., alike, any one of whom has it in his power to afford him grievous annoyance and trouble if he is so disposed. When all these things are taken into account, it is not so much to be wondered at that a difficulty in procuring Masters for the numerous packs should exist, as that any persons sufficiently disinterested to undertake the duties and responsibilities inseparable from such a position should be forthcoming. There is an old saying, that 'a Master of Hounds must ever have his hand in his pocket, and a guinea at the bottom of it'; and this is true enough.

Unlike other sports, it will be seen by the foregoing remarks that, in the matter of fox-hunting, those who derive pleasure from it do so very much through the generosity of our Masters of Hounds, who are sufficiently disinterested to devote their time and money to the maintenance of the packs with which they are connected; and if this is the case, it surely behoves the hunting public to afford them all possible support, not only by subscribing as liberally as their means will admit, but also, by their behaviour in the field, to lessen rather than increase the labours and anxieties which they so cheerfully encounter.

If all hunting men were true sportsmen, I take it that the labours and anxieties of a Master of Hounds would be lessened by half. Unfortunately it must, I fear, be admitted that the true sportsmen are very much in the minority. It is all very well for a man to be able to ride well, be well mounted and turned out; but something more than this is requisite, viz., some knowledge of the science of hunting—at all events, sufficient to enable him to know what the hounds are doing, and what they are desired to do. This is but the A B C of hunting, and without this very superficial knowledge, I fail to see how such an individual can lay claim to the title of sportsman, when he is altogether ignorant of the first rudiments of the sport in which he participates. Yet how many there are in every field to whom the actual working of the pack is but as a sealed book! They can frequently ride well, and, as it is termed, 'go well,' when hounds are running; but there are, alas! too frequently those who, by reason of their ignorance, sadly trouble the Master by pressing and mobbing the hounds, and the commission of other enormities of a like nature. 'Gone away!' rings out cheerily from the top corner of the covert, and they are happy enough so long as the pace is good and lasting; and who can blame them for being so? Not I, certainly; for what greater happiness can mortal man experience than when, well-mounted, he sits down and rides across the green pastures of an English shire?

After all, the madding crowd is soon thinned, and it is not for those who only hunt to ride to see the end of a severe run. One may take it for granted that those who have gone the straightest, and lasted to the end, have kept careful watch on the hounds throughout the line. Let the novice remember these golden rules : To ride wide of hounds; to take his own line, and stick to it; as soon as he lands in one field, to instantly determine the place where he intends to get out of it; to save his horse in every way he can with due regard to keeping his own line; to avoid doing damage to crops ; and last, but by no means least, never to maltreat his horse at any time, especially in the hunting-field. To brutally punish an animal is ungentlemanly and cowardly. Oftener than not the poor brute is made to err through the ignorance of its rider, and even if this is not the case, the hunting-field is not the place for breaking horses. It is fortunate that the hunting public have ceased to tolerate the insensate exhibitions of cruelty which were at one time by no means infrequent, though chiefly confined to a certain class of persons.

Under no circumstances is the character of individuals more apparent than in the hunting-field, and if good qualities are requisite in a hunter, equally so are they in the man who bestrides it. Alas, how often is it that the animal possesses the greater share! The hunting-field is no place for the mean man, the coward, or the nerveless drunkard ; and I cannot believe that, provided he could afford to hunt, any man has ever been justly able to assert that, barring accidents, he has ever been anything but the better, both physically and morally, for having participated in a sport which is so thoroughly English and manly.

A FEW WILD-FLOWERS:

THEIR LEGENDS AND USES.

Instruction of Children in Natural History and Botany—Waste of Wild-flowers—Beauty of Wild-flowers—Gradual Extinction of Rarer Wild-flowers—Beauty of some of the Commoner Wild-flowers—Cow Parsley—Meadowsweet—Milkwort—Orchises—Saloop—Autumnal Wild-flowers—Dropwort—Aconite—Forget-me-not—Ragged Robin—Scarlet Poppy—White Campion—The Comfrey—Greater Willow-herb—Lesser Willow-herb—Devil's-bit Scabious—The Yarrow—Wild-mignonette—The Elder-tree—Traveller's Joy—Agrimony—Common Avens—Water Avens—Red-berried Bryony—Yellow Broom—Yellow Bedstraw—Burdock—Buckbean—Bindweed—Brooklime—Betony—Butcher's Broom—The Common Camomile—Colt's-foot—Cowslip—Cuckoo-pint—Dandelion—Dodder—Broad-leaved Dock—Elecampane—The Eyebright—Foxglove—Fritillary—Field Gentian—Wild Garlic—Herb-Robert—Henbane—Wild-hop—Wild-hyacinth—Ground Ivy—Yellow Iris—Purple Loosestrife—Yellow Loosestrife—Lily of the Valley—Marsh Mallow—Common Mallow—Moneywort—Mullein—Deadly Nightshade—Woody Nightshade—The Great Nettle—List of British Orchises—Peppermint—Pennyroyal—Scarlet Pimpernel—The Great Plantain—The Hoary Plantain—The Ribwort Plantain—The Water Plantain—The Rest harrow—The Shepherd's Purse—The

Silver-weed—The Succory—The Speedwell—The Snapdragon—The Spurge—Solomon's Seal—The Tansy—The Teasel—The Wild-thyme—The Yellow Toad-flax—The Common Valerian—The Wood Sorrel.

THE lap of Nature, so amply stored, is ever open, and displays treasures the richest and rarest; yet how few there are for whom they possess sufficient attraction to induce them to turn aside to view the world of wonders which is theirs if they but choose to avail themselves of it! The pursuit of what they have not got and cannot see is, apparently, preferable to them. Birds, beasts, flowers, etc., and all the countless riches which should interest us, are unheeded by the many. Birds may sing their sweetest, and the wild-flowers pleadingly put up their heads to be noticed; the songster, if not altogether unheeded, is unknown; the flower is but a flower. It seems somewhat strange that in the present day, when education is so highly esteemed, so much ignorance should still exist regarding the many natural objects which surround us. It would surely be well for the children in all our schools to learn something of the natural history of the country in which they live. Nor is this want of knowledge confined to children of the poorer classes alone; it exists to a very great extent in all classes, among children and adults alike. There are numbers of people who, though well informed on most subjects, are content to pass their lives without experiencing the least desire to learn something of the life around them, and without which the world would be so dull and dreary, or of the flowers which so add to its beauty. Where instruction is given to children on these subjects, it is, too frequently, so scientifically instilled as to pall rather than please. Long names, useful and necessary as they may be for scientific purposes, and dull, dry text-books, offer but small inducement to any but the more serious students. It is not the subject which lacks interest, but the treatment of it.

With the acquisition of some knowledge of natural history and botany, a new world, previously unheeded because unknown, a world of wonders, which daily appears more marvellous as our knowledge of it increases, presents itself to us. The daily walk becomes no longer a mere measured mile, traversed solely for the sake of exercise, but, as it were, a journey into wonderland; each bird and flower, each leaf, each blade of grass, has something to say to us, and throughout the four seasons of the year there is no single hour of daylight, save in inclement weather, in which a country walk may not be productive of interest to those who know where and how to seek for it. To withhold instruction from children on such subjects is to do them great and grievous wrong, and to rob them of half the pleasure of life. Thanks to the printing-press and the superb collections and museums nowadays open to the public, it is within the power of any intelligent student to become a naturalist. Were children, generally speaking, more carefully and wisely instructed in these subjects, it would be to their advantage, and afford them interest and amusement, not during the days of their childhood alone, but also throughout their whole lives; and such instruction could hardly fail to indue them with a true love and respect for bird and beast and flower. A true lover of Nature is incapable of cruelty to her children, and very surely do the latter repay tenfold the benefits which increased consideration for their welfare may accord them. By the term respect, as applied to birds, animals, and flowers, I mean such a measure of regard for them as may suffice to afford protection to each and all. Because certain wild-flowers may chance to grow in profusion in certain places or districts, that is no reason why they should therefore be ruthlessly gathered and wasted. Some few years ago I was travelling on the South-Western line in Hampshire; it was spring-time, and the earlier wild-flowers were at their best; the platform at one of the stations was crowded with the members of a girls' school, of the class known as 'young ladies,' who had evidently been spending the afternoon in the neighbouring woods. Each one of them was carrying either a basketful or a large bundle of wild daffodils, and the platform was strewn with the golden flowers which had fallen from their overcrowded hands, and were lying crushed and trodden underfoot. Such wanton waste was without excuse and distressing to witness, being far beyond all possible need.

Of all flowers, wild-flowers ever please me most, nor, to my mind, can any products of the garden or hot-house, beautiful though they may be, lend themselves as gracefully and readily for decorative purposes. And how few there are of either sex able to arrange flowers to advantage! Too often are they crammed into some jar or vase altogether unsuitable in colour and form for their reception, and made to present as unnatural an appearance as possible. Wild-flowers demand especial care and taste in their arrangement, for half their beauty lies in the free lightness of their growth; to crush them is to murder them. Buttercups and stitchwort, cow parsley and ragged robin, corn-cockle or devil's-bit scabious, and moon-daisies, etc., form the most charming combinations of colour when artistically and lightly arranged. Hot-house and garden flowers, when used in over-profusion for decorative purposes, are calculated to oppress rather than gratify; the excess of colour is apt to bewilder, and savours of the heat and glare of the flower-show tent. Flowers should charm and refresh, not irritate and confuse.

Many of our rarer wild-flowers are rapidly becoming well-nigh extinct, owing to the ruthless treatment which they receive at the hands of excursionists and collectors of botanical specimens, who are frequently not satisfied with a specimen flower, or even plant, but who greedily tear up all they see, flowers, roots, and all. The best fate which can befall their hapless spoils is to linger out a miserable existence in some sunless suburban garden. Far too frequently are they discarded ere they have faded. It is not so many years ago that the fritillaria, meadow snowflake, grass of Parnassus, and yellow loosestrife, flourished in the neighbourhood of Oxford. The first and last named may still be found in the water-meadows of the Cherwell, though sadly reduced in number, and they bid fair to become altogether exterminated ere many years have passed; but I much doubt if the most scrutinizing search would discover a single specimen of the other two beautiful flowers in that part of the county. A rapid increase of the population has occasioned a correspondingly rapid decrease of wild-flowers in the district. The case ought to be reversed. It is the wanton waste of wild-flowers which is so grievous; and yet no steps are taken to prevent it. The same deplorable custom prevails in the vicinity of all our large towns and popular holiday resorts. Nothing escapes the rapacity of the Graball class, who annex everything they see lest others should do the same.

Many of our commoner wild-flowers, frequently unheeded because they are common, are the most beautiful. The cow parsley grows in profusion in well-nigh every hedge. Surely none of our wild-flowers can surpass the grace and beauty of its slender, star-like blossoms of purest white! For decorative purposes, it is a most adaptable flower, its sprays, when mingled with other wild-flowers, giving an effect of extreme elegance and lightness. I not long ago was witness to what an extent it can be utilized for decorations, being present at a wedding in a country church which had been adorned with nothing else. The effect was singularly beautiful and light; masses of the tall white flowers lined both sides of the aisle up to the altar-rails, which were similarly decorated—a truly fitting adornment for a bridal! The meadowsweet can be also used in the same manner as the cow parsley, but its perfume is apt to be somewhat overpowering, and is said to be very deleterious in a close room, and to have proved the cause of illness when kept in a bedroom.

There grows amid the herbage of the chalky downlands a small and unpretentious little flower, yet in former days held in no small repute, having been used to form garlands during Rogation Week, and thence called Rogation flower, but nowadays better known as the milkwort. During the months of May and June it blooms freely in masses of the purest sapphire blue. Of all our wild-flowers, this is, perhaps, one of the most exquisite. Although most commonly of a blue colour, it may be found in shades of pale lavender, steel-gray, white, and pink. It is impossible to accurately describe the exact colour of the blue variety, for it is of such surpassing depth, being neither blue, purple, nor sapphire, but a combination of the three.

On some of the downland hillsides, more especially those which, receiving the soakage from the higher ground, remain more or less moist and spongy until dried up by the summer sun many of the rarer kinds of orchises may be found. A friend of mine informed me that he has gathered on one such hillside in my own neighbourhood every one of the rarer kinds of this curious and beautiful plant, of which there are no fewer than fifteen varieties. Many years ago a decoction prepared from the root of the orchis was sold in the streets of London and our larger towns, much as coffee is sold nowadays. This decoction was termed salep or saloop; the grain to which the root was reduced before cooking was imported from the East, and prepared from the root of the orchis, the variety employed being that known as *Orchis mascula*—the early purple orchis of Britain. This beverage is stated by good authority to be extremely nourishing and digestible, and would, doubtless, be used at the present time were it not for the moderate prices at which tea and coffee are retailed. The early saloop-seller was, in former days, a well-known feature of the London streets. It is, however, doubtful if one saloop-merchant could now be found in any part of Britain.

A few years ago—and it was late in October—

WILD-FLOWERS OF EARLY SPRING

I gathered on a hillside of the Wiltshire downs more than forty varieties of wild-flowers, amongst them some cowslips in full and healthy blossom; and last year, when rabbit-shooting on a neighbouring down, on nearly the same date, I found wild strawberries in fruit, and also a single cowslip, but a few yards apart from each other.

Not the least beautiful of our summer flowers, often blooming late into October, is the common dropwort (*Spiræa filipendula*), the pink unopened buds pleasingly contrasting with the soft and creamy flowers.

When the branches of the elm-trees are turning purple, and the willow-rods grow crimson in the woodlands, the aconite fearlessly pushes its way through the still cold earth, and, nothing daunted, unfolds its yellow petals in the weak, wintry sunlight. The north wind may whistle and blow chill, but through fair and foul alike the brave little flower, the harbinger of lengthening days and returning spring, still holds its own. Then come the snowdrops, their graceful, downcast petals fair in white robes trimmed daintily with green. They, too, can thrive and flourish, despite the bitter blast which, searching each crevice in the thickest hedge, rasps the dead leaves against the sapless boughs; and ere these have faded and turned brown, lords-and-ladies, as the country-folk term the wild arum, begin to assert themselves and take their accustomed places; while here and there, from amid their fresh and clustering leaves, the primrose flowers appear, shyly at first, then, growing bolder, crane their long, graceful stems to view the scene. Where the rays of the spring sun rest on the southern banks, the blue, and still sweeter-scented white, violets peer through the short grass, at first so 'wee and modest' that one may pass them by unseen or crush them under foot. Tall sprays of white blossom in the hedgerows mark where the blackthorn warns us that the Frost King, 'in his ice-embroidered robes,' has not yet laid aside his sceptre. The daffodils, which are bursting into bloom, must needs have their 'mouthful of snow,' or the summer will be short and sunless. The kingcups, too, are growing impatient, fearful lest they should be too late to see the world, and be elbowed out by the grass which has already covered over the crimson fairy-goblets in the hedgerows.

The bluebells are mingling with the delicate white flowers of the wood-sorrel in the copses, and the cow-parsley is growing tall and rank, but ere long each spray will be tipped with starry splashes of white, a veritable wealth of summer snow. The buttercups, the most spring-like of all wild-flowers, grow apace with the grass, and are yellowing the pastures with their fresh and burnished blossoms.

When the bushes are white with the sweetly-scented May-blossoms, the flowers of the forget-me-not gleam in many a water-meadow and by the riverside. A little later and the yellow iris, ragged robin, red and white campions, purple loosestrife, blue and white comfrey, meadow-sweet, willow-herb, St. John's wort, and a host of other flowers, follow each other in rapid succession, till all the meads are 'flowery vales.' The hillsides are clothed with every shade of softened green, here and there relieved by large patches of crimson-hued trifolium and the pink-flowered sainfoin.

Too bright to last, and when at their brightest and best, most of them doomed to fall under the scythe. There they lie, dead and dying, in long swathes, side by side—sweet in their lives, and even when dying 'diffusing fragrance round.'

With the hay-harvest, the fields grow gray till the fresh grass springs again; but in the meadows the beauty of the year has gone. Scarlet poppies and blue cockles come to deck the corn; mullein and toad-flax, bugloss and scabious, yarrow and hawk's-bit, adorn the banks and hedgerows, and here and there patches of wild mignonette wave in the summer wind; the thistles lengthen, bloom, and fall away, strewing the ground with tufts of softest down. The starlings are feasting merrily on the purple berries of the elder-trees; the long, graceful clusters of the traveller's joy glisten green and red in the sunlight, till, ripening, they turn to old man's beard, from which the autumn dew-drops hang like 'tears of sorrow' shed for the flowers of summer which have passed away.

To the very few wild-flowers to which I have

so briefly referred, some special interest, either legendary or real, is attached; where one may be a deadly poison, another is a useful herb, possessing peculiar medicinal virtue, while some tale or superstition has served to immortalize a third; and so on throughout our British flora there is in each and all something to attract our attention.

The forget-me-not, the emblem of constancy and love, is said to have been raised to honour by Henry of Lancaster, who during his exile added a jewelled forget-me-not to the ornamentations of his golden collar, with the initial letter of his watchword, 'Souveigne vous de moi.'

The ragged robin is also called the cuckoo flower, from its blossoms being most plentiful at the time of year when the notes of the cuckoo are most frequently to be heard.

The white campion, the vesper or evening flower, receives its second name from its lack of fragrance until the sun has set.

The comfrey is said to be valuable for medicinal purposes, yielding a mucilage which forms a serviceable emollient. The purple variety is also grown as a crop in some parts of the country, and is held in high esteem as food for fattening swine.

The greater willow-herb is also known by the name of codlins-and-cream, from the fruity aroma of its blossoms; and the lesser willow-herb is used on some parts of the Continent for the brewing of ale.

The mullein is said to be a specific for ague, while to the yellow toad-flax innumerable virtues are inscribed, not the least of which is its utility as a fly-destroyer, the flowers being for this purpose dipped in milk, though it must be added that, since the plant is, when used medicinally, a powerful drug, its use as a remedy for the destruction of flies demands some considerable caution.

The devil's-bit scabious owes its name to the legend that 'the devil bit its root out of envy, because it was a herb possessing so many virtues, and was so useful to mankind'; though what those virtues may have been prior to the satanic onslaught is not recorded. The leaves, when dried, were, however, occasionally used for the purpose of dyeing.

From the yarrow an astringent ointment is prepared, and yarrow-tea was formerly recommended by the herbalist doctors, though I am unable to state for what complaints it was supposed to be a specific; but a friend of mine informed me that it was a favourite remedy with their old family nurse, who insisted on the children partaking of it periodically (as a tonic, I presume), and that its flavour was too disgusting for words. Hence, perhaps, its supposed virtue.

The wild mignonette, so common on the chalky downlands, turns its long, graceful stems towards the sun during its course.

The uses of the elder-tree are numerous. The heavily-scented flowers, when distilled, form a valuable and soothing lotion for the skin, and the virtues of elder-flower-water are well known and appreciated as an adjunct to the toilet of the gentler sex. Elder wine is made from the berries, and the latter also supply many of our birds with food, the starlings being especially fond of them, gorging themselves until the red juice drops from their bills. The wood is useful for the manufacture of mathematical instruments, and other purposes for which hardness and lightness are requisite. The plant itself, when used alone as a hedge, forms a valuable shelter in bleak situations near the sea, for inasmuch as the tender points of the branches are killed by the wind and saltness of the air, the lower portions thereby grow all the stronger. Its growth is also extremely rapid in soil which is suitable for its reception.

Nor is the wild clematis, the traveller's joy, without its value as well as its beauty, the long, trailing stems being used abroad in the manufacture of baskets, beehives, etc.

Of other plants—their virtues, vices, and the many legends which are connected with them—volumes have been and might be written. Want of space prevents my referring to more than a few, and I propose to take these as they occur alphabetically, rather than in their true order, it being neither my desire nor intention to treat of them botanically.

The agrimony, a plant so frequently to be seen

AGRIMONY AND THE COMMON AVENS

growing by the roadsides during the summer months, has, if the many useful properties ascribed to it are merited, been well named the all-heal. Its yellow-golden flower is so small and unpretentious as readily to escape observation. Its chief beauty consists in the shape of its leaf, which is said to be the most beautiful of all our wild-flower leaves. Nor are its flowers altogether scentless, yielding, when bruised, a sweet and fruity aroma. This plant is still used by herbalists as a tonic gargle for sore-throat, and also as a remedy for certain complaints of the liver.* In olden days it was held to be an efficacious cure for snake-bites. Its name is derived from the Greek word αργεμα, from αργος (white), the plant being supposed to cure a disease of the eye known as the 'web' or 'pearl'; and a decoction made from the leaves of the plant was frequently administered as a febrifuge.

Both the common and the water avens were formerly used medicinally. The yellow flowers of the former are familiar to many of us. When the petals fall, a small, round, prickly ball is apparent. And of the many good qualities ascribed to this plant, by no means the least are the pleasing scent and the moth-repelling powers of its root. In olden days it was esteemed a sacred flower, amongst its many other appellations being those of herba benedicta, herb bennet, star of the earth, etc.

* The cottagers in my own village make use of this plant, drying the flowers, and making a kind of tonic tea from them.

The water avens, as its name indicates, is most frequent in water-meadows and marshy localities. It is especially common in the counties of Hants and Wilts, being found in almost every water-meadow. It is a singularly beautiful and graceful flower, and somewhat curious withal, the flower-stalk of one flower frequently protruding through the centre of another flower above it. The colour of the petals is of a dull madder, with a yellowish centre. The root was formerly used as an astringent medicine.

A friend of mine attempted to cultivate this plant, but although when placed in rich garden soil it attained dimensions four or five times greater than those in its ordinary wild condition, it never flowered.

The red-berried bryony, whose trailing clusters and silvery shoots add so greatly to the beauty of our hedgerows, was formerly a well-known and powerful drug. I am, I believe, correct in stating that the nauseous medicine known as jalap, the terror of children, is extracted from this plant or a variety of it. A well-known botanist mentions that the roots of this bryony were formerly sold in Covent Garden Market as a specific for the cure of black-eyes. At the present time we may congratulate ourselves upon being less quarrelsome than our forefathers, since there is, apparently, no demand for the root for this purpose nowadays.

The yellow broom, the badge of the Plantagenets, waves its golden blossoms in the early summer breezes on many a sandy heath and roadside bank. A graceful and free-flowering shrub, it is also not without its uses; the young buds when picked are said to be an excellent substitute for capers, and the tender branches were formerly of medicinal value; the wood, when matured, is also useful for various purposes. When it is considered how many plants there are which were formerly used either for culinary or medicinal purposes, and how many others have been found to be deadly poisons, we can but come to the conclusion that the knowledge which our predecessors gained regarding the qualities, good and bad, of our British plants and flowers cannot have been acquired without some very considerable risk and loss of life, and we have, therefore, much reason to be grateful to them for their apparently disinterested and enterprising botanical researches and experiments.

The yellow bedstraw, otherwise anciently called Our Lady's bedstraw (scientifically, *Galium verum*), grows in clustering masses on many a bank and hillside. Small, fine, and delicate, as its name implies, it was none the less at one time in considerable request, being, when boiled, used for the same purposes as rennet in curdling milk. The Cheshire dairy-farmers found it of value in the manufacture of cheese. A valuable dye of a rich madder-colour is obtained from the roots of this unpretentious little plant. In the Highlands of Scotland the plant is still used both for milk-curdling and also as a dye, salt and nettles being added to it for the former purpose. Its scientific appellation of *Galium* is derived from the Greek γαλα (milk), by reason of its milk-curdling property. There are no fewer than sixteen varieties of the bedstraw in Britain, amongst them being included the plant known as the bur, the seeds of which are said, when roasted, to be a good substitute for coffee, though I am personally unable to endorse the assertion.

Most of us are familiar with the burdock, and which of us has not experienced a close acquaintance with its prickly and tenacious seed-pods? Nor have we far to go to seek for the derivation of its name, 'bur' and 'dock' being sufficiently suggestive in themselves. I have seen it stated that these burs are at times used by the village boys for the purpose of catching bats, by throwing them up into the air; the bat, darting at it in mistake for a moth or fly, becomes entangled with its thorny spines and falls helplessly to the ground. During the later months of summer the plant puts forth its flowers, which are of a purple-lilac colour. It was at one time used medicinally as a salve for wounds, and inwardly as a cure for rheumatism and pectoral complaints.

The bogbean, erroneously termed the buckbean, is amongst the most beautiful of our British wild-flowers. It is also known as the marsh trefoil. As the latter and its truer appellation infer, it is a marsh plant. A description of the beauty of its waxen-looking flowers, which make their appearance in June and July, can hardly be exaggerated. The roots, which are bitter, are, I believe, still used as a vegetable tonic, and also as a cure for rheumatic affections. I have seen this plant growing in profusion by the banks of the river Test in Hampshire, and it also grows moderately in some of the Wiltshire valleys.

Despite the annoyance which the bindweed is capable of inflicting upon the gardener, it is none the less one of the brightest and most delicately-coloured of all our British wild-flowers, and, it may be also added, one of the sweetest-scented. It grows everywhere, and, as a weed, is most difficult to eradicate; its growth is exceedingly rapid, and if but the smallest portion of its long and shining white root is left in the soil, it is sufficient to speedily produce a strong and vigorous plant; indeed, it may be said to be well-nigh ineradicable, since its roots are endless. It is known by a variety of names, the most common amongst the country-folk being that of withywind. Of the Convolvulaceæ, of which the bindweed is a representative species, and all of which are more or less beautiful, there are several varieties, the large white kind, so well known in our hedgerows and gardens, being one. The black bryony is also at times called the black bindweed, and, indeed, during the earlier period of its growth it is not very dissimilar from the true bindweed of the hedgerow, though its leaves are larger than those of the common bindweed or withywind. It is stated that from one of the Convolvulaceæ (*Convolvulus cissus*) a description of paper, known as bindweed paper, has been manufactured; the same plant has also been used for the stuffing of chairs and mattresses, as well as by rope-makers. The root of the common bindweed was also supposed to have its medicinal value, though for what special purpose I am unable to state.

The brooklime, so often, and with such serious consequences, mistaken for the watercress, alongside of which it grows, is, nevertheless, when the two plants are compared, in many respects so unlike as to render it difficult to understand how such a mistake can arise. The leaf of the brooklime is more fleshy, of a ranker green, more glossy, and of a different shape to that of the watercress. The flower of the one (the brooklime) is blue, that of the watercress white; the flavour of the former is acrid, pungent, and nauseous to a degree, yet, notwithstanding, it was formerly esteemed as an antiscorbutic. Botanically speaking, the watercress belongs to the genus Nasturtium, being the *Nasturtium officinale;* whereas the brooklime, otherwise called the beccabunga, a name derived from the German (*bach*, a brook, and *bunga*, a basket for catching fish), is one of the tribe of Veronica. Strange to say, wherever the watercress grows, the brooklime is nearly always to be found flourishing by its side.

The virtues of the wood betony were formerly believed to be so numerous as to have given rise to more than one proverb. 'Sell your coat and buy betony;' 'He has more virtues than betony,' etc., serve to show how highly it was esteemed, and it is doubtless not without some medicinal value as a mild tonic. Not the least of its supposed good qualities was the power it was credited with of being an efficient charm against the influence of evil spirits, and for this purpose it was often planted in churchyards. Gout, dropsy, jaundice, palsy, convulsions—for each and all of these, and ever so many more ailments, it was believed to be a sovereign remedy. In olden times 'faith-healing' must have flourished exceedingly, since the use of the betony, and the majority of the plants in which so much confidence was anciently reposed, is now almost abandoned. The red-purple flowers of the betony are conspicuous in most of our woods and moorlands from June to August.

The butcher's broom is nowhere very common in England, and chiefly to be met with in the Southern counties, where the soil is sandy and gravelly. The red berries of this shrub are as brilliant as those of the holly, though less numerous, and less visible by reason of their peculiar growth, being borne on the leaves themselves, and not on the stems of the plant. The name of butcher's broom is derived from the sprays having been used by butchers for the purpose of sweeping their blocks; it also is termed knee-holly, Jews' myrtle, etc., though its first appellation is the most common. The berries, when crushed, were believed to be a useful application for fractured bones, and the roots, boiled with honey, were supposed to be good for various complaints of the chest and lungs. The flowers, which make their appearance early in the spring, are of a greenish-yellow.

The wild camomile was formerly used as a tonic medicine, and much for the same purposes as is the cultivated plant at the present day. The name is derived from the Greek words χαμαι, on the ground, and μελον, an apple. The flowers were also used as a cure for jaundice, and it was very probably found to be an efficacious remedy for that complaint; but it is somewhat strange that, 'in old medical writers, an external mark or character on a plant was supposed to cure particular disease or diseases of particular parts. Plants with yellow flowers were said to cure the jaundice. Some plants bear a very evident signature of their nature and use.' The above quotation is taken from the work of a well-known authority, and refers to an ancient theory termed 'The Signatures of Plants'; of course, it is needless for me to add that such a theory is absolutely groundless. The Spaniards term the wild camomile *manzanilla;* hence we may conclude the origin of that name as applied to a certain kind of sherry.

The colt's-foot, so called from the shape of its leaves, is a conspicuous plant in our stubble-fields, especially when the leaves are turned up by the wind, thereby exposing their silvery under sides to view. It is one of the commonest of all British plants, and by no means the least valuable. The leaves, when dried, are still used at times, when mixed with tobacco, as a cure for asthma and other similar complaints. It is said that the down from the seed-vessels was formerly, when steeped in saltpetre, used as tinder, and, when simply dried and beaten out, for the purpose of stuffing cushions and pillows. It flowers in early spring.

Cowslip-time may well be regarded as the brightest time in all the year, for everything is, or should be, surely then at its best and gayest. The golden flowers are ever welcome to all save the farmer, who can hardly be expected to regard with any especial degree of favour the profusion of a plant which is indicative of poverty of soil; and this the cowslip invariably denotes, since it thrives best where the soil is worst.

The cowslip was formerly supposed to possess certain medicinal virtues for the cure of paralysis and similar affections, being believed to stimulate and strengthen the brain and nerves. A cosmetic was also prepared from this plant, and the leaves utilized as a salad. Cowslip wine is an excellent home-made wine, and cowslip-tea is by no means to be despised; the latter is said to be a sedative drink. The cowslip is also, in certain districts, termed the 'paigle,' a name the derivation of which I have never been able to discover.

The cuckoo-pint, wild arum, or, as I have

previously termed it, lords-and-ladies, is one of our earlier spring plants, and perhaps one of the most curious of all our wild-flowers. It is known scientifically as the *Arum maculatum*, or spotted arum, by reason of its leaves being frequently spotted with black or yellow, and it is also known by various other appellations, such as arrow-head, its leaves being of that shape; arrow-root and starch-root, the latter name having reference to the powder obtained from the roots when baked and ground—a powder which is said to be nutritious and to afford an excellent starch, which was much in vogue for the stiffening of the ruffs, coifs, and pinners formerly worn by ladies. The roots also afforded a kind of soap. During the Irish potato famine they were baked, ground, and made into bread, for which purpose they appear, by all accounts, to have answered admirably. When raw, the roots are not only nauseous to the taste, but said to be poisonous, the scarlet berries, which are so plentiful in autumn, especially so, and thence called 'poison berries.' Birds are able to consume them with impunity, and in hard winters dig them up. The banks in autumn are frequently covered with the berried stalks of this plant. The starchy powder prepared from the root of the wild-arum was also known as Portland sago, and was an article of commerce. It may be further added that the roots of all the several known varieties of the arum are especially pungent to the taste;

moreover, the name arum signifies 'fire,' 'heat.' The plant itself, when in flower, is curious, and possesses especial attraction for children, who not infrequently extend their acquaintance with it to the extent of eating it, the results being at times fatal to them. They should therefore be specially cautioned regarding this flower.

The name dandelion is so peculiar a corruption that few would suspect its derivation to be from the French *dent-de-lion*. Common though it may be, it is none the less a valuable plant, being possessed of considerable medicinal virtue in certain ailments of the liver, and well known as taraxacum. Dandelion coffee is frequently sold as a liver tonic, and is considered by some persons to be not only equal, but superior to ordinary coffee. The young leaves mixed with hops are also said to produce good beer. A chemist informed me that the great merit of the dandelion as a medicine consists in the freshness of the roots, for when old and stale they are comparatively valueless, and that he employed a number of boys to procure the roots for the requirements of his own trade. The dandelion and the hawk's-bit are so much alike as to be frequently confounded with each other. There is, however, some considerable dissimilarity between these flowers, which is noticeable on closer inspection. In their shape, length, and union with the base of the flower, the petals of the dandelion and the hawk's-bit will be seen to differ.

A curious parasitical plant may frequently be observed growing upon the furze, nettle, or clover, twisted round their stems and attached thereto by small suckers, which, as it were, drain the very life out of the plants to which they thus affix themselves. This is the dodder, a leafless, crawling, serpent-like little parasite, yet trembling with every breath of wind. It is of the genus botanically known as Cuscuta, one species of which is not inaptly designated 'hellweed.' Like the majority of plants, especially those which are remarkable for some special peculiarity, it was not without its supposed value as a herbal medicine in times past, being used as a remedy for swoonings and fainting-fits. It is so small and delicate-looking a plant as to readily escape observation. When the suckers have fully established themselves, the parent stem dies away, the plant deriving its sustenance entirely from that to which it may have elected to attach itself.

The broad-leaved dock is among the commonest of our field and hedgerow plants. There are some dozen different species of the dock in Britain, including the various kinds of sorrel, all of which belong to the genus Rumex. The broad-leaved varieties are termed docks, and the small-leaved sorrels. The common or broad-leaved dock to which I refer is well known as a remedy for the sting of the nettle. Propagating itself by means of its seeds, which are widely

THE DOCK AND THE ELECAMPANE 433

scattered over the surrounding ground, the dock is a serious nuisance to the farmer, more especially since it invariably selects the most fertile ground for its habitation, refusing to thrive in poor and worthless soils. The leaves are frequently utilized for the purpose of packing butter, and hence its second appellation of butter-dock. It is an enemy to the farmer not only as a weed, but as being utilized as a lodgment for the turnip-fly, which finds a suitable breeding-place amongst its broad and shady foliage. The root, when dried and reduced to powder, is said to be used in the manufacture of tooth-powder, and to be valuable for that purpose. The flowers, which make their appearance in July and August, are of a reddish colour.

The elecampane was well known and highly prized by the ancients. Its name is stated by Pliny to be derived from the legend that the plant sprang from the tears of Helen. It is not so many years ago that the sweetmeat sold under this name was procurable in some few of our more primitive village shops. As far as I can remember, it was a very sugary compound made into round, flat cakes. The plant is found in moist meadows and pastures, more especially those in the vicinity of houses, from which it may be inferred that it was formerly cultivated for the sake of its value as a remedy for coughs and colds, and it is also probable that the sweetmeat manufactured from the root of this plant was procurable only in those villages where the soil and situation were alike suitable for its cultivation. Looking back on the days of childhood, such I remember to have been the case in the neighbourhood of the village in which the shop I patronized was situated. The root is said to be useful for various other purposes, and to have been formerly in some considerable request amongst shepherds for their flocks, though for what special disease of sheep it was a specific I am unable to state, nor whether it was the root or the oil extracted therefrom which was used.

As its name implies, the eyebright was formerly, and is still, used by herbalists as a remedy for certain diseases of the eyes. Its white blossoms are more or less visible throughout the summer months among the herbage of our hedgerows. It is a small and unpretentious little plant, barely a foot in height, the leaves and root alike possessing a strong and astringent flavour.

The foxglove, so brilliant and conspicuous a flower during the fuller summer months, derives its name from a somewhat curious corruption of 'folks' glove' ('fairies' glove'). The following extract from a well-known author describes the valuable properties of this plant, scientifically named *Digitalis purpurea*, although the white-flowered variety is frequently to be met with : ' It is the most stately and beautiful of our herbaceous plants, and one that has had great reputation as a medicinal plant, being applied externally to ulcers and scrofulous tumours, and internally as a sedative, narcotic, and diuretic, in diseases of the heart and dropsy.' Another authority states that the use of this plant is highly valued in Paris, and that the flower is often painted upon the doorposts of an apothecary's house.

It is from the leaf of the foxglove that the medicine known as digitalis is procured. In some parts of the country it is known by the name of 'finger-flower,' hence the derivation of the name of digitalis (*digitus*, a finger).

It is impossible to pass by the graceful fritillary without some few remarks, although there is apparently neither special legendary interest nor virtue attached to it. It is one of our rarer British wild-flowers, though in some districts in which it is to be found it was formerly plentiful, and doubtless would be so at the present time were it not for the ruthless greed of the wholesale collectors of botanical specimens and the swarms of excursionists, who have done their best to exterminate it. It is more commonly in the Eastern and South-Eastern counties of England that the fritillary thrives best, and although when transplanted it will at times live and flower annually, I have observed that it does not increase in numbers, as is the case when it is left to flourish in its native water-meadows. I have made some five or six attempts to transplant this flower, but without success. It has either become gradually smaller year by year, or has refused to blossom at all, and yet, knowing the flower and the description of soil which it frequents, I had every reason to hope for its welldoing in some two or three instances, as every requirement was apparently present. Compared with the size of the flower, the bulbous root is excessively small.

Although I have never so found it myself, the fritillary is said to grow occasionally in some of our woods. Such localities are probably moist, since it is a plant to which moisture seems a necessity. There are two distinct varieties of this flower : the one, that most common, of a greenish-yellow, chequered with purple, the other pure white. In shape they are very similar to a small tulip, about twelve inches in height.

I have seen it stated that the fritillary is a particularly easy plant to grow in one's garden. Now, this assertion I cannot endorse, since I am well aware that to successfully cultivate it is very exceptional, even under the most apparently promising conditions. Strange to say, in the one and only instance which I can remember of its transplantation having been entirely successful, both soil and situation seemed most unsuitable for its reception. I have known the plants to which I refer for very many years, and although, as I have before remarked, they have not increased in numbers, the flowers which they annually produce are finer and more perfect in every way than any which I have ever seen growing wild. I may add that they are of the white variety.

It is truly distressing to see the large baskets of the roots, as well as bunches, of this flower which are annually exposed for sale in the streets of Oxford during the month of April. In the water-meadows of the Cherwell and Isis, which were formerly brilliant with their blossom, it is now often a matter of difficulty to find a single flower.

The name fritillary is derived from the Latin *fritillus*, a dice-box, having reference to the peculiar chequered markings on the petals of the flower. The plant is also known as the snake-head, chequered daffodil, turkey hen.

The purple-blue flowers of the wild gentian are conspicuous on nearly every hillside pasture during the earlier autumn months, and even at times late into October. As its second name of bitterwort implies, it is possessed of tonic properties, though it is from the *Gentiana lutea*, a native of the Swiss and German mountains, that the drug which is used by chemists is procured. The Swiss also prepare a kind of fermented tonic drink from the root, which they call 'gentian-wasser.'

Few of our wild-flowers can equal, and none can surpass, the wild garlic in grace and beauty; but at the same time it must be regretfully admitted that to no product of the field or hedgerow can the epithet of *stinking* be more truthfully applied. Yet, notwithstanding, this flower has of recent years found a large and ready sale. During the months of April and May the wild garlic may be found growing in profusion in many a woodland and on the steep banks of many a valley. A few years ago, when fishing in Cumberland, I saw it growing in the greatest profusion on the banks of the river Lowther. One spot in particular, where the ground rose abruptly from the edge of the stream, was, for the distance of nearly a hundred yards, completely covered with the white flowers of this plant. Where it is at all luxuriant it is by no means a friendly herb to the farmer, for so strong is its flavour, that the milk of the cows which have fed upon it is rendered unsaleable, and the flesh of their calves is said to be also tainted, a flavour which may possibly enhance its value in the estimation of the garlic-loving foreigner, but which would militate against its sale in an English market.

The florists, in order, I presume, to advance its sale, have given it the name of star-flower. It is also known by the name of bear's garlic. The leaves were formerly used as a vegetable by the country people, though nowadays the practice is discontinued, since they are able to grow onions and shallots in their gardens and allotments, and those, too, often of a size and quality unattainable by the gardeners of their richer neighbours.

The origin of the appellation of herb-Robert is, apparently, unknown, although some authors have suggested that it is derived from a St. Robert whose festival is commemorated about the time when this plant first flowers, viz., at the end of April or the beginning of May. The festival of this St. Robert, who was a Benedictine abbot, occurs on April 29, and so it has come to pass that the supposition has arisen. This plant, as also the crane's-bill, stork's-bill, and others, is one of the geraniums, so called from the shape of their seed-vessels, which resemble the bill of a crane, the Greek word γερανος signifying a crane.

The herb-Robert is also called the stinking crane's-bill, by reason of its rank and unpleasant smell; and it is also known as the wild-geranium. But both flower and leaves are not without their beauty, more especially when in the later months of summer and early autumn the latter turn to a crimson hue. Nor was this plant formerly without its supposed medicinal virtues, possessing certain astringent qualities; the leaves were also used to repel insects.

The henbane, from which the well-known drug hyoscyamus is procured, is chiefly interesting by reason of the deadly poison extracted from its leaves, and which has rendered it so famous an ingredient of the 'hell-broth' supposed to have been brewed by witches. It, however, possesses the merit of being a useful plant to the chemist, furnishing a valuable narcotic medicine. Its purple-yellow flowers make their appearance in June, and continue more or less throughout the summer. Although poisonous to mankind, horses and cattle, it is said to be innocuous to sheep, goats, and pigs, and it is also in some localities termed hog's-bean. Like the woody and deadly nightshades, it belongs to the genus Solanum, of which genus the potato is also a member—the fruit so poisonous, the root so useful and nutritious an article of our daily food.

The beauty of our hedgerows is not a little enhanced by the graceful trailing clusters of the wild hop, a plant indigenous to this country, but, until the sixteenth century, uncultivated. It was during the reign of Henry VIII. that the culture of the hop was first commenced in England, and since that period its value has gradually increased; for inasmuch as the plant requires soil of a special nature in which to thrive, the area of its cultivation, in this country at all events, must necessarily be very limited. Kent, Sussex, parts of Surrey and Herefordshire, are the principal hop-growing counties. It is the female flower which is used in the brewing of ale.

The wild-hop is by no means a useless plant; the roots are said to possess tonic and blood-purifying properties. The young shoots, when boiled, are excellent as a vegetable; the stalks and leaves are said to yield a good yellow dye; and, apart from their value to the brewer, the flowers, when placed in a bag and used as a pillow, act as a narcotic. Hop-pickers are apt to suffer at times from the sap of the flowers poisoning their hands, any previous sore place on the latter being liable to fester severely.

With the appearance of the purple-blue flowers of the wild hyacinth, the spring may be said to be well established; nor do any of our many wild-flowers add more to the fresh brightness of our woodlands and hedgerow-banks. Where it grows it does so in profusion—not here and there, but it literally 'clothes the grass of the field.' With the classic fable of Hyacinthus, from which the plant is named, everyone is doubtless well acquainted. It is often, most erroneously, termed the bluebell, a name belonging exclusively to the harebell.

From the root, which yields a strong, glutinous substance, a kind of starch was formerly manufactured. A well-known botanical writer states that this starch was used for stiffening muslin, fixing the feathers to arrows, etc.; and also that the flowers of the plant were worn by the Grecian maidens at bridals, a custom which gave rise to the term 'hyacinthine locks.' The plant has, apparently, no real or supposed medicinal virtues.

The ground ivy, otherwise termed gill, alehoof, cat's-maid, etc., may be found by the sides of many of our roads and hedges, or by some crumbling, ruined wall. A kind of tea is often made from this plant by the country people, who use it as a tonic. It is also said to be of service as an eyewash. The whole plant is strongly, and by no means unpleasantly, scented.

Wherever sedges are abundant by the sides of

our rivers, the yellow iris is generally to be found, and very beautiful and bright are its blossoms. There is a saying that 'no bouquet is complete without some yellow in its composition,' and such may be also observed of the flowers which deck our fields and hedgerows. The yellow iris is, perhaps, seen at its best when growing on the margin of some river-bend or still backwater in which the reflection of its graceful stems, surmounted by their brilliant, yellow blossoms, is mirrored in the stream. Beautiful as it is, it fades so rapidly when gathered as to be useless for decorative purposes, and so it may as well be spared to grace the riverside.

This flower is also called the fleur-de-lis or flag-flower; it is from the *Iris florentina* that iris, or, as it is corruptly termed, *orris-root*, is procured. The root of the iris, when chewed, is said to cure toothache, and to be a powerful astringent. The seeds of this plant, when roasted, are also stated to be a substitute for coffee.

The purple loosestrife is common by the sides of most of our English streams. It is often confounded with the willow-herb; but a comparison of the two plants will at once suffice to show the differences which exist between them, not only in the shape and colour of the blossoms, but also in their arrangement, those of the purple loosestrife being more truly purple, more compactly arranged, and smaller than those of the willow-herb, whilst the long spike of blossoms is pyramidal in its form;

the flowers of the willow-herb being further apart. In former days a decoction prepared from the purple loosestrife was esteemed valuable as an eyewash.

If the purple loosestrife and the willow-herb are unlike each other, a still wider difference exists between the former and the yellow loosestrife, though both plants are to be found frequenting similar situations. A far greater similarity exists between the yellow loosestrife and the smaller variety of the St. John's wort.

Though a less imposing and smaller plant than the purple loosestrife, the yellow loosestrife is perhaps the more graceful and beautiful flower of the two. It is, however, by no means as common as the former; it may, indeed, be regarded as one of the less common of our wild-flowers. I have, nevertheless, seen it growing in great profusion on the banks of the river Test in Hampshire, and was very regretfully forced to trample much of it under foot on one occasion, the demands of a fresh-run salmon admitting of no alternative. A peculiarity of this plant, which may suffice for its identification, is that the leaves grow amongst the flowers. It blooms during July and August, and is never found elsewhere but by the side of a stream.

The lily of the valley is, unhappily, now so rarely to be found in its wild state that it can hardly be included in the list of ordinary British wild-flowers. It is, however, still to be found growing wild in some parts of the country, and some few years ago I received a large basketful which had been gathered in a wood in the neighbourhood of Birmingham, where, for aught I know to the contrary, it may still be found, though I withhold the exact locality for obvious reasons. A considerable similarity exists in the appearance of this flower and the wild garlic. Of the two, the latter is undoubtedly the more beautiful, but its ill savour more than nullifies any advantages it may possess as far as its appearance is concerned; indeed, I am of opinion that the wild garlic is best left alone. It is said that the flowers of the lily of the valley were formerly dried and reduced to a powder, which was, when used as snuff, found an efficient cure for headache. In Germany the flowers, when steeped in wine, are still used for the same purpose. It is, perhaps, the extreme beauty of the flower, its purity, and its delicious fragrance, which in olden time rendered it an object of reverential regard.

There is, perhaps, no one of our wild-flowers which has been more deservedly lauded for its many virtues than the marsh mallow. A well-known writer remarks of this flower: 'Every part of this plant is useful.' As its name implies, it is a marsh-loving plant, and by the sea-shore and amongst the salt-marshes its pink blossoms and downy leaves may frequently be observed during the later summer months. Both the root and leaves of this plant are used in medicine in decoction and syrup, and it is from the root that the sweetmeat known as *pâté de guimauve* is prepared. No plant is more generally useful, and its value is fully appreciated.

The common mallow, a plant which is to be found in every hedgerow and piece of waste ground, though less valuable, perhaps, than the marsh mallow, is not without its uses. From it the mauve dye is procured. The leaves, when boiled, form an excellent poultice for superficial cuts, wounds, and sores, and a decoction, also made from the leaves, is used by the country people as a fomentation for the same purposes. It is not by any means common in Scotland.

A small, lowly trailing plant may often be observed growing by the sides of the smaller ditches and drains in our water-meadows. During June, July, and August it is bright with yellow flowers. This is the moneywort. When not in flower, it is easily overlooked amid the long grass which surrounds it, and with which its long stems are confused. After hay-harvest, or when the first grazing of the meadows has been completed, it is most conspicuous. Although it naturally prefers a damp situation, it will also thrive exceedingly well in the garden, and the long golden trails form a brilliant and graceful addition to many a window-box in our towns and suburbs. Its name is said to have been derived from the shape of its leaves, which are round, like pennies, and situated in pairs, though graduating in size throughout the length of its stem, the flowers springing from their axils; both leaves and flowers turn themselves towards the light. This plant is also known by the name of creeping Jenny. Strange to say, no legend or special medicinal virtue appears to have attached to it.

The bright yellow flowers of the mullein are common in most of our banks and hedgerows from midsummer to September, and very handsome they are, especially when, as is so frequently the case, growing side by side with the devil's-bit scabious and the yarrow, with which they so charmingly contrast. The leaves are exceedingly soft and downy, the down being formerly plucked and used as a substitute for cotton lamp-wicks. The word 'mullein' is said to be derived from the Latin *mollis*, soft.

Many medicinal virtues were formerly ascribed to this plant, the root, the flowers, and the seed alike contributing to cure various ills. The first, when boiled, was said to cure the toothache, cramps, and convulsions; the second, when distilled or dried, were supposed to be efficacious for the gout; while the seed, boiled in wine, was used as a poultice for thorns, etc.

Two plants bear the name of nightshade, the one being distinguished by the name of *deadly*, the other by that of *woody*. The former is somewhat rare, the latter common. It is but a few days ago that a specimen of the deadly nightshade was brought to me for identification; it was found growing in a garden a short distance from my house. It is from this, the most poisonous of all our British plants, that the preparation known as belladonna is procured. It is botanically known as the *Atropa belladonna*, and is otherwise styled the sleeping nightshade, and the dwale, the latter appellation being probably derived from the French *deuil*, grief, mourning, though the French term it the *morelle mortelle*.

The difference between the two nightshades is very marked. The species in question bears large heart-shaped leaves, free from any indentations on their edges, and deeply veined, growing to a considerable height (the specimen to which I have referred being between five and six feet high); the flowers bell-shaped, and of a purple colour; the berries large, and black when ripe. The whole aspect of the plant is significant of its poisonous nature. Its value as a drug is considerable; oculists use it largely on account of its power of dilating the pupil of the eye. The origin of its botanical name is Italian, as it was formerly used by the Italian ladies as a cosmetic.

The woody nightshade, or, as it is sometimes termed, the bittersweet, from its peculiar flavour, is little less poisonous than the deadly nightshade, and also possesses certain medicinal properties. Both plants, in common with the potato, tomato, capsicum, and henbane, belong to the genus Solanum. The leaves are lance-shaped with two distinct lobes on either side of their base; the flowers, which are deep purple, are somewhat small; the petals turned back; the anthers yellow; the berries are, when ripe, of a crimson colour, though previously yellow, and at first green. It may be found in every hedgerow, and is, perhaps, most luxuriant when growing by the riverside. Trout are especially partial to the shade afforded by its overhanging branches, a fact of which fishermen are not slow to avail themselves.

Any description of the nettle would be superfluous, but it may at the same time prove of some interest to the reader to know that, rank and offensive weed though it may be, it is nevertheless a most useful plant in a variety of ways. When boiled, the young shoots form an excellent vegetable food; uncooked, it is by no means a despicable provender for cattle. A decoction made from the leaves is a good astringent gargle for sore throat; the seeds, when ground, are stated to be a cure for goitre. The stinging power of the leaves has even been turned to account as a cure for paralysis. I was once much amused by an old man in our village telling me how he had cured himself by the use of stinging-nettles. He had been for a long time suffering from cold feet, and to such an extent as to interfere with his rest. One night he could stand it no longer, so, getting out of bed, he made his way into his garden, and, gathering a bundle of nettles, beat his feet with them as long as he could. He assured me that he had never since then been similarly troubled. It is, of course, perfectly possible that by this

NETTLES AND ORCHISES

rough-and-ready treatment he contrived to effect a cure, by exciting the nerves to increased action.

Nettle-leaves rubbed into wooden vessels, tubs, etc., prevent their leaking, the juice of the stems and leaves coagulating, and so filling up any interstices. Paper and linen have also been manufactured from the fibres of the nettle, and nettle-cloth may still be procured in some parts of the Continent. The caterpillars of the tortoiseshell, peacock, and red admiral butterflies feed largely on the leaves of the nettle; indeed, the scientific name of the first-named is *Vanessa urtica*. Three species of the nettle are more or less common in Britain, viz. : the great nettle, the small nettle, and the Roman nettle. It may be seen from the above that the nettle, if a plant to be avoided, is, nevertheless, by no means to be altogether despised.

Without entering into any detailed account of the various British orchises, it may prove useful to the reader to give a list of those which are to be found in this country, and which includes the following fifteen varieties :

1. The bee (Ophrys apifera).
2. The late spider (O. arachnites).
3. The spider (O. aranifera).
4. The fly (O. muscifera).
5. The green-winged meadow (Orchis morio).
6. The early purple (O. mascula).
7. The dwarf dark-winged (O. astulata).

8. The great brown-winged (O. fusca).
9. The military (O. militaris).
10. The lax-flowered (O. laxiflora).
11. The marsh (O. latifolia).
12. The spotted palmate (O. maculata).
13. The pyramidal (O. pyramidalis).
14. The monkey (O. tephrosanthos).
15. The lizard (O. miricina).

It is from the roots of the green-winged and early purple varieties of orchis that the preparation known as saloop was formerly obtained.

The purple-lilac-coloured flowers of the peppermint are visible on many a river-bank and marsh in the later months of summer. The uses of the plant are too well known to require any special reference. The essential oil from which the various preparations are procured is found on the calyx and leaves.

The pennyroyal, or, as it is sometimes termed, the pudding grass, is also another useful medicinal herb, and various medicinal preparations are procured from it. Both this plant and the peppermint belong to the genus Mentha. Its scent is less powerful than that of the peppermint. It is unlike the latter plant in the character of its growth, its leaves being small and oval, and the stems long and trailing. It flowers earlier than the peppermint; the flowers are of a purple colour. It is also known as the hop marjoram.

The scarlet pimpernel, weed though it be, may nevertheless lay claim to being one of the most charming and interesting of all our wild-flowers. It is ubiquitous, so much so as to be a source of no little trouble to the gardener, but none the less does the simple, bright-coloured little flower appeal to our sympathy. It is a truthful little timepiece, and its brilliant scarlet blossoms expand themselves from spring to autumn. Throughout the sunnier hours of the day, so regular is it in its habits, that it has earned the name of shepherd's clock, shepherd's barometer, and poor man's weather-glass. In cloudy, sunless weather it refuses to unfold itself, but when the sun is shining its petals are opened from 7 a.m. till 2 p.m., and this with such regularity as to enable a very fairly correct estimate of the time to be declared from its movements. Nor was it formerly without its supposed medicinal virtues —near sight, epilepsy, dropsy, the bite of a mad dog, being but a few of the ills for which it was esteemed a valuable and efficacious remedy.

The great plantain, so common and so familiar a weed, is not without some interest, since it was formerly used as a remedy for ague, the sap from the roots being expressed, and it was also used as a specific for other ailments. Their ribs having been removed, the leaves were bruised and applied as a cure for the stings of bees.

The leaves of the hoary plantain, which is common in all chalky districts, are said to make a good astringent lotion, and the seeds of the ribwort plantain, which are of a mucilaginous nature, are used in demulcent drinks instead of linseed or marsh mallow.

The water plantain is one of the many plants which have been supposed to be a cure for hydrophobia.

By the edges of the ploughed fields, as well as by the roadside, the pink flowers of the rest-harrow may be often observed throughout the summer months, and it is also by no means an uncommon object among the chalky cliffs of our Eastern and Southern coasts. The stems of this plant are frequently covered with sharp, thorny spines. Its name is said to be derived from the toughness of its long roots, which are said to impede the progress of the harrow, a derivation which appears to be somewhat far-fetched. It was formerly believed to be so obnoxious to snakes as to keep them from frequenting the localities in which it is abundant, and it was also supposed to possess medicinal virtue in cases of delirium.

The shepherd's purse, a weed so troublesome and familiar in gardens, was, when the culture of vegetables was less understood than at the present time, boiled and used as a substitute for greens, and also was supposed to possess certain medicinal properties. It was also styled the St. James's wort.

The silver-weed, which is conspicuously abundant on many a waste ground and grass-grown by-road, is remarkable for the beauty of its leaves, both as regards their shape and their cool silvery-gray colour, further enhanced during the summer months by its bright yellow flowers. Scientifically it is termed the *Potentilla anserina*, and is in certain districts known as the goose grass, though, apparently, without any particular reason, since geese do not feed on it, certainly not in preference to any other herbage. It is said to indicate poor pasturage, and to be most frequent in moist, low-lying lands. I have also seen it in the greatest luxuriance on dry, thirsty uplands. The exquisite shape of the leaf of this plant is hardly surpassed by that of the agrimony, and it may be recognized on the head of many a carved stall in our older churches and Cathedrals. So striking a plant was, of course, not without its supposed medicinal virtues in former days, being used as a specific for ague, sciatica, etc. The root, which is long and somewhat similar to that of the parsnip, is said to contain a considerable amount of nourishment when roasted. Unlike the majority of wild-flowers, the leaves retain their beauty and freshness when dried.

The succory may be reckoned as one of the most useful of our wild-flowers, and, apart from its utility, it is also one of the most beautiful. This plant is said to be identical with the garden endive ; and it is also from its roots that chicory is procured, though the supply of this article is mainly obtained from Germany. The succory thrives best in those localities where the soil is of a light, chalky, or gravelly nature.

The flowers, which are white before they are fully expanded, turn to a lavender-blue colour when matured, this transition being attributed to the action of the acid contained in the plant. The succory (supposed by some writers to be the horehound referred to in the Bible) is said to have been one of the five different herbs which the Jews were permitted to eat at the Passover.

The speedwell or common veronica is one of the most frequent of our garden weeds ; it is often found growing side by side and entwined with the pimpernel. Unobtrusive as is its small blue flower, it is none the less not without its share of comeliness. It may be said that, although the removal of these two lowly little plants from our gardens is urgently necessary, the necessity is nevertheless somewhat grudgingly admitted, by reason of the beauty of their flowers. The speedwell was at one time used as a substitute for tea, and was believed to possess tonic properties. It may be said to flourish in every locality, and in any description of soil.

The snapdragon (*Antirrhinum majus*) is also known in various districts by various names, such as toad's-mouth, rabbit's-mouth, etc. It is a plant which flourishes nearly everywhere, where there are old or ruined walls, to which it frequently attaches itself. Thrusting its roots into the crevices, or bravely flaunting itself on the very topmost ridge amid the crumbling mortar of the coping, in such situations it thrives equally well as in the deeper and richer soil of the garden. Wherever its seeds can find a lodgment, no matter how slender, there they take root. The Russians cultivate this plant for the sake of the oil yielded by its seeds. The flowers of the wild snapdragon are mostly red or white.

The spurge is another plant well known as a garden-weed, and ever thriving best where its presence is least desirable. Its curious green flowers appear soon after midsummer, and continue until the autumn. It is known locally as cat's-milk, wolf's-milk, wart-weed, etc., the last appellation being derived from the caustic nature of its juice, which was used as a cure for warts, as also for the wound caused by the bite of an adder, and, when rubbed behind the ear, as a remedy for toothache.

Although it cannot be regarded as one of our commoner wild-flowers, and is more frequently to be seen growing in some herbaceous border of the garden, the Solomon's seal is, nevertheless, to be found in several parts of England, its long and gracefully-drooping stems, adorned with white pendent flowers, being at their best during the earlier months of summer. Other plants belonging to the same genus, viz., Convallaria, are also known by the name of Solomon's seal. The lily of the valley is one of these. The variety to which we refer frequently attains to three feet in height, and is sufficiently remarkable to attract the eye wherever it may be growing. In olden days the roots, when pounded and steeped in ale, were supposed to possess the power of uniting broken bones, and, like the leaves of the garden lily, were used, when bottled in spirits, as a cure for bruises and cuts. The roots are also stated to supply a nutritious flour when dried and ground.

The tansy is a plant which may be seen growing by nearly every riverside throughout the kingdom. Wherever the willow-herb and meadowsweet abound, there the orange-yellow flowers of the tansy are almost sure to be visible, asserting themselves amidst the lowlier plants like large golden-coloured balls. I find mention of its having been used as a stomachic bitter, and given as a remedy for the gout. The same authority states that this plant also was supposed to have been one of the bitter herbs of which the Jews partook at the feast of the Passover.

When the autumnal leaves are falling, and the hedgerows are becoming thin and bare, the long stalks of the teasel, surmounted by their broom-like heads, are conspicuous in the banks and waste places. During the leafy days of summer the purple flowers are discovered amid the tangled growth of long grass, nettles, and thistles which surrounds them. Other names, more or less apt, have been given to the teasel. In some localities it is known as Venus' cup, by reason of the large quantity of water which the leaves are capable of containing; as much as half a pint is said to have been collected from one leaf. The growth of the leaves is peculiar, their bases being united, and so forming a kind of natural cup. The common teasel is not the plant which is used by fullers for carding wool, the latter being a cultivated variety known as the fuller's teasel, the seed-vessels being furnished with hooked spines; the flowers are also of a lighter hue. Though somewhat similar to a thistle in its growth and appearance, the teasel is distinct from the thistle, the former belonging to the genus Dipsacus, the latter to that of Carduus, the common teasel being the *Dipsacus sylvestris*, the fuller's teasel *Dipsacus fullonum*.

The wild thyme may be found on every bank and hillside pasture in the United Kingdom, and is familiar to all. Though inferior to the cultivated variety, which is not a wild British plant, but an importation from South-Western Europe, the wild thyme is, nevertheless, by no means without its good qualities. Bees feed eagerly on its flowers. Virgil, who knew as much about agriculture, etc., as any modern farmer, and something about everything, refers to the value of thyme in the vicinity of a bee-farm in the fourth book of the 'Georgics,' in the lines thus rendered by Dryden:

'Wild thyme and savoury set around their cell,
Sweet to the taste, and fragrant to the smell.'

Nor are other of the ancient classics unmindful of

the wild thyme; Horace thus makes mention of it:

> 'Impune tutum per nemus arbutos
> Quærunt latentes et thyma deviæ
> Olentis uxores mariti.'

Its praises have been sung by well-nigh every poet, not so much, perhaps, from any particular admiration for its modest purple blossoms, as from the sweet fragrance of its leaves. And thyme was held in high repute for various ills, being supposed to be especially valuable as a remedy for lung diseases, headache, etc., and doubtless not without reason, since a certain amount of camphor is said to be contained in the plant.

The yellow toad-flax is a common object during the later summer months, its yellow flowers adorning the tops of the field-banks. The name of toad-flax has been, apparently, derived from the fact of the plant, not the flower, being somewhat similar to the flax plant. The prefix of *toad* probably owes its origin to the curious shape of the flower, which is similar to that of the snapdragon, or, as it is otherwise called, the toad's-mouth; indeed, the toad-flax is locally termed the wild snapdragon.

The common or great wild valerian grows abundantly by the riverside and in moist places throughout the country, intermingled with the sedges, willow-herb, and dropwort. The flowers, though graceful and delicate in their colouring, emit a faint, unpleasant scent.

THE WOOD SORREL

The root is used medicinally as a nerve tonic, and has a peculiarly strong and disagreeable smell. It is said, though I have never witnessed it, that cats eat the leaves and the root of the valerian greedily, and become apparently intoxicated by them.

The wood sorrel, or wood-sour, as it is locally termed, may well be regarded as one of the most beautiful and delicate of all our earlier spring flowers. Nor are the leaves less beautiful than the flowers. It appears to have been a plant which was formerly regarded with some veneration, probably from its being a trefoil, and so considered as emblematical of the Trinity. It was also called cuckoo's meat (by the French, *pain de coco*), and 'alleyluya' by ancient writers. The leaves contain oxalic acid, and were formerly used as an antiscorbutic medicine. The scientific name of the plant is *Oxalis acetonella*.

WATERCRESS-FARMING.

EVERYONE is well acquainted with the cry of the watercress-seller, though it is, perhaps, rather amongst the by-ways and lanes of the large towns that he seeks his customers than in the more fashionable quarters. The inhabitants of the latter would hardly elect to purchase from the shabbily-dressed and none too cleanly-looking individual whose stock-in-trade is generally carried in a hamper slung to his back by a piece of cord, both as dilapidated as himself; but the cresses within look fresh and green, notwithstanding; they may have been gathered by fingers guiltless of soap, and their vendor may be a most unsavoury mortal, but none the less some of the fresh little bunches may perchance find their way to the table of his Grace the Duke, who lives in the big house at the corner of the square, while others may serve to adorn that of some hard-worked artisan, or the cabman who lives in the mews off the side-street: for Sprouts, who keeps the greengrocer's shop close by, was formerly in the service of his Grace, and is permitted to supply the family, when in town, with vegetables of the commoner sorts, and, buying in the cheapest market and selling at an exorbitant profit, contrives to earn a very respectable livelihood. He and our tattered friend transact a considerable amount of business during the year; at one time it is 'creases,' at another 'musherooms,' groundsel for cage-birds, etc., and so the little green bunches find themselves transferred from the old hamper to all sorts and conditions of men, and as his basket grows lighter, the heart of the vendor grows lighter, too, and when he shambles homeward, wherever that may be, his broken and clouted old shoes applaud him as they flap the pavement, and the coppers in his pocket jingle merrily. He has had a hard day's work, has, perhaps, tramped many a mile to fill his basket, and many more in order to empty it. Who could be hard-hearted enough to grudge him the modest pint in which he indulges as he trudges wearily home?

It is during the earlier months of the year that watercresses realize the best prices, for they are then scarce, and the labour of gathering them is greater, for their stems are short and the water is icy cold. They require to be picked carefully, or the stock will suffer. Altogether, watercress-gathering is as cheerless and wet a job as anyone could desire; to paddle about in the cold spring-water, sockless, and well-nigh bootless, to say nothing of the keen north wind whistling through every hole in threadbare and tattered garments, best described as a number of holes sewn together, is as miserable and unenlivening an occupation as can well be imagined. Then, when they have been gathered, the cresses must be tied up and trimmed, and, in order to ensure them from damage, as well as to admit of their being more closely packed, this work must be performed on the spot.

The water-keepers hate the 'creasers,' lay all sorts of crimes to their charge, and aver that they poach the fish, etc. If the spawning season has been a bad one, it is all due to 'them creasers a-messing about.' If a jack has got off the trimmer, it is 'one of them dratted creasers who stole it,' etc.; and so the poor wretches, who work really hard for their living, and are far oftener sinned against than sinning, get hunted off here, warned off there, until it becomes a matter of greater difficulty each year to procure a sufficient supply of cress for their needs, and they are forced to travel further and further afield in order that they may do so unmolested.

The demand for watercress, especially during those months in which salads are scarce, and consequently dear, is so great that, of recent years, its culture has formed an industry of considerable importance, and where the conditions are favourable for its cultivation, it has been found that the cost of its production is capable of yielding a very satisfactory return. What these conditions are, and how it is cultivated, I will endeavour to explain.

Firstly, the supply of water must be constant and steady, and the nearer the beds are to the spring-head, for spring-water is ever preferable for the purpose, the better; secondly, the soil must be of a suitable nature; thirdly, the bottom of the beds must be hard and sound.

As regards the first of these essentials, no matter how carefully the beds may be prepared and tended, cress grown in beds supplied with water from a river will ever be inferior to that grown in those supplied with spring-water, and in a hard frost, the one thing, perhaps, most dreaded by the watercress-farmer, the crop may entirely fail, or, at all events, its growth be very seriously retarded. When such weather prevails, the plants are beaten down under water by means of long light switches, or besoms made for the purpose, and are so kept comparatively safe until the return of a more genial temperature.

As regards the soil most suitable for the growth of watercress, chalk appears to be the best of all; for whilst it is capable of forming a good sound bottom for the beds, it is also porous, the plants readily take root and spread, and are thereby less liable to be washed out. The young cress shoots from the stool of the plants, and is not propagated from the seed alone.

That the beds should be hard and sound is necessary, not only because they can be more easily attended to, but also because the general depth of water which is requisite is more easily maintained. This depth should never exceed six inches, and at times may have to be reduced to little more than one inch ; but whatever the depth required, the flow of water must be constant and gentle.

The beds are usually cut out into large squares, divided by means of low earth embankments, the water flowing from one bed to the other through drain-pipes or miniature sluices. Where practicable, these are arranged in tiers one above the other until the level of the spring-head is reached. Needless to remark, the beds must be kept scrupulously clean, and free from weeds or any rooty growth, and where the bottom is sound and hard this becomes an easy matter.

When the beds are planted, the best plants are selected, preference being given to those taken from other soil ; the roots are cut off and thrown away, and the cuttings thus obtained are scattered thinly and broadcast over the bed in about an inch or two of water. Where the flow of water is at all over-strong they are kept in their places by means of stones laid on them. This planting generally takes place during July, August, or September, according to the time when the crops may be required, each bed being annually freshly planted. The cuttings soon strike, and grow vigorously, and when in bloom bear a small white flower. Plants laid in July will yield a fair crop in the autumn, but it depends very much on the distance from the market, demand, etc., as to whether it is worth while to cut and convey it away for sale, for it is the earliest spring cress which yields the best return. During the early summer cress is cheap enough, for every brooklet yields its store. The cress-growers aim at producing plants with good long stalks, and maintain that the latter are a greater delicacy than the leaves ; moreover, such plants are more easily cut, and, being more bulky, yield a better return, in a pecuniary sense, than the smaller, shorter-stemmed specimens.

Any waste portions of a field, where there is a good spring and the soil is suitable, can, with a very trifling expenditure and comparatively little labour, be readily utilized for the formation of a watercress-bed; the return is rapid and sensible, especially if near to a good market or a railway-station, and the beds, when once made, require but occasional attention to secure the crop, which, when gathered, is trimmed with long, sharp knives, packed in square hampers styled 'flats,' shaded with some sacking, and placed in running water until the cart is ready to take them away.

It may be of interest to some of my readers to know what the value of a watercress-bed may be. From the information which I have collected, probably much below the mark, I am given to understand that every rod of ground may be expected to yield two flats at each cutting. A flat is about thirty inches in length, two feet wide, and a foot in depth, and is capable of containing some two hundred large bunches—at least twelve bunches, such as are usually retailed in the shops at a penny apiece, or two for three-halfpence, could be made out of each of these larger bunches. It is, therefore, possible to form some estimate of the value of each flat, labour and cost of carriage included, and it will readily be seen that a very satisfactory sum may be left to carry over to the credit side of the account. Of course, the greater the extent of ground cultivated, the larger the profit will be, as the men employed can be retained throughout the year, unless their services can be used for other work on the farm.

It is curious how many people are annually poisoned by mistaking brooklime for watercress, for the two plants are very unlike, and the flower of the former is blue, that of the latter white; moreover, a very superficial experience of the flavour of the brooklime should be quite sufficient to deter anyone from a desire to extend it further, for nothing can possibly be more nauseous. Wherever cress will thrive, osiers can also be profitably grown, and as these are useful for making the flats, the village basket-makers profit by the industry.

Living in a district where cress-growing is carried on to a considerable extent, I take no little interest in the various operations connected with the crop; nevertheless, I cannot say that my pleasure in so doing is unalloyed, for cress-growing has been found to pay so well that every available hole and corner in the parish has been turned to account, much to the detriment of the trout-fishing, the stream being tapped in every direction; moreover, when the fish run up to the beds, as they do for the purpose of spawning, they fare hardly at the hands of the 'creasers,' and year by year they are diminishing in number. The river, never too constant in height where water-meadows abound, is rendered still more unsteady, and constantly fouled and thickened during the planting and cleaning of the beds, one or other of which operations is for ever going on. Then, again, the soft, marshy spots so dear to snipe are gradually being cut out and drained. War is also waged against the moorhens, these unfortunate birds being held in abomination by the cress-growers, though they inflict no harm on the cress-beds further than by swimming about in them and eating the slugs and water-snails which adhere to the stems and leaves of the plants. I fear that ere long the moorhens, snipe, and trout will have altogether vanished from the scene.

INDEX.

A.

A DAY with the rabbits in Downland, 393
A favoured spot, 169
A *rara avis*, 118
A shower of crystals, 116
A strange 'right and left,' 274
A year with the birds, 157
Aconite, The, 415
Agrimony, The, 420
Alcidæ, The, 349
Allowance, 381
Among the golden reed-beds, 171
Anatidæ, British, 318
An idle hour with the birds, 169
Animals, The love of, 2
    British wild, 3
An old-fashioned day, 388
Ashdown, Former days at, 21
Auk, great, The, 350
    little, The, 352
Avens, common, The, 421
    water, The, 422
Avocet, The, 289

B

Badger, The, 5, 395
Badgers and foxes, 7, 8
Bag, A mixed, 85
Bat, Barbastelle, The, 82
    Bechstein's, 84
    common, The, 80, 81
    Daubenton's, 83
    great, The, 80
    hairy-armed, The, 84
    greater horseshoe, The, 81
    smaller horseshoe, The, 81
    long-eared The, 81
    mouse-coloured, The, 84
    notch-eared, The, 83
    parti-coloured, The, 84
    reddish-gray, The, 83
    serotine, The, 84
    whiskered, The, 83

Bats, British, 79
    British, Common, 80
    Rare and common, 82
    Rarest, probable importation, 85
    Table descriptive of, 87
Bedstraw, The yellow, 423
Betony, The, 427
Bettws-y-Coed, 4
Bindweed, The, 425
Bird collectors, 212
    language, 113
    stuffers and taxidermists, 178
Birds affected by their surroundings, 121
Birds, Bracing of, 99
    British varieties, Reference to the, 146
    Caged, 94
    Caterpillars and, 130
    eggs, Act for protection of, 93
        Disproportionate size of, 142
    Food-supply of, 121
    Garden, 123
    Making observation on, 157
    Migration of, 274
    Nests and destruction of, 91
    on passage, Mortality amongst, 275
    Protection of garden produce from, 112
    songs of, Difficulty in detecting, 136
    Training of, by brace-board, 100
    useful, Destruction of, by keepers and gardeners, 111
Bittern, The, 266
Blackbirds, Utility of, 112
Blackbirds, Warning notes of, 113
Blackcap, The, 162
Blackcock, The, 239
    Measurements of, 242
British warblers, 154

INDEX

Brooklime, The, 426. 466
Broom, butcher's, The, 427
   yellow, The, 422
Brute creation, The, 2
Bryony, red-berried, The, 422
Buckbean, The, 424
Bullfinch, The, 95
   British varieties of, 97
   Tamed, 96
Bullfinches, Caged, 97
   Preference of, for dry situations, 96
Bunting, cirl, The, and yellow-hammer, 148
Bunting, common, The, 149
   snow, The, 152
      peculiarity in change of plumage, 152
Buntings, The, 147
   reed and black-headed, The, 151
   Songs of, 150
Burdock, The, 424
Bustard, The, 117
Bustards, Flight of, 119
   Size of, 120
Butt and Ward, Messrs., 180
Buzzard, common, The, 210
   honey, The, 211
   rough-legged, The, 210
Buzzards, The, 210
   Protection needed for, 212

C.

Camomile, common, The, 428
Campion, The, 418
Capercailzie, The, 238
   measurement of, 242
Cat, diving, A, 109
   wild, The, 3
      True colour of the, 5
Cats, wild, 5
Cats, wild, Domestic, 5
Cheiroptera, The, 85
Chiffchaff, The, 163
Chough, The, 188
Cocktails, 20
Colt's-foot, The, 428
Comfrey, The, 417, 418
Coot, The, 256
Cormorant, common, The 363
Cormorants, The, 363
Cow-parsley, The, 412
Cowslip, The, 429
Crake, corn, The, 248
   little, The, 249
   spotted, The, 249
Crippled game, 383
Crossbill, The, 98
Crow, The, 189
   family, The, 190
   Indian, An, 190

Crow tribe, The, 188
Crows, rooks, and jackdaws, 189
Cruelty of bad shooting, The, 380
   of long shooting at hares, 380
   to wounded game, 383
Cuckoo, The, 138
   Egg, deposition of by, 139
   Mound bird and the, 142
   Nests utilized by the, 141
   Note of the, 140
   Peculiar formation of back of young, 139
   pint, The, 429
   pipit's nest, Preference of for the, 143
   rearing its young, 138
   Thrush feeding young, 141
Cuckoo's eggs, Varying colour of, 139
   mate, Name of, 137
Cuckoos, Birds feeding young, 142
   Migration of, 138
   young, Rearing of, 141
Curlew, The, 301
   sandpiper, The, 305
   stone, The, 116

D.

Dandelion, The, 431
Diver, black-throated, The, 355
   great Northern, The, 353
   red-throated, The, 354
   white-billed Northern, The, 355
Divers, The, 353
Dixon on migration of birds, 274
Dock, broad-leaved, The, 432
Dodder, The, 432
Dotterel, The, 284
Dove, ring, The, 232
   rock, The, 236
   stock, The, 233-236
   turtle, The, 236
Doves, British, 232
Dropwort, The, 415
Ducks, List of British, 318
Duck, common wild, The, 321
   gadwall, The, 325
   garganey, The, 334
   golden-eye, The, 329
   goosander, The, 332
   long-tailed, The, 330
   pintail, The, 325
   pochard, The, 327
   red-breasted merganser, The, 323
   scaup, The, 328
   sheldrake, The, 320
   shoveller, The, 323
   scoter, The, 330
      surf, The, 332
      velvet, The, 331
   smew, The, 333
   teal, The, 323

Duck, tufted, The, 327
Dunlin, The, 300

E.

Eagle, golden, The, 215
    white-tailed, The, 216
Eagles, The, 214
Eels, Quodding for, 76
Elder-tree, The, 419
Elecampane, 433
Eyebright, The, 434

F.

Falcon, Greenland, The, 223
    gyr, The, 223
        heron and, Fatal encounter between, 263
    Iceland, The, 223
    peregrine, The, 223
        heron and, Fight between, 262
    red-footed, The, 229
Falconidæ, British, 213
Ferret, gipsy, A, 47
    lost, A, 48
    Curious recovery of a, 46
Ferrets in houses, 49
    Probable origin of, 44
Field-gentian, The, 437
Flycatchers, Spotted and pied, 173
Forget-me-not, The, 418
Fowls, Indian method of cooking, 72
Fox-cubs at play, 17
Foxglove, The, 434
Fox-scented plant, 9
Foxes, English, 16
    Foreign, 15
    Impudence of, 19
    Poultry and, 11
    Rabbits and, in same earth, 17
    Scotch greyhound, 15
    Tame, 18
    Varieties of, 14
Fox-hunting, 400
    on foot, 15
Foxy story, A, 12
Fritillary, The, 435

G.

Gadwall, The, 325
Game-birds, British, 237
Game, Disposal of, in a larder, 40
Gannet, The, 365
Gapes, Cure for, in poultry and pheasants, 135
Garganey, The, 334
Garlic, wild, The, 437
Geese, British wild, 313
Gipsy's curse, A, 64
Godwit, bar-tailed, The, 311

Godwit, black-tailed, The, 305
Golden-crested wren, The, 186
Golden-eye duck, The, 329
Goldfinch, tame, A, 101
Goldfinches, Increase of, in England, 101
Goosander, The, 332
Goose, bean, The, 315
    bernacle, The, 317
    brent, The, 316
    gray-lag, The, 314
    pink-footed, The, 315
    red-breasted, The, 316
    snow, The, 316
    white-fronted, The, 314
Goshawk, The, 216
Grayling-fishing, 371
Grebe, eared, The, 357
    great crested, The, 356
    lesser crested, The, 357
    little, The, 358
    red-necked, The, 356
Grebes, British, 355
Greenshank, The, 311
Grosbeak, pine, The, 97
Grouse, The, 240
    Measurements of the, 242
Guillemot, common, The, 351
    black, The, 351
Gull, black-backed lesser, The, 345
    brown-headed, The, 343
    common, The, 344
    glaucous, The, 345
    herring, The, 344
    Iceland, The, 345
    ivory, The, 347
    kittiwake, The, 346
    little, The, 343
    Sabine's, 342

H.

Hare-calls, 30
Hare, cooking, A recipe for, 27
    distant, A, 21
    hunting, 25
    shooting, 27
Hares and their ways, 22
    Gradual decrease of, in England, 20
    hunted, Daring of, 25
    Netting, in gateways, 30
    Poaching of, 28
    Positions selected by to form, 25
    Solitary habits of, 24
    Timidity and ferocity of, 24
    Travelling powers of, 25
    Utility of, 27
Harrier, Hen, 208
    Marsh, 208
    Montagu's, 209
Harriers, British, 208

INDEX

Harriers, Jeffreys', Mr., 26
Hawking Club, Old, The, 217
Hawks, Destruction of, by keepers, 113
Hedge-potterers, 144
Hedgehog, The, 71
   Cruelty to the, 73
   Gipsy method of cooking a, 72
   not an ugly animal, 73
Hedgehogs, Torpidity of, in winter, 73
Henbane, The, 439
Herb-Robert, The, 438
Heron, The, 259
Herons, British, Varieties noticed in, 265
   Destruction of, in fisheries, 253
Heron's feathers, Use of, 264
Heron as food, 264
Hobby, The, 227
Home surroundings, 109
Hop, wild, The, 440
Hyacinth, wild, The, 441

I.
Indian crow, An, 190
   hot season, An, 191
Instruction of children in natural history, etc., 408, 409
In the moonlight, 252
Iris, yellow, The, 442
Ivy, ground, The, 441

J.
Jackdaw, The, 190
Jackdaws, rooks, and crows, 189
Jackson's *Oxford Journal*, Extract from, 125
Jays and magpies, 193
John Peel, 14

K.
Kestrel, The, 221
   lesser, The, 229
Killed in the open, 16
Kingfishers, 129
   Anecdotes respecting, 128
   An enemy to, 125
   Destruction of, in fisheries, 252
   feathers used for salmon-flies, 127
   Indian and British, 127
   mortality during prolonged frost, 124
Kite, black, The, 230
   red, The, 222
Knot, The, 308

L.
Landrail, The, 248
Laridæ, The, 336
Larinæ, The, 341

Lark, French lines on, and translation, 146
Larks, Pipits and, 144
Leveret, 'star,' A, 23
Lily of the valley, The, 443
Linnet, Redpole and, compared, 104
Linnets, Beauty of, 106
   Large flock of, 105
Loosestrife, purple, The, 442
   Yellow, 443

M.
Magpies and jays, 193
Mallow, common, The, 445
   marsh, The, 444
Marsh harrier, The, 208
Martens, 50
Meadowsweet, The, 413, 417
Merganser, red-breasted, The, 323
Merlin, The, 227
Mignonette, wild, The, 419
Migrants, Summer and winter, 103
Migration of birds, 274
Milkwort, The, 391, 413
Mole, The, 68
   catching, 71
Moles, Foxes feeding on, 70
   Underground dwellings of, 70
   Utility of, 69
Moneywort, The, 445
Montagu's harrier, 209
Moorhen, The, 254
   shooting, 255
Moorhens, Destruction of, in fisheries, 253
Mound bird, The, 142
Mullein, The, 417, 446

N.
Ned Powell, 99
Nerves or straight powder, 379
Nettle, great, The, 448
Nightingale, Beauty of the, 107
   Nest of the, 108
Nightingales, Too many, 140
Nightjar, The, 197
Nightshade, deadly, The, 446
   woody, The, 447

O.
Orchises, 414, 449
   British, List of, 449
Osprey, The, 230
   plumes, Wearing of, 231
Otter, The, 74
   Derivation of word, 78
   Ear of the, 78
   hunting, 374
Otters, Accusations against, 75
   asserted not to be fish-poachers, 76

Otters, fish-poachers, 76
   Inland and sea, 79
   Powers and pluck of, 78
   Size of, 78
   skin, Toughness of, 77
   Tame, 75
   Training of, 75
   Trapping of, 74
Ouzel, ring, The, 104
   water, The, 295
Owl, Ear of, 202
   long-eared, The, 205
   short-eared, The, 206
   scops, The, 201
   tawny, The, 204
   white or barn, The, 203
Owls, 200
   eggs, protection of in Oxfordshire, 129
   hawks and, Similarity between, 207
   Sight of, 201
Oyster-catcher, The, 283

P.

Partridge, The, 245
   French, The, 246
   shooting, 376
Peewit, The, 114
Peewits, solicitude for their nests, 115
Pennyroyal, 450
Peppermint, The, 450
Petrel, fork-tailed, The, 362
   fulmar, The, 359
   storm, The, 361
Petrels, The, 359
Phalaropes, The, 292
Pheasant, The, 243
   shooting, 386
Pimpernel, scarlet, The, 450
Pine grosbeak, The, 97
Pintail, The, 325
Pipit, meadow, The, 145
   tree, The, 145
   Varieties of, 145
Pipits, Larks and, 144
Plantain, great, The, 451
   hoary, The, 451
   ribwort, The, 451
   water, The, 452
Plover, golden, The, 281
   gray, The, 287
   Kentish, The, 283-286
   ringed, The, 282
Plover's eggs, 114
Plovers, British, 279
   nests, 116
Pochard, The, 327
Polecat, The, 43
Protection of garden-produce from birds, 112

Ptarmigan, The, 242
Puffin, The, 352

Q.

Quail, The, 247

R.

Rabbit-farming, 35
   poaching, 38
   shooting, 393-396
Rabbits, acute senses of hearing and smelling, 32
Rabbits at play, 37
   Black, 35
   Breeding season of, 32
   Condition of, when born 36
   Counties most suitable for, 34
   disease caused by overcrowding, 34
   Distribution of, to the poor, 39
   Effect of, on pastureland, 36
   English, crossing of with foreign, 40
   Hedge, stated not to burrow, 36
   Liver disease of, 33
   once domesticated said not to burrow, 35
   Profligacy of, 32
   Restocking a manor with, 34
   Soil suitable for, 33
   Tame, 35
   Wild white, 35
   Wood, and ferreting, 37
Ragged robin, The, 411, 417
Rampick-tree, A, 64
Rat-bite, Poisonous effects of, 54
   black, The, 55
      Disappearance of, 57
   brown, The, 56
      The, Goldsmith on, 56
      and water-vole, Fight between, 61
Rats, 54
   Black and brown, 57
   method of keeping out of a house, 49
   Snakes and, 59
Raven, The, 189
Razorbill, The, 350
Redpoles, Siskins and, 100
Redshank, The, 300
   dusky, The, 304
Restharrow, The, 452
Retaliation, law of, The, 130
Retrievers, 384
Ring-ouzel, The, 104
Rodents, 62
Rook, The, 190
   court-martial, A, 192
   shooting, 372
Rooks, crows, and jackdaws, 189

INDEX

Rooks, Destructiveness of, 112
  fishing, 192
  washing, 192
Ruff, The, 306

S.

Salmon-fishing, 366
Saloop, 414
Sanderling, The, 309
Sandpiper, common, The, 307
  curlew, The, 305
  green, The, 309
  purple, The, 310
Scabious, Devil's-bit, 419
Scaup, The, 328
Scolopacidæ, British, The, 297
Scops owl, 201
Scoter, The, 330
  surf, The, 332
  velvet, The, 331
Shag, The, 364
Shearwater, great, The, 360
  sooty, The, 361
  Manx, The, 361
Sheldrake, The, 320
Shepherd's-purse, The, 452
Shoveller, The, 323
Shrew, common, The, 65
  Characteristics of, 66
  compared with the mole, 67
  oared, The, 67
  origin of the word, 65
  Varieties of the, 63
  water, The, 67
  The, 62
  Mortality amongst, 65
  Persecution of, 63, 64
  Pugnacity of, 66
  Superstitions regarding, 63
  Teeth of, 66
Silverweed, The, 452
Siskin, The, 102
Siskins, Redpoles and, 100
Skua, great, The, 348
  long-tailed, The, 349
  Pomatorhine, 348
  Richardson's, 348
Skylark, French lines on, and translation, 146
Skylark, Woodlark and, 144
Smew, The, 333
Snakebird, Name of, 138
Snapdragon, The, 454
Snipe, British varieties of the, 270
  common, The, 269
  Crouching, 271
  flushed, returning to same spot, 272
  jack, The, 268
  shooting, 270
  Indian, 271

Snipe, shot, difficult to find, 271
  solitary, The, 269
Solomon's seal, 455
Sparrow, Beauty of, 106
  hawk, The, 218
  tree, The, 106
Sparrows, Starlings and, 111
Speedwell, The, 454
Sport and cruelty, 77
Spurge, The, 455
Squirrels, 51
Stercorariinæ, 347
Stilt, black-winged, The, 292
Stint, little, The, 303
Stoats, Weasels and, 45
Stonechat, The, 195
Stone curlew, The, 116
Succory, The, 453
Summer and winter migrants, 103
Swans as food, 264

T.

Tansy, The, 456
Taxidermists, Naturalists and, 179
Taxidermy, Provincial specimen of, 179
Teal, The, 323
Teasel, The, 456
Tern, Arctic, The, 340
  black, The, 338
  white-winged, The, 338
  black, common, The, 341
  little, The, 341
  roseate, The, 339
  Sandwich, The, 338
Thyme, wild, The, 457
Tit, bearded, The, 184
  blue, The, 183
  coal, The, 183
  family, The, 181
  great, The, 182
  long-tailed, The, 182
  marsh, The, 183
Tits feeding in winter, 183
Toad-flax, yellow, The, 458
Traveller's joy, The, 417, 420
Tree-creeper, Nuthatch and, 193
Tree-sparrow, 106
Trout-fishing, 368
Tufted duck, The, 327
Turnstone, The, 287

V.

Valerian, common, The, 458
Village cats and village birds, 109
Vole, water, The, 60
Vulpecides, 18

W.

Wagtail, gray, The, 176
  pied, The, 175

Wagtail, white, The, 175
  yellow, The, 176
Warbler, garden, The, 161
  reed, The, 166
  sedge, The, 166
  willow, The, 165
Warblers, British, Common, 156
  common, Classification of the, 158
  Difficulty in distinguishing certain, 156
Warde Fowler, 'A Year with the Birds,' by, 157
Watercress-farming, 460
Water ouzel, The, 295
  rail, The, 250
Wheatear, The, 196
Whimbrel, The, 304
Whinchat, The, 195
Whitethroats, The, 159
Widgeon, The, 326
Wild animals, British varieties of, 73
  Birds Protection Act, 89
  duck, The, 321
  ducks, herons and, Destructiveness of, in fisheries, 114
  flowers, Autumnal, 391, 417
    commoner, Beauty of some of the, 412
    rarer, Gradual extinction of, 411
  Waste of, 410, 412

Wild geese, British, 313
Willow-herb, greater, The, 418, 442
  lesser, The, 418
Wires, Poachers' and keepers', 28
Woodcock, Drawing a, 276
  first, My, 272
  flushed, returning to same spot, 276
  snipe and, Shooting and taking, 237
  carrying their young, 277
Woodcock's feathers, Uses of, 277
Woodcocks, Migration of, 273
Woodlark, Skylark and, 144
Woodpecker, greater spotted, The, 134
  green, The, 132
  lesser barred, The, 134
Woodpeckers, The, 131
  British varieties of, 132
  in Devonshire, 133
  wrynecks and, Observations on, 136
Wood sorrel, The, 459
Wren, golden-crested, The, 186
Wryneck, The, 136
  Eggs of the, 137
  neck of, Peculiar structure of, 137
  Plumage of the, 137

Y.

Yarrow, The, 419

THE END.

BILLING AND SONS, PRINTERS, GUILDFORD.
J. D. & Co.

www.ingramcontent.com/pod-product-compliance
Lightning Source LLC
Chambersburg PA
CBHW051846300426
44117CB00006B/283